D1601139

CHARISMA
AND SOCIAL
STRUCTURE

CHARISMA AND SOCIAL STRUCTURE

A Study of Love and Power, Wholeness and Transformation

RAYMOND TREVOR BRADLEY

PARAGON HOUSE

New York

Published in the United States by

Paragon House Publishers
90 Fifth Avenue
New York, New York 10011

Copyright ©1987 by Raymond Trevor Bradley

Designed by Paul Chevannes

Library of Congress Cataloging-in-Publication Data

Bradley, Raymond Trevor.
  Charisma and Social Structure.

  Includes index.
  1. Leadership.   2. Social structure.
3. Power (Social sciences)   I. Title.
HM141.B825 1987   303.3'4   86–30461
ISBN 0–913729–03–5

To Kathleen and Arthur,
my parents,
whose love and wonder for all living things
long ago sparked a little boy's curiosity

To Nancy,
my dearest friend and partner in life,
whose unfaltering love and belief
fires a journey on a new path

There is only one problem, namely our resistance to seeing things as they truly are, or more accurately, seeing the wholeness as it is.

Willis W. Harmon

When we try to pick out anything by itself, we find it hitched to every-thing else in the universe.

John Muir

CONTENTS

PART THREE: SUBSTANTIATION

PART FOUR: TRANSCENDENCE

PART FIVE: NEXUS

APPENDICES

FOREWORD

Raymond Bradley has presented us with a remarkable piece of work in this book on charisma. The work is remarkable on two counts: method and content. Opinions abound that the social sciences do not deal with society but with trivia and that their methods are anything but scientific. Here is a book that shows that social science can be sound in both method and content.

What is so impressive about the method Bradley uses is his meticulous description of every step in his argument, every step in his data gathering, and every step in his analyses. One may have reservations about this particular application or that, but one *knows* what was done and can act accordingly. Agreement is not the grist of the scientific mill; sharing one's observations and thought process is. Bradley comes off as a superb scientist in this volume.

What Bradley has discovered is equally encouraging. The best of methods applied to the most interesting of problems is of no avail if nothing is discovered. The painstaking analyses of relations at the dyadic, triadic, and global levels by which Bradley took to understand the network of relationships within fifty-seven entire communities yielded a rich harvest. Should the findings prove generally valid for other social organizations — and I believe there is a good chance they will — this volume will become a ground-breaking classic.

Bradley finds that there are two rather different types of order which operate within the groups he has been studying. One of these is heterarchical and the other hierarchical. The heterarchical order, which is essentially egalitarian and network-like, is responsible for generating energy, defined as the potential for doing work. The hierarchical order deals with power, the structure which translates this potential into actual work.

Bradley is especially concerned with the discovery of the heterarchical order since this is ordinarily hidden from casual observation. He points out that heterarchy entails an enfolding of the total order in each of the units — individuals and relationships — that make up the whole. Information is thus distributed over the entire group much as it is in a holographic representation which stores the potential for reconstructing the image of the whole. The whole is represented in each of its parts and the part represents the whole.

This enfolded, implicate ordering is holistic in an entirely different sense from the ordering that characterizes hierarchy. In hierarchical wholes the sum is greater than and different from the sum of its parts. In a heterachical, holonomic order the whole becomes to some extent enfolded in all of its parts so that each part can act in lieu of the whole.

Both orders are necessary for transformation. The holonomic order energizes while the hierarchical order empowers. This fits with the physics: the energy/momentum domain is potential; the space/time domain is where the action is. The two domains are related by way of a Fourier transform (a holonomic transform). It is the invertibility of the transformational process, the going back and forth between the two orders, that makes the entire process go.

Why, in the groups Bradley has studied, the holonomic heterarchy should be the source of energy for the group remains to be investigated. As Bradley correctly assumes, it is "love" that constitutes the generative process. But what is the essence of love? Can the techniques so successfully applied here be taken a step further to answer this question so critical to our very survival?

It has been a privilege to read this seminal work and I hope others will enjoy it as much as I have. I hope too that Bradley can continue his explorations and that he will someday be able to resolve the puzzle that constitutes the relationship we call love.

Karl H. Pribram
Stanford University

PREFACE

As a powerful force for change in the world, charisma is something that everyone must contend with. Today, more than ever before, the tremors triggered by charisma reverberate around the world, often dramatically altering the lives and destinies of many people.

In part, this widening scope of charisma's impact is a result of the growth in global interdependence. The expansion and deepening of political, economic, and cultural bonds has made the world a smaller place. The unsettling impact of charisma from a distant region has been felt many times in the twentieth century. Reverberations are still echoing from charisma's most recent eruption with Khomeini in Iran.

But the widening scope of charisma's impact is also due to changes in its appeal as an instrument for influence and change. No longer is it something that holds an attraction only for the marginal elements of society, who see charisma as a means for revolution and change. Now charisma is something valued and desired by the respectable. Not only are its powers of persuasion sought by world leaders, and the leaders of all kinds of national, political, and social movements, but charisma is also sought by leaders in the local community. Indeed, charisma's appeal has even reached the corporate world where some view it as a managerial tool for mobilizing employee commitment to raise productivity. In short, charisma has come of age as a legitimate source of power in the modern world.

Yet despite charisma's growing importance, social science has made little progress in unraveling the enigma of charisma beyond that achieved by Max Weber over half a century ago. The results of the research reported in this book offer what I believe is a new and fruitful understanding of charisma. In presenting this understanding, I have endeavored to make the sociological rationale explicit and have also sought systematic empirical validation.

The results of my investigation are summed up in two models that sit on a desk in my office. Each is made with ten polystyrene balls and lengths of wire. In one, the ten balls are completely interconnected to one another by forty-five wire links to form a polyhedron — a many-sided, three-dimensional structure. In the other, the ten balls are linked in a hierarchy extending down a number of levels from a single ball at the top in the shape of an ellipsoid. At each level, the balls are directly connected by the wire to all balls at the lower levels. Both are models of the same charismatic commune in which members are represented by polystyrene balls and social relations by wire links. The models typify two patterns of social organization that, in this study of 57 urban communes, I find co-exist whenever beliefs acknowledging the presence of charisma are held by a group.

In the first model, the wire links represent social bonds highly charged with communion. Communion is the power plant that generates the enormous amounts of collective energy a charismatic group requires to accomplish a radical transformation of social structure. In the second model, the wire links represent power relations. Because the energy liberated by communion is highly volatile and has a destabilizing effect on the group, a strong, robust power structure acts to contain the energy. Harnessed and regulated this way, the energy is used to mobilize group members for the awesome task of transforming an established order into a totally new form of social organization.

This book describes how and why I have come to view charisma this way — to believe that charisma is best understood structurally, as a distinctive pattern of social relations. It describes the path of investigation that led me, first, to question the notion that charisma is simply an exceptional talent for leadership possessed by an individual. The data are more congruent with the idea that charisma is a property of the group: a set of beliefs held by a collectivity attributing extraordinary powers, of a supernatural origin, to a particular person or social position.

Probing beneath the surface of these beliefs I found, in contradiction to Weber, a structure involving many elements of formal and routine organization, with an elaborate division of labor, a stable economic base of self-sufficiency, and much delegation of authority. These elements of social organization enable charisma to be more than a momentary expression of collective desire. But it was only as I probed more deeply into charisma's structural foundation, that I discovered the relational forms that provide charisma with its awesome power as a vehicle for radical social transformation: namely, a heterarchy of communion and a hierarchy of power. When cojoined as complementary orders, these relational systems not only account for the stability of charismatic groups, but the evidence suggests the same interrelation is a requisite for the survival of noncharismatic systems.

To locate and describe these relational forms, I have employed the perspective and methods of network analysis. This approach, by focusing on the nature and form of the social bonds that interconnect social actors, enables the researcher to build images of the relational structure of a group. However, description of the relational images alone does not provide a compelling, let alone valid, empirical demonstration of charisma's structural foundation. Such an inference requires evidence of an *emergent* order in the way social relations are arranged — showing that the organization of relations cannot be explained by attributes of the structure's parts.

Paradoxically, however, the data show that not only is the whole (the group) different from and greater than the sum of its parts (individuals and relations), but also that part and whole are one — that they are interrelated in a *holonomic* order. So that while the whole is constructed from the parts as a manifest, emergent order, each part contains the whole as an implicit, encoded order. It is this postulate of holonomic social order that empirically explains the patterns of communal global organization constructed from mappings of discrete dyads in this study.

In short, the journey of discovery we undertake in this book will not only lead beyond charisma to questions about the fundamental nature of social organization, but also to some striking parallels between social order and structure at other levels of reality.

ACKNOWLEDGMENTS

In the course of writing this book I have received valuable help from many people. While there is not the space here to mention everyone by name, I want to express my deep gratitude for their assistance and support. Whatever has been accomplished was made possible by their special talents and contributions.

The early foundations for my work were laid as a student at Victoria University of Wellington in New Zealand. I owe so much to Allan Levett and his enthusiasm for sociology. First as a challenging, dedicated teacher, and then as an inspiring colleague and good friend, Allan fired my sociological imagination, guided my fledgling research efforts, and introduced me to network analysis. I also learned much from Harvey Franklin and Peter Webster. It was their fascination with social and economic development that kindled my interest in social change.

It was while a graduate student at Columbia University, that these interests in social change and network analysis took

XX CHARISMA AND SOCIAL STRUCTURE

root. There, Ben Zablocki provided me with both the initial inspiration and also the opportunity for the research that this book is based on. His classic ethnography of a rural commune, *The Joyful Community* (Zablocki, 1971), pointed to a critical relationship between communion and power that has become the central concern of my work. With the Urban Communes Project (funded by a grant from the National Institute of Mental Health [1 RO MH 25525-01MP]), he created the larger study out of which my own work grew. A panel study of sixty urban communes (1974 through 1976), sampled from six American cities, the Urban Communes Project reflects Ben's great skill for establishing fertile empirical ground in which new sociological understanding can take root. In addition to his own definitive work, *Alienation and Charisma* (Zablocki, 1980), and my research reported here, this rich data base has yielded other interesting studies (Aidala, 1980; and Carlton-Ford, 1986). This book owes much to Zablocki as my teacher and to his extraordinary foresight as a researcher.

I also have a deep gratitude to the members of the Urban Communes Project: for field work and data collection, Angela Aidala, Nina Housman, Jane Ferrar, Mimi Leonard, Michael Ort, Debbie Podus, Howard Schneider, Charles Sprague, Ernest Vollin, and Ben Zablocki; for computer programming and data file maintenance, Michael Manhardt, Betty Sheets, and particularly Peter Messeri for *DAMP* and *STAM* (the relational analysis programs); for coding and data management, Lee Cokorinos, Miriam Davis, Milcha Mrema, James O'Toole, Emily Singer, Jamie Sunderland, and Tom Thirlwall; for taped interview coding and transcription, Wendy Bradley, Jane Kingston, Claudia Lawrence, and Jamie Sunderland; for project administration and secretarial responsibilities, Wendy Bradley, and especially Jane Kingston and Claudia Lawrence. This is a rare group of individuals; their special talents, professional dedication, and boundless energy made my job as Project Director an enriching experience full of fond memories.

As an Assistant Professor at the University of Minnesota, Minneapolis, I received help and support from a number of individuals. Alexa Albert, Ron Anderson, Harold Finestone, Bob Fulton, Pat Lauderdale, Ian Maitland, Don McTavish, Jeylan Mortimer, Joel Nelson, Ira Reiss, Paul Reynolds, Roberta Simmons, Steve Spitzer, and the late Greg Stone extended a warm colleagueship that I appreciated during my time at Minnesota. At a technical level, Mark Mongiat, Steve Carlton-Ford, and Terry Schmidt provided invaluable computer programming and data management assistance, while Barbara Lynch and Brenda Miller helped with library and editorial work. As Kathy Simon-Frank made an earlier version of the manuscript intelligible, Gloria DeWolfe typed it into a word processor. I also was lucky to have a number of exceptional graduate students who were generous with their help and criticism; Steve Carlton-Ford, Tim Owens, and Jane Silverman.

The manuscript evolved in three distinct stages and benefitted tremendously from being read by many individuals. As a doctoral dissertation at Columbia University (Bradley, 1980), the work was sponsored by a demanding committee; Herbert Gans, William Goode, Herbert Passin, Burton Singer, Sloan Weyland, and Benjamin Zablocki. My fellow students Craig Calhoun, Jane Ferrar, Peter Messeri, and Charles Sprague, too, made helpful suggestions. And the work also gained from comments by Peter Blau, Wendy Bradley, Harrison White, and the late Victor W. Turner.

Redrafted as a book, all or parts of the manuscript were read by Donald Campbell, Harold Finestone, Bob Fulton, William Goode, Charles Kadushin, Don Martindale, Bruce Mayhew, J. Clyde Mitchell, Jeylan Mortimer, Joel Nelson, Paul Reynolds, Nancy Roberts, Gerry Salancik, Arthur Schweitzer, Burt Singer, Ben Zablocki, and by my students Steve Carlton-Ford, Tim Owens, and Jane Silverman. Joel Nelson was particularly helpful with his thorough review — a catalyst leading eventually to the holonomic hypothesis of Part Four. And while I was visiting the University of Tasmania at this time, Rod Crook's probing questions helped me to see that my task was incomplete.

The final version of the manuscript gradually took shape and has been enormously improved as a result of critical input from Lois Erickson, Diane McGuinness, Joel Nelson, Karl Pribram, Nancy Roberts, Ben Zablocki and two anonymous reviewers. Encouragement and helpful advice also came from Michel Bougon, Riane Eisler, William Goode, Ron Haxton, David Loye, Louis Pondy, Bob Quinn, Bill Roberts, and Burt Singer.

Converting the manuscript into a quality publication has been in the capable hands of Ken Stuart and Helen Driller at Paragon House. The cartographic excellence of the more than fifty original figures, charts, and diagrams was created by my talented brother, Barry Bradley. He very generously donated most of this beautiful art work to the book.

I have been very fortunate to have had the support of wonderful friends during this process that, for so long, seemed to have no end. Wendy Bradley, Helen Carciofini, Dick Engerbretson, Bob Fulton, Mary Lundrigan, Joel Nelson, Midge Semans, Jane Silverman, Kathy Simon-Frank, and Judith Thomas, have each in their own precious way, nurtured me with kindness and understanding. Alice Bovard-Taylor and Bruce McBeath helped me with patience and sensitivity to know myself better.

But there are three individuals, in particular, to whom I am especially grateful. Lois Erickson, ever kind, generous, and thoughtful, has been a constant source of intellectual support and spiritual strength. Karl Pribram (who was not only instrumental in getting this book published, but also wrote the "Foreword") offered inspiration and encouragement, and shared the wisdom of his vast scientific knowledge and experience in a warm, stimulating friendship. And finally, my wife, Nancy Roberts, has supported me and nurtured my work with her love and inimitable patience. In shouldering the brunt of the burden, she has given and sacrificed much so that I could focus my full energy on bringing this project to fruition. Without their support, commitment, and love this book would not have survived these last long three years.

But it is my children, more than anyone else, who have given most to this project. For Therese, Kris, and Jonathan have lost precious moments from childhood — memories of special times with Dad that are now gone forever.

Finally, I would like to thank the members of the 60 urban communes, the subjects of this research. Without their commitment and cooperation this project would not have been possible. It goes almost without saying, though, that the flaws and failings of this study are mine — a product of "kiwi" obstinancy; an insistence on doing it "my way"; of following often misleading hunches rather than the conventions of expedience.

Institute for Whole Social Science,
Menlo Park, California

LIST OF
ILLUSTRATIONS

With the exception of Figures 2:1, 5:1, 5:N1, 6:1, 6:3, 9:1(b), 9:2(a), 9:2(b), 10:1, 10:N1, and A:N1, all illustrations are original and were drawn by Barry K. Bradley.

LIST OF TABLES

PART ONE

INTRODUCTION

The world is far too rich to be expressed in a single language. Music does not exhaust itself in a sequence of styles. Equally, the essential aspects of our experience can never be condensed into a single description. We have to use many descriptions which are irreducible to each other, but which are connected by precise rules of translations (technically called 'transformations'). Scientific work consists of selective exploration and not of the discovery of a given reality. It consists of the choice of questions which have to be posed.

Ilya Prigogine.*

---

*Quoted in: *The Self-organizing Universe*, Jantsch (1980: 303).

Chapter One

ENIGMA

Introduction

Charisma has its roots long ago in human evolution. From the advent of symbolically-oriented behavior, charisma has existed as a latent potential in all social systems. For with the creation of society as a shared order of abstract symbols and meanings came the belief in a supernatural reality (Durkheim, 1965). And from that followed the realization that there are alternative sources of knowledge and power to those of established moral order. With this, awareness of the possibility of a break with the current social order was born. It is in this seed of consciousness that the potential for belief in charisma lies.

As a structure that mobilizes enormous amounts of collective energy, charisma has brought dramatic and often discontinuous social changes to the world many times throughout human history. Even as we go about the mundane business of our daily lives in today's technological world, charisma's awesome power is still with us. And while it is rarely an element in our day-to-day consciousness, we are always vulnerable to its magnetizing force, and often have to contend with its serendipitous, long-term consequences.

3

Despite its long, dramatic presence, and its unparalleled power as a major, unpredictable force for change, charisma has eluded the light of scientific reasoning. It has continued to remain enshrouded in a mystique of irrationality and awe, defying social scientists in their efforts to render it to human understanding. It has remained an enigma.

My goal in this book is the demystification of charisma; to use the perspective and methods of sociology to construct an understanding that has theoretical utility and empirical validity. In this opening chapter, therefore, I want to introduce the study; to pose the problem, establish the research strategy, and introduce the data base to be used in this exploration. Let us begin the journey by stepping into the phenomenological world of charisma.

Phenomenon

Alabama Avenue[1] is a small, white, Christian commune located in a low income, transitional neighborhood of a southern city. Its six members are strongly committed to "spread the gospel of Jesus Christ and tell other Christians about the joy and liberty (they) find in Jesus." They want to "encourage the people of the area to find the new and living way through Jesus Christ." Aside from meeting together daily for dinner, to pray and sing, the group also holds Sunday religious services for its small congregation in a borrowed church nearby.

Will, the leader (formerly a priest in the Catholic Church), is seen by the group as having two roles. One is as an ordinary member: "As an individual, it's hard to say that he wields any authority. Most things are community (group) decisions, and God can speak through any member as well as Will." The other role is as the group's spiritual leader. Will is seen as "annointed by God" — he is the group's "top authority" with the power of veto over both collective and individual actions:

... God puts people into positions of authority and we as Christians are expected to submit to them as unto God. In other words, if Will told me to do something, even though I may not agree with it, I have to trust that God speaks to me through Will. ... If Will's vetoing whatever this thing is that I want to run out and do, there's a reason that God does not want me to do it. God can change your authority if your authority is wrong. ... God will change Will. I don't try to change Will. ... I submit to him (Will) as the authority, as unto God, knowing that God is ultimately in control.

The dual roles create a certain amount of strain and conflict between Will and the others: "A lot of times I could not separate him as a person from God's annointed authority. I had a real fear of him ... we had conflicts and blow-ups," one member explained.

As their spiritual leader, they see Will possessing special gifts of "knowledge," "teaching," "discernment," "prophecy," and "the Spirit of the Lord." Will also sees himself as possessing these abilities — "insight and discernment, a strong relationship with God, and the ability to teach and lead." To a lesser extent, the others believe that they have some of these "spiritual powers" as well, but Will, as the spiritual leader, is "The Authority." One of the group summed it up: "Will is God's annointed shepherd, and we are the flock."

To enter the *United Lotus Institute* is to enter a realm of serene tranquility: a place in which time seems suspended, purpose an illusion, and individuality unimportant. The Institute was founded by Yogi, an Eastern "spiritual master", in the late 1960s. Although located in different neighborhoods, its two households are seen as a single spiritual community with the center at the men's house. Most of the 23 members (17 are men) are between 20 and 30 years old and follow a strict daily routine of spiritual activities (meditation and yoga), chores, and jobs for the group (preparing the vegetarian meals, teaching yoga classes, running their natural foods store, etc.). The Community has some degree of formal organization with positions of responsibility assigned by Yogi, who lives elsewhere but keeps in regular contact and visits the Community three or four times a year.

The members see their major commitment as Yogi and the Community, and regard individual differences in personality and appearance as unimportant.[2] The group's objective is self realization by following the teachings of Yogi and serving others: "To emulate our teacher, Yogi; to learn to give to others unreservedly; and to become loving and fully aware." The basis of Yogi's authority is found in their perception of him as a "Spiritual Master" who possesses special powers and abilities: "power of perception;" "awareness;" "a master of himself;" "has recognized the goal of life and has the ability to inspire;" "is completely enlightened":

> He is someone who is completely dedicated to God. ... Every vibration that he gives off and every atom of his being is love, and service to God, and through God, service to man. ... I see that spirit, I feel it, and I just know that it's there.

Workers of the World, the last commune we will introduce here, is a political group under the influence of a leader of national repute. The group included in this study is one of a network of communes extending across many large American cities. The Union and the communes, under the direction of their leader, Tony, seek better working and living conditions for disenfranchised workers and their families. Demonstrations, pickets, and boycotts are used to politicize the workers' cause and to put direct pressure on the employers involved.

Workers of the World had ten members in 1974, at the time of the first wave of data collection, and has undergone very high membership turnover since its founding two years earlier. Most of the group's members are between 20 and 30 years old — many from the workers' families. The commune is formally organized with its leader, office manager, and other positions of responsibility assigned by Tony. But there is dissatisfaction and tension among members over the organization of household chores and discontent about their House Leader, Steve, Tony's brother. They feel Steve is "weak," "unsupportive," and "too strongly influenced" by his wife.

With food, shelter, and clothing provided, the members are expected to devote their complete time and energy to the commune's political activities. They find little time for any personal life or outside interests:

> You knew you were going to have to do without a lot of things for the Union. But the reason you're here, doing any sort of social action type work, is because there is something bigger to think about than yourself. ... The whole thing with the Union is one of self-denial: that if anything is to succeed, you just have to immerse yourself in whatever, and work, and work, and work. And you don't really think too much about yourself.

This dedication and commitment to the workers and the Union's political struggle, despite the very tense interpersonal relations in the group, is maintained by the members' belief in, and devotion to, their absentee leader, Tony. He has become their hero: an "extraordinary individual" — someone who, despite overwhelming opposition from employers, "led (them) from exploitation, repression, and powerlessness," to become the "best organized Union in the labor movement." He is seen as a person of "incredible strength" and "complete dedication" to resolving the workers' plight. And, as a national political figure, he is seen as their "voice" — someone who is "able to communicate with a broad spectrum of people and get the message across." It is these special abilities that they believe have enabled Tony to accomplish "the impossible."

Problem

In *The Theory of Social and Economic Organization*, Max Weber defines charisma as:

a certain quality of an individual personality by virtue of which he is set apart from ordinary men and treated as endowed with supernatural, superhuman, or at least specifically exceptional powers or qualities. These are not accessible to the ordinary person, but are regarded as of divine origin or as exemplary, and on the basis of them the individual is treated as a leader. ... What alone is important is how the individual is actually regarded by those subject to charismatic authority, by his 'followers' or 'disciples' (Weber, 1947:358-359).

By this definition, there can be little doubt about the presence of charisma in the three communes. It is clear, for example, that the members of Alabama Avenue believe Will has many exceptional spiritual powers, and further, that these are special gifts from God. Thus, because he is seen as "God's annointed shepherd," the group submits totally to Will as "The Authority." Similar beliefs are held by the members of United Lotus about Yogi. Believed to be a "Spiritual Master", endowed by God with exceptional powers of perception and enlightenment, the group has granted Yogi complete authority over its life. These same elements of belief exist in the Workers of the World, despite the underlying tension and dissatisfaction among members. Tony, too, is seen as possessing exceptional abilities, although these are political — the talents of an "ideological virtuoso" — rather than spiritual.[3] The group feels these extraordinary talents have enabled Tony to organize and lead the workers to accomplish the "impossible."

We can see, just from these three communes, that there is quite a diversity among charismatic groups in terms of size, ideology, goals, activities, and so on. What sets these groups apart from other communes in this research, though, is that authority is based on beliefs about an individual's possession of exceptional powers of a divine or supernatural origin.

Yet, we must ask, is charisma more than a belief system? To what extent can it be better understood, sociologically, as a distinctive pattern of social organization? By studying the nature and form of the social bonds among those in a charismatic group, we aim to identify charisma's *structural foundation* — to show that charismatic beliefs adhere to a particular arrangement of social relations. In other words, our goal is to show that charisma is an emergent system with properties that are independent of the characteristics of individuals.[4] However, as we will see in Part Four, this quest will lead beyond charisma to a new understanding of social organization itself.

Study Design

That a sociological approach to charisma[5] should be more concerned with the nature and structure of bonds among participants than with their personal and social characteristics, has been argued by a number of researchers (Turk, 1971; Schiffer, 1973; and Worsley, 1968). This, of course, was Weber's original formulation.[6] Despite this, little work has been undertaken, either theoretically to build a structural understanding of charisma, or empirically to identify the distinguishing properties of charismatic social organization.[7]

Most previous work has focused on large-scale settings such as social movements (egs.; Worsley, 1968; Fabian, 1971; Wallis, 1977; Theobold, 1980) institutions (eg., Hill, 1973), formal organizations (egs.; Etzioni, 1961; Shils, 1965), and societies (egs.; Cell, 1974; Madsen and Snow, 1983; Schweitzer, 1984; Willner, 1984). But in such settings physical limitations and the enormity of these systems have meant that only fragments of a whole charismatic structure can be examined. There has also been a fascination with charisma's more exotic manifestations in the liminal regions of society (egs.; Lofland, 1966; Zablocki, 1971; Kanter, 1972; Johnson, 1979; Leger, 1982; Galanter, 1983). In this twilight zone of communes and cults, problems of visibility and accessibility make systematic research difficult.

Typically, researchers have looked at only that part of the structure occupied by the charismatic leader and those individuals who are visible and socially proximate. Moreover, they have been concerned primarily with the more dramatic occurrences of charisma, focusing almost exclusively on "super charismatic" leaders (egs.; Willner, 1968 and 1984; Schlesinger, 1970; Burns, 1978; Schweitzer, 1984). There has been much less interest when charisma occurs more mundanely in smaller settings, unheralded by the media, and without the drama of revolution or death (Zablocki (1980) and Roberts (1985(a)) are exceptions).

An important weakness of such approaches is that charisma is not seen as a variable social property with a range of manifestations differing in size, scale, and intensity. It is often assumed, instead, that "genuine" charisma only occurs in large social collectivities, on a broad scale, with electrifying intensity, and producing consequences of historical significance (egs., Schlesinger, 1970; Schweitzer, 1984). In doing so, the sociological significance of charisma, as a mode of radical transformation is overlooked — a potential in all social collectivities that provides an alternative to gradual, evolutionary change. Until efforts are made to view charisma as a variable social property, to deal with its full range of empirical diversity, a more general, more valid understanding cannot be developed. By studying charisma in communes, this inquiry aims not only to broaden our knowledge, but also to demonstrate the strategic importance of research in smaller, less dramatic settings.

A more basic limitation of previous approaches, is that the focus on the large-scale occurrences of charisma, by its very nature, precludes the possibility of studying the social organization of the charismatic collectivity as an entity in itself. To do this, a researcher must have access to *whole* social systems, with readily identifiable boundaries, and enough of them for comparative analysis.

In my opinion, this is the great advantage of using communes as a research site. Communes are strategic for the study of charisma: they are small, diverse, bounded, and more-or-less total institutions of voluntary membership, catering to virtually all of the individual's physical, emotional, and social needs. While they are not microcosms of larger social units (see Zablocki, 1980:6), they may nonetheless shed light on common underlying patterns and processes. But most importantly, communes are collectivities that, as social wholes, are accessible to research. It is possible to establish the boundaries of a commune; to enumerate all members and study the organization of social relations that connect them. Consequently, this study is able to be much less concerned than previous research with the individuals' (both leaders and followers) personality, background, and social characteristics, and focus directly on the social bonds among members. The ideal results from this research, therefore, would be to identify the distinctive emergent properties of charismatic organization.

Of special interest in this regard, is the extent to which a relational theory, presented in Chapter Three, is supported by data gathered from the 57 communes examined in this study. In this theory, I spell out the nature and structure of relations that underlie collectively held beliefs about the presence of charisma. Specifically, I postulate that highly interlocking bonds of communion will coexist with a strong power structure. It is predicted that, while communion mobilizes the extraordinary levels of collective energy needed to achieve radical social change, power will act to control this volatile energy, thereby stabilizing the charismatic group.

Structural Imperatives

To verify this theory, we must confront the most basic methodological implication of structuralism: namely, empirical demonstration of an emergent order. To accomplish this we must show that the distinctive properties of charismatic organization are not reducible to the lower order elements from which social structure is constructed (Nagel, 1955; Piaget, 1970).

The methods of network analysis offer us a way of enumerating the organization of a charismatic system.[8] By systematically mapping ties among group members, we can obtain detailed empirical images of the patterning of relations in the communes.[9] But for valid inference of emergent structure, we must achieve certain structural imperatives in the operational process.

From a networks perspective, the components of social structure are social actors occupying social positions that are interconnected by social relations. Emergent structure is a particular arrangement of these elements that produce properties that exist only for the group as a whole; these properties are not reducible to the aggregated characteristics of the actors, positions, or relations themselves (Blau, 1981).

Emergent structure has two relational dimensions. The first is a persisting pattern of relations among social positions across different kinds of bonds. This is the usual meaning of social structure (Laumann, 1973; Mayhew, 1980). But there is a second dimension to be considered. Separate from the question of social relations as channels linking social positions, is the issue of interrelations among the diverse contents that flow in these bonds. This second aspect of social structure, multiplexity, involves understanding how different contents are interrelated in various contexts (Gluckman, 1955; Nadel, 1957). In this study of charisma, it concerns the interrelation of communion and power.

Operationally, an accurate mapping of emergent structure requires measuring both of these dimensions. Since the patterning of ties and contents only can be seen by viewing *all* relations in a structure, mapping dyads is the minimum way by which this can be accomplished. For small, bounded social units such as communes, where network sampling is not necessary, complete enumeration of all possible dyadic relations across all contents of theoretical interest is both possible and essential (see Appendix A). Without it, valid inference of emergent structure could not be achieved (Wellman, 1980).

But relational mappings of social structure are highly susceptible to problems of measurement error, missing and incomplete observations, and structural bias in the methods of analysis employed (Hallinan, 1974).[10] Unfortunately, due to the fundamentally interdependent nature of relational data, these problems can introduce serious distortions even when present at very small levels.[11] Moreover, in analyzing these data we are faced with the relativity of relational models: that potentially, our data may contain many alternative images of "social structure". It is thus crucial to be able to differentiate valid images, with real sociological significance, from spurious patterns.

One solution to this problem is to be very specific in our substantive theory of charisma's structural foundation. By doing so, we can give the abstract concept of emergent structure a more concrete sociological meaning — a "testable theory of a system of appearances" (Goode, 1975:71). In addition to explicit verification criteria, our substantive theory also will provide specific sociological criteria to guide the operational process (Blalock, 1982).

A second way we have attempted to minimize spurious results is by employing a multi-methods approach. Multiple sources of data help the detection of measurement error and enable an assessment of the implications of missing and incomplete observations. Because almost any socio-matrix representing ties among social actors, can be interpreted as possessing substantively-meaningful structure, corroboration from other data increases the likelihood of valid inference.

A final imperative, is to show that the relational properties of our charismatic communes are not reducible to characteristics of the members or the attributes of dyads. Multi-level analysis offers us a way of controlling for such lower-order effects (Falter, 1978; Wallace, 1983: Chap. 6). Our aim will be to demonstrate the existence of an independent structural residual that is associated with charisma.

Methodology

In the Urban Communes Project,[12] out of which this research grew, sixty communes were chosen for study in the following way. First, a commune was defined operationally as: a minimum of three families, or five nonblood-related adults who shared, to some degree, common geographical location, voluntary membership, economic interdependence, and some program of common enterprise (usually spiritual, social-psychological, political, cultural, or some combination of these). Next, six Standard Metropolitan Statistical Areas (Atlanta, Boston, Houston, Los Angeles, Minneapolis-Saint Paul, and New York), broadly reflective of differences in geographic location and urban context, were selected. In each city, at the start of the summer of 1974, a commune census was undertaken by fieldworkers to establish contact with as many communes as possible and build a profile in terms of size, membership composition, ideology, organization, duration, and location.[13] From this census, ten communes in each city were chosen that were both representative of the overall characteristics of the communes enumerated, and also reflective of commune differences among the six cities.[14]

Data collection for the Urban Communes Project, following a panel design, took place over the summers of 1974 and 1975. A combination of formal and informal data gathering techniques were employed. Intensive fieldworker contact was maintained with each commune for three to four months each summer. During this time extensive ethnographic material on the structure and activities of each group was collected in fieldnotes, and by taped interviews with commune informants.

Using the ethnographic material as a guide, a number of formal instruments were constructed and administered to all members 15 years and older.[15] Taking sex, position, and length of membership into account, five members from each commune were given in-depth standardized interviews (two to three hours long) to gather personal background data and information about communal participation. While a much shorter version of this instrument (a 15 minute questionnaire) was administered to virtually all other members, a questionnaire of 100 attitude items covering a variety of topics (alienation, anomia, self-esteem, urban and communal life) was less successful. Finally, to map the pattern of social bonds in each commune, a sociometric questionnaire was administered to all adults.[16]

To measure charisma, a three-step, qualitative procedure was developed.[17] First, for each commune a list was constructed from the ethnographic data of all individuals the members believed possessed extraordinary powers or abilities of a divine or supernatural origin. Then, more systematic corroboration was sought from questionnaires and taped interviews, to assess the extent to which these beliefs were held in common by everyone in the group. These materials also were scrutinized for evidence that the authority granted an individual for leadership was based on the group's recognition of the individual's charismatic qualities. When both of these conditions were met, a commune was classified as charismatic. Finally, independent validation for the classification was sought from the commune's fieldworker. This procedure resulted in 28 communes being classified as charismatic and 29 noncharismatic. (Three communes have been excluded from this study because membership involved an element of coercion.)

The sociometric questionnaire, mentioned above, was used to measure the nature and structure of informal relations among the members of each commune. In this instrument, every member was asked to answer a set of questions about his or her relation with each resident who was 15 years or older. The aim was to map all possible dyadic relations among group members across a variety of different kinds of social bonds. This meant that each person had to complete a set of standardized questions for N-1 members (where N = the number of permanent adult members).[18]

This procedure generated an exhaustive mapping of the N(N-1) dyadic relations in a group.

A final matter concerns the significance of patterns of relations revealed by this analysis of the commune data; how far can findings be generalized beyond the communes sampled? This is the question of statistical inference. A powerful set of statistical tools is available so long as the assumption of statistical independence can be met: that knowledge of the occurrence of a given event will not aid the prediction of another (Blalock, 1960:105). However, when entities such as dyads, rather than discrete individuals, are the units of analysis, this assumption is no longer met; these relational elements are *interdependent*, not independent. Consequently, the concept of statistical independence can neither accurately describe the distribution of relational entities, nor even be regarded as a reasonable hypothetical first approximation.[19]

Until more precise statistical procedures are developed for calculating degrees of freedom for populations of relations,[20] this question can be more appropriately handled by the use of substantive sociological theory.[21] Rather than risking spurious inferences based on invalid tests of significance (Hallinan, 1974; MacFarland and Brown, 1973), when interpreting the statistical analyses conducted in this research, I have relied more heavily on corroboration from other sources of data and sociological criteria (Lieberson, 1985).[22]

Urban Communes Sample

Altogether, a total of 566 adults, 15 years and older, were residing in the 57 communes at the time of the first wave of data collection in the summer of 1974.[23] As one would expect, the commune sample is comprised mainly of young adults (see Table 1:1), but with slightly more men than women. Most in the sample were raised by both parents, lived in a small family with fewer than three siblings, and most grew up in urban locations in middle class circumstances. Although the

majority have Protestant religious backgrounds, Catholic and
Jewish religions also were well represented. Naturally, given
the young age, only a small proportion have ever married and
few report having had a child. Being a well educated group,
most report a white collar or professional occupation, with a
full-time salaried job. While similar to the national population on employment status and class affiliation, it is the
smaller family of origin, the greater probability of a middle
class background, higher education, and a non-blue collar
occupation, that distinguishes the commune sample from the
American population as a whole.

In terms of communal involvement, three fifths of the sample report previous experience with communal living. While
a third are founding members of their present commune, half
had been members for less than a year. Most said they had
joined either for ideological reasons or for more practical con-
siderations of convenience.

Generally, the respondents are quite involved in their commune. Nearly half hold a formal office or position of responsibility, and most said they spent almost all of the three days
prior to being interviewed in or around the communal household. They are also quite committed; more than half feel they
would "definitely reject" an offer of $10,000 to leave their
commune.

As far as the communes themselves are concerned, they
range in size from five[24] to 67 members, with an average of ten
adults. While nearly half had been in existence for two years
or longer, a quarter were founded in the same year the study
started. One out of ten had been established four or more
years earlier and one group was in its ninth year. Fifty
percent were found in inner city slums and transitional
neighborhoods and, although another third were located
within city limits, twenty percent were, somewhat unexpectedly, located in suburban areas. A little over half of the sample
is almost equally divided into Christian/religious, political,
counter-cultural, and household ideological types. A further
quarter has an Eastern religious ideology, and the remaining

twenty percent is equally divided into family and personal growth ideological orientations. Fieldworkers report that the ideological orientation is regarded as "important" by most of the groups.

Nearly all communes have special conditions for admission as members: half want people with certain personal traits or insist on "seeing" the prospective member; a third require a period of trial membership. While, in three fifths of the sample, individuals had a private room, in some of the religious communes five or six members shared the same sleeping space. Most groups employ various elements of formal organization: half rotate or assign communal chores and jobs; virtually every commune has at least a "few" rules that must be followed by everyone — nearly half have "some" or "many" rules; all but two groups have a collectively sanctioned procedure for making decisions about the group; and almost half (mainly those with a religious ideology) are formally affiliated with a larger organization. Finally, most communes require that members share at least one daily meal together.

TABLE 1:1   SOCIAL CHARACTERISTICS OF URBAN COMMUNE SAMPLE COMPARED WITH NATIONAL POPULATION*

	Urban Commune Sample Population (N = 545)	National Population	
		NORC 1974 (N = 1,481)	U.S. Census
Median Age (over 15 only)	25 yrs.	42 yrs.	37 yrs. (1976)[a]
Percentage Male	54%	45%	49% (1975)
SOCIAL BACKGROUND			
Percentage who grew up with both parents in the home	90%	76%	—
Percentage with ≤ 2 siblings in family of origin	73[b]	34	—
Percentage who grew up in rural area or small town (< 50,000 pop.)	29[d]	—	—

TABLE 1:1 SOCIAL CHARACTERISTICS OF URBAN COMMUNE SAMPLE COMPARED WITH NATIONAL POPULATION* — *(continued)*

	Urban Commune Sample Population (N = 545)	National Population	
		NORC 1974 (N = 1,481)	U.S. Census
Percentage who have moved residence 3 or more times	50[e]	—	—
Percentage whose father's occupation is service, farm, or blue collar	28%	71%	—
Religious background:			
Percentage Protestant	44	66	—
Percentage Catholic	26	28	—
Percentage Jewish	19	3	—
Percentage other, mixed	11	3	—

PRESENT SOCIAL STATUS

	Urban Commune Sample Population (N = 545)	NORC 1974 (N = 1,481)	U.S. Census
Percentage single, never married	72%	12%	43% (1974)[c]
Percentage who have had one or more children	20	78	—
Education: percentage with college diploma	50	14	24 (1974 est.)
Percentage with service, farm, or blue collar occupation	27	49	51 (1974)
Employment: percentage not in full-time jobs (regardless of whether seeking one)	54	57	—
Percentage with "middle-class" self-definition:	48	46	—
Religiosity: percentage "strongly agree" that "solution to today's problems is Christ"	30[f]	—	—

---

*Source: adapted from Zablocki (1980), Table 3-1.
[a]Calculated on population over age 14.
[b]N = 211; a subsample who were given indepth interviews.
[c]% of those in age group 18-29 years.
[d]N = 424; valid responses to this item on the Long Form or Short Form.
[e]N = 458; valid responses to this item on the Long Form or Short Form.
[f]N = 346; valid responses to this item on the Attitudes Questionnaire.

Looking Ahead

The book is divided into five sections. Following this "Introduction", Part Two seeks the theoretical tools that we will use in our endeavor to "demystify" charisma. Because his work is still regarded as the foundation for a sociological understanding, Chapter Two undertakes an assessment of the validity of Max Weber's account of "pure" (nonroutinized) charisma. However, not only is Weber's model of charismatic social organization contradicted by the commune data, it is also based on questionable sociological reasoning. Chapter Three, therefore, builds a new theoretical framework.

Using hierarchic logic, two levels of charisma are distinguished — the normative, charisma as a social category; and the relational, charisma as a relationship of rule. Both are validated by the commune data. A third structural level of charisma is postulated — charisma as a distinctive pattern of social organization. It is argued that while communion generates the energy required for social transformation, this energy is highly volatile and must be aligned by power if group stability is to be maintained.

"Substantiation" of this thesis is the concern of Part Three, and the analysis moves in four chapters from simple to increasingly more complex dimensions of social structure. Chapter Four leads off by selecting, from the 13 relational contents mapped in this study, those contents that most differentiate the charismatic from the noncharismatic communes. The analysis is further narrowed by identifying the kind of dyadic bonding that characterizes each content.

Moving from treating each content as a discrete dimension of social structure, Chapter Five examines the nature and form of interrelation among three clusters of relations: first, the contents of positive affect, as the relational components of communion; second, the contents of love, intimacy, and fraternity, to establish the fraternal (nonromantic) nature of love as communion; and finally, the contents of love and power, to show the coexistence of communion and power in charismatic groups.

In Chapter Six, the global organization of these relations is analyzed. Here the unit of analysis changes from dyads to triads, and Holland and Leinhardts' (1976) triadic analysis is used to detect the different patterns predicted for relations of positive affect and power in the charismatic and noncharismatic communes. Multi-level analysis is then employed to verify that these relational patterns are structurally emergent. Finally, the possibility of a spurious association with charisma is checked by examining the relationship between other variables and power and communion.

Chapter Seven completes Part Three by examining evidence on the causal effect of these relational patterns on the stability of charismatic groups. We aim to show that the volatile bonds of communion must be counterbalanced by a strong, collective power structure if stability is to be preserved. Using panel data to test this proposition, our results show that both the structuring and interrelation of power and communion are strongly related to group survival over time.

Part Four moves beyond charisma to address a more general question that our findings raise about the fundamental nature of social organization: namely, to explain why coherent images of global structure can be derived from mappings of discrete dyadic relations. In Chapter Eight, four existing sociological theories are tested; historicist, interactional, normative, and stratificational. However, not only do measures of these theories possess little explanatory power, but the data point to a very different interpretation.

Chapter Nine explains our discovery of coherent global order from mappings of dyads by postulating that social organization is holonomic: that the parts (the dyads) contain information about the organization of the whole (the group). Testing this hypothesis with membership turnover suggests the possibility of a collective order that, while it transcends individual awareness, is enfolded into the mind of each group member. There is also evidence that coherent global structure may be causally related to both group stability and individual behavior.

Chapter Ten (Part Five) concludes the book with a review and some broader speculations. The major findings not only point to an interrelation between love and power that seems fundamental to social organization in general, but also they reveal some striking parallels with forms and processes at other levels of reality.

NOTES

1. The names of all communes and individuals mentioned in this book are pseudonyms to protect the identities of the subjects of this research.
2. This is reinforced by their plain white robes.
3. In an analysis of Weber's usage of charisma in his "Sociology of Religion and the Sociology of Domination," Roth (1975:151) defines the "ideological virtuosi" as: "that minority of persons whose spiritual needs and passionate commitments cannot be satisfied by piecemeal social amelioration or political compromise ... (they) ... embrace a moralistic absolutism that rejects established authority, whether religious or political, and the status quo. These persons are charismatic not only because they claim a legitimacy of their own, but also because they endeavor to form their own groups."
4. One point should be made clear at the outset. My definition of charisma is similar to Zablocki's (1980) in a number of important respects — as exemplified in the emphasis placed on its structural and variable aspects. However, our two definitions also contain points of difference. His is based primarily upon a dynamic conception of the changing boundaries between the self and the collectivity. Mine is based upon a concept of the collective will as manifested in the patterns of relationships among units of the collectivity.
5. There has been some recent interesting work on the psychological and social-psychological dimensions of charisma that lies outside the scope of this research. See Hummel (1974 and 1975), and Stark (1977); and Schiffer (1973), Bord (1975), House (1977), and Swanson (1978), respectively.
6. This is his discussion in the section, "The Principal Characteristics of Charismatic Authority and Its Relation to Forms of Communal Organization," in Weber, 1947:358-369. Weber's model is assessed in Chapter Two.

7. A recent exception is Schweitzer (1984).

8. The traditional approach of survey analysis cannot capture emergent structure, because its units of analysis are discrete, independent entities. It does not directly measure the relations nor relative positions among social entities, and so cannot reveal how the entities are organized. The best we can obtain is a profile of the aggregated characteristics of a system's components. Consequently, valid inference of emergent structure is not justified when this approach is employed (Wellman, 1980).

9. See Berkowitz (1982) or Knoke and Kuklinski (1982) for an introduction to the perspective and methods of network analysis. More advanced discussions are presented by Rogers and Kincaid (1980), Burt (1980), and Leinhardt (ed., 1980). Mitchell (ed., 1969) and Barnes (1972) are still important for the substantive significance of social networks. Nadel's classic, *The Theory of Social Structure* (Nadel, 1957), is an essential source for relational and structural theory.

10. Maureen Hallinan (1974:23-24) defines "measurement error" as the difference between the "true" relational structure and the pattern of responses to a sociometric instrument. "Structural bias" results when measurement operations favor certain relational configurations over others.

11. See the example in Chapter Four (Figure 4:3, page 93) and also the discussion of this problem in Appendix A.

12. Directed by Benjamin Zablocki, the Urban Communes Project evolved from a decade of pioneering research on the changing boundaries of the self and the collective in rural communes. With the Urban Communes Project, Zablocki extended this research to urban communes to investigate with more formal research techniques, many of his early insights.

13. The enumeration of communes was more complete in the smaller cities of Atlanta, Houston, and Minneapolis-Saint Paul. In the larger cities, especially New York and Los Angeles, only a relatively small proportion of the commune population was able to be contacted.

14. Although probability sampling methods could not be employed, due to the vast size of the larger cities and the low profile most communes adopt in urban situations, the Urban Communes Project is confident that the sixty communes sampled are at least representative of those in the six cities and probably representative of urban communes in America (see Zablocki, 1980:371-377). However, because probability sampling procedures were not followed either in choosing the communes

or in selecting subsets of individuals for the administration of some of the data gathering instruments, tests of statistical significance are inappropriate here (Blalock, 1960).

15. See Bradley (1980) for these instruments.

16. See Appendix B for a copy of this instrument.

17. See Bradley (1980:103-116) for a more detailed description of these procedures.

18. To accomplish this mapping, all group members were assembled together. Then the instrument was completed by each person under strict fieldworker supervision to ensure there was no collaboration among members in answering the questions. The lack of such collusion is necessary to establish conditions of independent measurement (Hallinan, 1974).

19. The assumption of statistical independence is immediately violated in two respects. First, a relation is a property that links two elements and, as such, its presence or absence is dependent upon the existence of both elements in the first place. Second, it cannot be assumed, among a given population of relations, that any one relation is necessarily independent of any other relation.

     A brief illustration of the nature of this problem can be given here. The number of dyads possible in a network is $N(N-1)/2$, where N is the number of actors. But information missing about the relations held by any one actor, immediately influences the potential information that can be gathered about each other actor's relations. For example, a population of 10 social actors has $10(10-1)/2$ possible dyads, or 45. Thus, if each individual indicates a relation with the other nine members, and they reciprocate, there will be 45 different dyads. However, if any one individual decides not to hold a relation with the other nine members which, even if they hold a reciprocated relation with one another, there can only be $[(10-1)(10-2)]/2 = 36$ dyads. In those cases where the conditions of statistical independence are met, as in the case of random samples of individuals, the number of degrees of freedom, with no restriction, is equal to the size of the population, N. But, for dyads the degrees of freedom fall somewhere in the range of $\geq N$ or $\leq N(N-1)/2$. Consequently, in our example, the degrees of freedom lie somewhere between ten, the number of social actors, and 45, the number of possible dyads.

20. Until recently, relatively little work had been undertaken on this problem. On the sampling side of this issue, an early effort was made by Goodman (1961) and more recently by Granovetter

(1976). Frank (1978; 1979), Holland and Leinhardt (1981), and Feinberg and Wasserman (1981) have been working to develop statistical models to solve this problem.

21. Expected probabilities for different relational patterns can be derived from the empirical validation of specific models of network structure under varying social conditions. This will establish at least some kind of base-line that is founded on sociological reasoning, and one that can be revised and improved, as necessary, from the results of repeated empirical verification.

22. This question is discussed at greater length in Chapter Six (see pages 142–143) in reference to "triadic analysis" — the particular structural analysis technique employed in this research.

23. This is the total for the 57 communes in which membership is totally voluntary. It excludes three communes with a goal of rehabilitation since membership involved an element of legal coercion.

24. A size criterion of five adults was used in selecting communes for the study. A subsequent check on the exact membership disposition of every adult in all groups reduced the actual number of permanent residents to four adults in the case of two communes.

PART TWO

DEMYSTIFICATION

Spontaneous communitas is nature in dialogue with structure. ... Together, they make up one stream of life, the one supplying power, the other alluvial fertility.

Victor W. Turner, *The Ritual Process* (1969: 140).

Chapter Two

WEBER'S LEGACY

Introduction

Our search for an understanding of charisma's structural foundation should start with an examination of the current sociological accounts of charisma. But, because his work is still so influential,[1] the primary aim of this chapter is to assess the theoretical and empirical validity of Max Weber's conception of charisma. Such an assessment is especially important, for of the many concepts Weber developed, there are few, if any, which have generated so much confusion over meaning and utility. Indeed, some researchers have gone so far as to reject charisma altogether as a hopelessly confused and, therefore, useless concept (Nettler, 1957; Schlesinger, 1960; Etzioni, 1961; and Worsley, 1968). For example, after a long discussion, Worsley asserts that:

> ... there is little hope that we will get far in our efforts to develop and enrich sociological theory with such a blunt instrument as the concept of charisma as a part of our theoretical tool-kit ... (Worsley, 1968: 1iii).

He concludes that charisma's only utility is that by "thinking about its ambiguities ... (it) ... may help us clarify our minds."

But this kind of counsel, if taken literally, has serious consequences for sociological theory. To abandon the concept of charisma, without replacing it with a more useful tool, risks losing the study of important, unique phenomena that the idea of charisma alone singles out for attention (Schweitzer, 1984). Without a concept of charisma, how can we account for the dramatic births and rapid development of modern Russia and China? How can we understand Germany's reawakening following the First World War, the Nazi invasion of Europe, and the events of the Second World War? How do we make sense of the periodic eruptions of the masses — whether under a Kennedy in the developed world, or under a Khomeini in the developing nations? Without the concept of charisma, how, then, can we explain the most tumultuous events and changes of the twentieth century (Bradley, 1985(b))? Clearly, abandoning the concept is just not reasonable; it will only leave sociological theory even more impoverished. A more fruitful approach, and the one I will pursue, is to start over and attempt to build a completely new set of concepts and understanding of charisma. First, however, we must show why Weber's approach has little utility and must, therefore, be put aside.

Charisma as Authority

Types of Authority

For Weber, charisma is one of the three pure types of legitimate authority — the others being traditional and rational-legal. His concept of legitimate authority rests on his concept of imperative coordination, which he sees as the probability that the commands from a given actor will be obeyed by a group (Weber, 1947: 152). Although obedience by group members may be based on ulterior motives or genuine acceptance, the sufficient condition for a reliable and stable system of imperative control, is belief in the legitimacy of the basis and source of control. Consequently, every system attempts to establish and cultivate belief in its legitimacy. And, because the kind of legitimacy is directly associated with different organizational forms, and has important social consequences both for individuals and the group, it is useful to classify the types of authority by the kind of claim to legitimacy typically made by each:

> What is important is the fact that in a given case the particular claim to legitimacy is ... treated as 'valid'; that this fact confirms the position of the persons claiming authority and that it helps to determine the choice of means of its exercise (Weber, 1947: 327).

Using the validity of claims to legitimacy as the differentiating criterion, Weber distinguishes among three pure types of legitimate authority. The first is *rational-legal authority* and is based on a belief in the legality of universalistic, normative rules. The rules are impersonal and apply not to individuals but to specified positions of authority. It is the rules that give the incumbents of such positions the right to issue commands to subordinates within the scope of the authority vested in the position. Compliance by subordinates, therefore, is based on their recognition of the legality of the person in authority to issue orders. This type of authority, Weber suggested, is found primarily in the bureaucratic organizations of the industrialized world.

Traditional authority, his second type, rests on custom: an "established belief in the sanctity of immemorial traditions and the legitimacy of the status of those exercising authority under them" (Weber, 1947: 328). Obedience in this system is personalized and, because of accustomed obligations, is owed to the "person" of the chief who occupies the traditionally sanctioned position of authority. Because legitimacy is based on established customs, both the person in authority and the person subject to authority are bound, within its sphere, to each other by tradition. The positions and the authority relationship between them are ascribed. Weber sees feudal and preindustrial societies as characterized by this form of authority.

The third type is *charismatic authority*, and rests "on devotion to the specific and exceptional sanctity, heroism, or exemplary character of an individual person, and of the normative patterns or order revealed or ordained by him" (Weber, 1947: 328). The legitimacy of charismatic authority depends upon the recognition of the charismatic qualities ("the gift of grace") that the leader is believed to possess and which have to be repeatedly "proved" to the followers. As a consequence, legitimacy lasts only so long as the followers' belief in charismatic inspiration remains. As a revolutionary force, charismatic authority is an instrument for social change. It is a transitional form — a temporary and unstable phenomenon in which the problem of leadership succession requires the transformation of charismatic authority into either a traditional or rational-legal type.

For Weber, then, charismatic authority stands apart from both rational-legal and traditional authority because it is not a routine system of social organization; it is different from the former because it does not establish a formalized body of universal, impersonalized rules; it is different from the latter because, by repudiating the past, it is opposed to custom and tradition.

"Pure" Charisma

Having differentiated charismatic from traditional and rational-legal types of authority, Weber goes on to construct a detailed model of the social organization of "pure" (personalized and nonroutinized) charisma. In addition to being very clear about what he regards as the "principal characteristics" of pure charisma, Weber is also quite explicit about those elements that are specifically *not* charismatic (see Figure 2:1). Since Weber reasons that the charismatic group is communal in form, the communes' data provide an ideal site in which to test his theory.

Organizational Imperatives:	DEFINITELY CHARISMATIC	DEFINITELY NONCHARISMATIC
DIRECTION	Recognition and legitimation of leader's authority based on 'sign' or proof of divine grace. Followers recognize duty of complete personal devotion.	Clearly defined hierarchy, scope of authority, and spheres of competence.
ORGANIZATION	Recruitment, selection of administrative staff, and allocation of tasks by leader, according to individual's "charismatic qualities."	Recruitment based on technical skills. Standards for promotion, dismissal, and salary. Routine organization, specialized division of labor, and an administrative apparatus.
REGULATION	By formal divine revelations, decrees, and judgments of leader.	Formal rules, legal principles, and judicial procedures.
SUSTENANCE	Communalistic with leader. Means of support by voluntary gifts and booty.	Regularized means of support.
* Derived from Weber, 1947: 358-363.		

2:1 *Weber's "Principal Characteristics of Charismatic Authority"**

Weber's model of pure charisma rests on two postulates:

1: That there exists among followers some need, goal, or aspiration that is unfulfilled by the existing order.

2: That the followers submit to the leader, based on a belief in his or her possession of charisma, expecting realization of their unfulfilled wants.

Because the leader is seen as sole possessor of the means (the exceptional powers) for achieving the charismatic promise:

Proposition 2:1 There is a minimal delegation of power and authority by the leader to the followers.

Since there is little delegation of authority:
Proposition 2:2 Each follower is directly accountable to the leader; there is a direct, personalized relationship of authority between the leader and each follower.

The absolute control and authority of the leader means that:
Proposition 2:3 The leader holds complete control over the allocation of positions (recruitment, selection of lieutenants and staff, task allocation, etc.). These are assigned on the basis of the individual's "charismatic qualities".

The disaffection with the existing order and repudiation of routine organization, including economic enterprise and material acquisition, means that:
Proposition 2:4 Sustenance needs will be met by a communistic, subsistence economy based on gifts, booty, etc., involving few economic activities with a minimal division of labor.

With little delegation of authority and division of labor, there is also:
Proposition 2:5 A minimal amount of hierarchy and formal structure concerning positions of authority and responsibility. Hierarchically, the structure has three levels: the leader; his/her lieutenants, staff and disciples; and the followers.

The limited hierarchy and formal structure means that:
Proposition 2:6 There are no formalized rules, institutions, or legal-judicial procedures. All judgments are made by the leader on a case-by-case basis as proclamations or decrees.

Insofar as the followers continue to believe in the leader's charisma, and given the absence of any formal or routine organization:
Proposition 2:7 The whole structure (duties, activities, and organization) can be changed by a decree from the leader.

Finally, because the durability of charismatic leadership depends upon the leader's repeated proof of continued possession of the "gift of grace", Weber concluded that:

Proposition 2:8 Charismatic leadership is a temporary and unstable phenomenon, always contingent upon the leader's ability to prove his charismatic powers to the followers. To become a stable and permanent relationship, charismatic leadership must undergo routinization to become a traditional or rational authority structure, or a combination of both.

In essence, then, Weber's model of charismatic organization is that of a communal social form, with few elements of formal organization, little division of labor, nonregularized economic activity, and minimal hierarchy under the absolute authority of the charismatic leader.

Empirical Assessment

The data presented in Table 2:1, however, provide a very different picture of charismatic social organization than Weber's model. They show, in contradiction to Proposition 2:4, that the charismatic communes[2] spend much time and energy building a viable economic base. Restaurants, food stores, clothing stores, bookstores, second-hand markets, car washes, and various personal growth classes are some examples of the variety of businesses owned and operated by the charismatic communes in this study. In some cases, this economic activity is also supplemented by members holding regular noncommune jobs and/or by odd jobs such as window washing, house painting, gardening, and lawn mowing. In one group (Love from Above), the members got so carried away with profit and economic success, that their charismatic leader had to remind them that economic activity was only a foundation for their real task of achieving and spreading "truth." The elaborate formal organization of this group can be seen in Figure 2:2.[3]

TABLE 2:1   SELECTED CHARACTERISTICS OF COMMUNES[1] BY CHARISMATIC GROUPING[2]

COMMUNE CHARACTERISTICS	Charismatic (28)*	Noncharismatic (29)	Total (57)
Mean size	12.4	7.6	9.9
Percentage founded during or before 1972	43%	41%	42%
Percentage upper-class or middle-class neighborhood	46	35	40
Percentage affiliated to larger organization	86	3	44
Percentage in which individuals have own room	25	90	58
Percentage with "strong" "'we'" group feeling	57	28	42
Percentage with "many" rules	39	3	21
Percentage assign or rotate chores	71	31	51
Percentage have communal business or jobs	25	7	16
Percentage have daily communal meals	89	62	75
Mean proportion of members legal or informal couple[3]	.19	.36	.28 (468)

ADMISSION REQUIREMENTS

	Charismatic	Noncharismatic	Total
Percentage requiring trait or exposure	29%	76%	53%
Percentage requiring trial membership or novitiate	46	21	33

IDEOLOGICAL ORIENTATION

	Charismatic	Noncharismatic	Total
Religious	71%	14%	40%
Political or counter-cultural	11	41	26
Personal growth or family household	18	45	34
	100%	100%	100%

IDEOLOGICAL STRENGTH

	Charismatic	Noncharismatic	Total
Percentage with "high" ideological consensus	71%	14%	42%
Percentage ideology "important" to group	89	69	79

	Charismatic (28)*	Noncharismatic (29)	Total (57)
LEADERSHIP TYPE			
Resident leader	14%	14%	15%
Absentee leader	79	3	39
Multiple leaders	7	24	16
No leaders	0	59	30
	100%	100%	100%
DECISION MAKING TYPE			
Percentage monarchical	36%	0%	18%
Percentage consensual/ democratic	39	100	51
Percentage anarchistic	7	0	4
MEMBER INVOLVEMENT AND PARTICIPATION[3]			
Percentage hold formal positions	52%	24%	41% (273)
Mean # hours spent in commune over last 3 days	55.7	43.3	50.7 (299)
MEAN # HOURS A WEEK SPENT DOING[3]			
Communal cleaning	3.7	3.0	3.4 (306)
Preparing communal meals	3.4	2.2	2.9 (304)
Washing dishes	2.5	2.4	2.5 (306)
Communal laundry & mending	1.0	0.3	0.7 (307)
Communal accounts	1.4	0.3	1.0 (307)
Spreading commune's message	6.8	0.9	4.1 (283)
Personal counselling	3.3	1.7	2.6 (299)

*N = ( )
1. The total percentages in this and later tables in this chapter may differ slightly from those presented in Table 1:1. This is because the earlier table is based on the complete urban commune sample of 60 communes used in Zablocki's (1980) study, whereas this and all subsequent tables are based upon the restricted sample of 57 groups used in this study.
2. The term "charismatic grouping," as used here and in a number of subsequent tables, means that measurement was made at the group level of analysis. Hence the number of cases will correspond to the number of communes in a given category. Exceptions involving aggregated individual-level data will be flagged by a footnote. Tables presenting analysis of data collected at the individual level, but aggregated by commune, will be designated by the term "charismatic affiliation."
3. Aggregated by commune.

The data also contradict most of the other propositions: jobs are often rotated than personally assigned by the charismatic leader (Propositions 2:3 and 2:5); members average more time, than those in noncharismatic groups, performing communal chores and tasks (Propositions 2:4 and 2:5); many of those interviewed hold positions of responsibility for which the power and scope of authority is clearly defined (Propositions 2:1 and 2:5); there are formalized rules and procedures that, in some of the larger charismatic communes, are codified in writing (Proposition 2:6); the process of joining a charismatic group is formally institutionalized, often requiring a period of trial membership or novitiate (Propositions 2:5 and 2:6); and decisions about the group are often decentralized through consensual or democratic decision-making procedures (Propositions 2:1 and 2:7). Moreover, field observations reveal that even the generation of collective energy through the shared experience of communion is ritualized and usually follows a formalized prescription (Proposition 2:5). In short, none of the six propositions derived from Weber's model we have considered here are supported by these data. And, when the appropriate data are examined, for Propositions 2:2 and 2:8 (see below, Chapters Six and Seven, respectively), support is found only for the former.

There are also theoretical problems with Weber's characterization. If, as he maintains, charisma is antithetical to formal organization and regularized economic activity, how can the charismatic group possibly sustain itself from such unpredictable and unreliable sustenance sources as gifts and booty? Surely, a first priority of a charismatic collectivity that has broken with the established order, must be provision for its members' basic physical, emotional, and social needs on a regular and predictable basis. Without providing for such fundamentals as shelter, food, clothing, protection, a sense of belonging and order, charisma cannot be anything more than a fleeting expression of collective desire. If a charismatic group is to be durable and able to work toward achieving the promised utopia, it must make certain that basic everyday

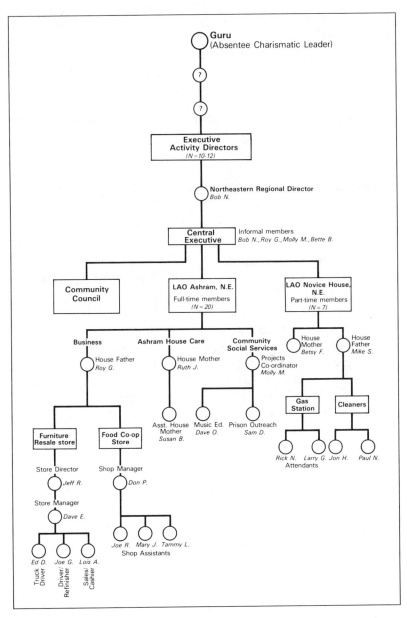

2:2 *Formal Organization in a Charismatic Commune (Love From Above, N.E.)*

needs are met smoothly and reliably. The task of implement-
ing the charismatic vision is a huge, all-consuming job which
requires that members are free from other worries and constraints to concentrate their energies on this purpose. Consequently, to persist, even for the short run, charisma must have
a rationalized, efficient organizational foundation that not
only provides for basic needs, but also can withstand problems and challenges from outside.

Temporally Bound?

Weber

Aside from the theoretical and empirical limitations we have
identified in Weber's model, there is another fundamental
aspect of his view of "pure" charisma that we must question.
This is the notion that charisma is temporally-bound — a
social form that is limited to premodern stages of social evolution and development. In contrast to the traditional and
rational-legal types of authority, Weber sees charisma as a
temporary, unstable form; a transitional bridge, involved in
the transformation from a pre-industrial to an industrial
social order. Unlike these more permanent and stable forms,
charisma is not an end in itself. Rather, it is a means to an
end: a structure by which radical social change can be
brought about.

By differentiating "pure" from "routinized" charisma,
Weber sees two stages in the process of change. The first is a
radical departure from established order and the creation of a
new pattern. The second involves institutionalizing the new
order into a regularized pattern of everyday activity. Pure
charisma, therefore, is a structure which can break the mould
of traditional order; routinized charisma is that which builds
an institutional mould to regularize and perpetuate the new.
For Weber, then, pure charisma is incompatible with rational-
legal order and, as a consequence, can occur only under pre-
industrial social conditions.

Shils

A variant of Weber's thesis is presented by Edward Shils (1968). He argues that charisma does exist in the modern world; but only in its routinized form as charisma of an office. He sees an increasing depersonalization of the social relations among members of large, complex, industrialized societies. This is a result of the continuous development and application of new technology, and the concommitant rationalization of social organization. While he also sees the demise of personalized or pure charisma in advanced societies, Shils suggests that the sheer size, complexity, and power of modern, bureaucratic organization engenders, in the individual, a sense of mystical wonder and "awe" toward those who hold positions of power and responsibility in these omnipotent systems. According to Shils, then, charisma has not died out in modern societies but, rather, as charisma of an office, it has adapted itself to the predominant social form of bureaucratic organization.

Wilson

More recently, Brian Wilson in his essay, *The Noble Savages* (Wilson, 1975) has contended that charisma is an attribute of traditional social organization. He argues that charisma emerges under "primitive" psychological and social conditions, where social relationships and social organization are personified, so that complete faith and trust can exist about the superhuman competence of a particular individual. As the "extreme exemplification of thinking in the personal idiom," charisma "is a relation of supreme trust in the total competence of an individual" (Wilson, 1975: 20-31). Because relations are depersonalized in modern societies, structured by rational-technological criteria to occur between "segmentary role performers", and not between "total individuals," charisma will die out as modern forms replace more traditional modes of social organization.

Underlying these views, is the idea that an important prerequisite for charisma is a belief that the present means for providing for human needs are inadequate, and that this problem cannot be solved by the application of "rational" knowledge — rational, that is, from the viewpoint of an established order, whether traditional or modern. Charisma involves means that go beyond the rationality of the existing order. Therefore, charisma is most likely when rational knowledge is inadequate and conditions of uncertainty exist.

By itself this seems a reasonable idea. It is supported not only by interview materials examined in this research,[4] but also by other studies.[5] Fundamental to this idea, however, is the assumption that modern society is characterized by an evergrowing body of rational knowledge that will increasingly satisfy human needs and thereby reduce uncertainty.

But for this to be true, one must further assume either a finite set of human wants and problems, and the achievement of a corresponding body of perfect knowledge, or that rational knowledge will at least keep abreast of social aspirations. Essentially, this means postulating that the rationalism of modern social order will provide the most effective way of orchestrating and achieving social change, and that it will also provide a socially satisfying interpretation of the reality and meaning of human existence. Therefore, charisma is unlikely in an advanced society because the rational-technological order provides the complete means for satisfying human needs, and charisma, as a consequence, becomes redundant. Charisma, thus, is temporally bound by its association with only particular stages of social development. For Wilson, it exists under certain primitive social and psychological conditions. For Weber, it occurs during the transition from a traditional to a rational-legal social order. For Shils, routinized charisma exists in bureaucratized contexts, while pure or personalized charisma is limited to earlier phases of social evolution.

Critical Assessment

The thesis that charisma is tied to a particular stage of social development is questionable on both empirical and theoretical grounds. Given the logic of the thesis, we should not expect to find pure or personalized charisma at all in the United States, since charisma should not exist under modern, rational-technological conditions. Consequently, the fact that all 28 of the charismatic communes are instances of pure charisma, in which the members believe that charismatic powers are possessed by particular individuals (personalized charisma) rather than adhering to positions of leadership (routinized charisma), is a direct contradiction of the thesis.

But even by a less stringent criterion, the thesis lacks compelling empirical support. For example, it is reasonable to expect that those commune members raised in and exposed to "higher" more "complex" forms of rationality and technology in the United States (those from higher socio-economic and urban backgrounds), will be less likely to join charismatic groups.[6] However, the data presented in Table 2:2 do not provide clear support for this expectation. The picture that emerges from this material is one in which individuals from either lower or higher socio-economic groups are susceptible to charisma. Thus, while a lower proportion of the charismatic members had a middle or upper class background, or have achieved middle-class socio-economic status, as many as 26% of them did grow up in a middle or upper class home, and that 43% are college educated or better, and that just as many have a professional, administrative, or managerial occupation.[7]

A second point emerges from Table 2:2. There are even fewer differences between the charismatic and noncharismatic members when other social characteristics are considered. Those in the charismatic communes are just as likely to be from a non-urban background, to have been raised in an intact family, to have moved residence three or more times, or to have had a strong religious background as those in the noncharismatic groups. And, finally, the likelihood of belonging to a charismatic commune is little influenced by sex, age, or marital status.

TABLE 2:2   SELECTED SOCIAL CHARACTERISTICS OF COMMUNE MEMBERS BY CHARISMATIC AFFILIATION[1]

	Charismatic	Noncharismatic	Total
Number of members	347	219	566
Percentage of sample	61.3%	38.7%	100%
SOCIAL BACKGROUND			
Percentage from rural/small town	31%	27%	29% (424)
Percentage grew up with both parents	87	93	89 (467)
Percentage moved residence 3 or more times	47	45	50 (458)
Percentage father's occupation professional/administrative/ managerial	26	47	34 (424)
Percentage religious past:			
Protestant	37	50	43
Catholic	33	24	29 (220)
SOCIAL STATUS			
Percentage males	58%	50%	54% (467)
Mean age	25.1 yrs.	25.9 yrs.	25.5 yrs. (461)
Percentage never married	75%	67%	72% (467)
Percentage never had kids	82	83	82 (455)
Percentage with college education or better	43	61	50 (447)

	Charismatic	Noncharismatic	Total
Percentage with full or part time job	65%	70%	67% (458)
Percentage with professional/ administrative/managerial occupation	43	65	53 (273)

COMMUNAL EXPERIENCE

	Charismatic	Noncharismatic	Total
Percentage with previous communal experience	63%	52%	59% (456)
Percentage joined commune in 1974-75	57	52	55 (459)
Percentage a founding member	29	49	37 (464)
Reason for joining: Percentage ideological	51	11	31
Percentage convenience	12	38	25 (208)

SELECTED ATTITUDES

	Charismatic	Noncharismatic	Total
Percentage "strongly agree" solution today's problems is Christ	45%	11%	30% (346)
Percentage "strongly agree" commune is a means not an end	58	31	46 (345)
Percentage "strongly agree" commune is family	57	18	40 (349)
Percentage "strongly disagree" distance between self and commune	78	54	67 (355)
Percentage "definitely reject" $10,000 offer to leave commune	60	48	55 (437)

1. The data in this table have been aggregated by commune.

Before we consider some theoretical problems with this thesis, it is worth noting that clearer differences do emerge when measures of communal involvement are examined (see Table 2:2). The charismatic members are less likely to have previously experienced communal living, or to be a founding member of their group, and they are more likely to have joined for ideological reasons. This greater ideological orientation is reflected in their stronger religious attitudes. They also are more likely to regard the commune as their family, and see their group as a means to a goal rather than an end in itself. Finally, as we saw above in Table 2:1, they tend to spend more time on day-to-day communal activities and spreading the group's philosophy.

Overall, then, it is apparent that the major differences in member characteristics are related more to the differences between the two types of communes than to the social backgrounds of individuals. These results provide some support for the idea that charisma is a potential in all social structures. The structure itself may become charismatic when a collectivity is under great stress, or survival is threatened and a new form of social organization is required. Under these conditions, virtually anyone may be susceptible to charisma's power and influence.

Beyond Rationality

The plausibility of the thesis that charisma is temporally bound also can be questioned on theoretical grounds. Basically, there seems no reason to assume that perfect rational knowledge of human needs is attainable by any social order, modern or otherwise, in the immediate future. If anything, just the opposite seems more likely: that while new knowledge provides solutions to current problems, it also expands the frontiers of the unknown by raising new questions, creating new aspirations and implications, and producing new possibilities for human development. Put simply, new knowledge both resolves and creates uncertainty.

While it is true that uncertainty increases dramatically during the period of transition from a preindustrial to an industrial order, this does not preclude a similarly dramatic social transformation in the future. Indeed, there seems a very real prospect of much uncertainty when, at some point in the future, humankind may be confronted with more advanced forms of life in the universe. If the rationality of any social order's system of knowledge is relative to the experience and the context of that order, and relative to other potential forms, then there seems to be no strong reason why, even in technologically advanced societies, rational knowledge will be perfect and uncertainty unknown. It is not reasonable, therefore, to contend that pure charisma is limited to the less developed stages of social evolution. Charisma is not a response to the past, but emerges as new needs are posed by the unknown future.

There is a comforting element to the thesis that charisma is temporally bound. It is reassuring to believe, in a modern society where the majority of people are highly educated and "rational" and, therefore, supposedly no longer embrace mystical beliefs, or magic, or superstition, that people are beyond the disruptive sway of charisma's powerful reach. It is more disquieting to entertain the thought that everyone, under the right circumstances, may be susceptible to charisma's awesome power.

In sum, there is little of Max Weber's thinking about pure charisma that is not questionable on empirical and theoretical grounds. It is time, therefore, to go beyond Weber and build a new understanding of charisma — an understanding that, in both of these respects, aims at greater validity.

NOTES

1. A recent example is Schweitzer's (1984) study of some fifty-five charismatic leaders of the twentieth century. Despite his strong criticism of Weber, which assails the core of Weber's theory of charisma, Schweitzer builds his own concept of "synergistic charisma" on a Weberian foundation (see Bradley, 1985b).

2. The reader is reminded that the procedures employed to measure charisma are described above in Chapter One (page 15). It is important to note here that all of the communes classified as "charismatic" are instances of "pure" charisma, in that the charisma was believed by the members to adhere to a particular person. None of the charismatic communes were far enough along in the process of institutionalizing charisma to a social position to be classified as "routinized" charisma. This is discussed at greater length in Chapter Three.

3. All of the individuals mentioned in Figure 2:1 (the names are fictitious) are members of the commune.

4. A major theme in the responses of the charismatic members to a question about their "reasons" for joining their commune, was that they had been unsuccessful in numerous attempts, in satisfying their needs and aspirations through more conventional societal channels.

5. See the studies reviewed by Worsley (1968) and by Wilson (1975).

6. Schiffer (1973: 7) presents another version of the thesis when he contends that the "irrational forces" that promote charisma depend upon the level of education achieved by a population.

7. Schweitzer's data on the geo-political distribution of twentieth century (national-level) charismatic leaders are pertinent here. More than a quarter (27.3%) of his sample of 55 charismatics are from the "advanced democracies"; this includes as many as eleven charismatic leaders from the United States. The percentage distributions across his other categories are: "early democracies," 21.8%; "military regimes," 20.0%; "communist regimes," 20.0%; "fascist regimes," 10.9% (see Schweitzer, 1984: Table 1.1, pp. 14–15).

Chapter Three

RETHINKING
CHARISMA

Introduction

In our everyday thinking we see charisma as a variable phenomenon. We recognize that it can occur in a variety of ways, at different levels in society, with varying degrees of intensity, producing a wide range of possible consequences. Most often the term is used to capture the inexplicable powers of persuasion that a particular individual is believed to possess. These powers represent a great potential for influence and change; they are in some special way, magical or mystical in nature. The person who possesses them is set apart from everyone else.[1]

At other times, we use the term to acknowledge that something more is present; that a powerful, all-encompassing relationship of leadership exists between the charismatic individual and a band of followers. So strong is the belief in the leader's charismatic powers, that the followers place their destiny in his hands. It is as if they have fallen under a magical spell; they become submissive, obedient, enraptured — blind in their absolute loyalty. His authority over them seems boundless.

Finally, we occasionally use the term charisma to describe a revolutionary structure boiling with explosive levels of collective energy and awesome in its power for social metamorphosis. We think of a charismatic structure in quantum terms: when it is successful, it can result in a radically new social order that represents a fundamental break with the past; or, if it fails, it may implode in a burst of self-destructive energy.

These common usages of charisma represent three distinct concepts: charisma as a social category, charisma as a social relationship, and charisma as a particular form of social organization.[2] Each concept corresponds to a separate level of social reality — the normative, the relational, and the structural — nested in a hierarchical order so that each incorporates the level preceding it. Aside from being grounded in our everyday notions of charisma, these concepts capture what is essential and clarify what is distinctive about the phenomenon in its different manifestations. These distinctions provide the foundation for a typology of charismatic groups and a relational theory of charismatic social organization that are developed in this chapter. But we seek more than theoretical utility; we also aim to show that these concepts have empirical validity.

I. A Social Category

Charisma must first exist as a social category in the normative framework of a group, as a social definition that identifies and labels certain qualities of an individual as "charismatic". It is only then, that beliefs can emerge to acknowledge the presence of charisma in a particular instance. In this sense, the social category of charismatic is part of the social structure — a "nominal parameter" in Blau's (1977) terms — and it exists independently of any particular person who may be seen this way. Whether or not the attributes labelled as charismatic actually exist is not important from a sociological view. What is important is that people believe them to be real, and in so doing, incorporate these qualities into the social construction of reality as a social category. Incorporated into social reality this way, the attributes signalled as "charismatic" thus have the potential for becoming the basis for social action (Berger and Luckmann, 1966).

Normative Elements

There are two normative elements in the attribution of charismatic qualities to an individual. The first is a belief that the individual is endowed with extraordinary powers and abilities; extraordinary, in that they are seen as exemplifying perfection and, accordingly, are rare (Roth, 1975). As we will see, such qualities are not solely, nor even primarily, special talents for leadership, but can be almost any highly refined talent or ability that a group may project on to an individual (Schiffer, 1973; Schweitzer, 1974/5).[3]

Alone, however, this first ingredient does not distinguish charismatic attributes from other qualities or talents that are also seen as exceptional or unusual. What must be present, in addition, is what Wilson (1975) has referred to as the "myth of charisma": the belief that there is a divine or supernatural basis to the exceptional powers (Friedrich, 1961). These special abilities are not available to the ordinary person; they are perceived as a "'gift of grace'" (Weber, 1947:360). It is this second ingredient that is the psychological basis of charisma's revolutionizing power. For it is acknowledgement of other sources of knowledge and power, beyond the bounds of prescribed rationality, that permits the individual to entertain the idea of an alternative social order. By recognizing that other realities are possible, an established order thus lays the seed for its own destruction and raises the spectre of a radically different social future.

Despite the theoretical justification for these criteria, a more restricted concept of charisma has emerged from research on so-called "super charismatic" individuals. The view from these studies is that charisma is based primarily

on the recognition of exceptional talents for leadership possessed by certain special individuals (for examples see;
Schlesinger, 1960; Burns, 1978; Willner, 1984).[4] From this perspective, then, we would expect more recognition of leadership abilities among the members of charismatic groups than
by those in noncharismatic groups. However, this is not borne
out by the evidence from the communes.

TABLE 3:1   ATTRIBUTIONS OF SELECTED SOCIAL
QUALITIES AMONG MEMBERS BY CHARISMATIC
AFFILIATION (RANK ORDER)[1]

Charismatic Mean[2]		Noncharismatic Mean	
.130	Supportive	.257	Supportive
.119	DECISIVE	.203	INFLUENTIAL
.113	Loving	.203	STRONG
.109	STRONG	.200	Loving
.100	INFLUENTIAL	.186	DECISIVE
.098	Intuitive	.158	Intuitive
.089	Passive	.153	Sexy
.083	DOMINANT	.132	DOMINANT
.075	CHARISMATIC	.117	Passive
.055	Dependent	.111	CHARISMATIC
.052	Holy	.098	Dependent
.050	Sexy	.092	Narcissistic
.042	Narcissistic	.058	Holy
.035	Motivates me	.035	Motivates me
N = ( )	(2291)		(1158)

1. Since these data are relational and violate the assumption of statistical independence, a rank
    order correlation cannot be used appropriately here.
2. Averaged by commune.

In Table 3:1 there is little to differentiate charismatic
members from noncharismatic members on a rank ordering
of leadership qualities (in capitalized type), and other personal characteristics they attributed to individuals in their
respective communes. While there is some difference in
the rank order of individual items, the top five qualities
(DECISIVE, INFLUENTIAL, loving, STRONG, and supportive)
are the same for both sets of members and include three of

the five leadership traits. The other two leadership characteristics *(DOMINANT,* and *CHARISMATIC)* are not seen as
salient and appear in the bottom half of the 14 qualities listed.
What is striking about these data is that the rank order for
both categories of members is so similar.[5]

It would appear, then, that such a restricted concept of
charisma is not able to capture what is distinctive. As a social
category, charisma is more than the recognition of exceptional
leadership talents and potential — no matter how extraordinary these skills may be in reality. Fundamentally, it is the
existence of a separate category in the group's normative
framework that creates a departure from the usual and
accepted way of thinking about leadership. This separate category institutionalizes the idea of a radical break with the
established social order by recognizing sources of knowledge
and power that lie outside a conventional, everyday reality.

Clear evidence of a supernatural dimension to the social
category of charismatic can be seen in Table 3:2. In reply
to an open-ended question, asking if there was someone
either in or associated with the commune whom they
believed possessed "special spiritual (or magical) powers or
gifts," 43% of the answers from the charismatic members
mentioned some kind of supernatural talent: "prophecy and
vision," an "ability to move to higher levels of consciousness," "able to see an outcome before it happens," has
"psychic healing abilities," "gifts of the spirit," etc. Only 14%
of these responses mentioned a leadership skill as a "special"
power or gift.[6] Furthermore, 59% of the 116 charismatic
members who answered this question cited at least one supernatural quality; only 24% and 17% said "no one" has special
talents, or listed abilities that did not contain a supernatural
element, respectively.

These results are in strong contrast to the noncharismatic
members; only 7% of their answers contained a supernatural
element, and these came from just 4% of the 105 who
responded. The noncharismatic members felt that either
"no one" had special powers or gifts (52%), or they named a

person to whom they attributed special but not supernatural talents or abilities (44%).[7] It is specialized knowledge or understanding, exceptional leadership skills, or unusually strong personal support for action in the existing social order, that is important to those in the noncharismatic groups. It is only when the conventional means for social action are seen as ineffective or inaccessible that knowledge and power from some alternative reality becomes salient.

TABLE 3:2   ATTRIBUTIONS OF "SPECIAL SPIRITUAL/MAGICAL POWERS OR GIFTS" BY CHARISMATIC AFFILIATION

SPECIAL POWERS & GIFTS[1]	Charismatic	Noncharismatic	TOTAL
Spiritual, divine, or psychic; or prophecy or vision	43.2%	6.5%	32.6%
Knowledge, discernment, or insight	21.6	32.9	24.9
Leadership, guidance, or judgement	14.1	21.1	16.1
Teaching or communication	12.4	9.2	11.5
Personal empathy & support	6.5	22.4	11.1
Unclassifiable	2.2	7.9	3.8
TOTAL	100.0%	100.0%	100.0%
	(185)*	(76)	(261)

1. These data are from the 221 members who were administered the Long Form interview schedule (five members from each group). Unfortunately, due to time and budget constraints, this instrument was not administered to the ten communes in Boston.
* N = ( ); multiple responses were given by some individuals.

The "Charismatic"

We have seen, then, that as a social category, charisma has two normative elements; the attribution of extraordinary powers or abilities to an individual, and the belief that these qualities have a supernatural basis. If we think of these as conceptual dimensions, within the belief in the supernatural hierarchically nested in the attribution of extraordinary powers or abilities, and examine the logical combinations, a typology of three distinct social categories is generated: the *ordinary* person, the *virtuoso*, and the *charismatic* (see Figure 3:1). The typology enables a clear differentiation of the charismatic from the virtuoso, with which it is sometimes confounded (see, for example, Schweitzer, 1974/5: 151-153).

The typology in Figure 3:1 poses two questions. The first, is whether a given individual is believed to possess extraordinary powers. If the answer is no, the individual is classified as an ordinary person. If the answer is yes, the second question is whether or not the exceptional powers also are believed to be derived from a supernatural origin. If the powers are not seen as having a supernatural basis, the person is classified as a virtuoso. If the powers are thought to have a supernatural basis, the individual is classified as charismatic.

To be regarded as a virtuoso is to be recognized as unusually learned and skilled in some special way — a person with talents that have been refined to the point of virtual perfection. Examples of the virtuoso are great thinkers such as Newton or Einstein, a great artist or playwright such as Michelangelo or Shakespeare, entrepreneurs or inventors such as Henry Ford or Thomas Edison. The virtuoso, then, is a special category reserved for unusually talented individuals. The key element that differentiates the virtuoso from the charismatic, is the belief that the former's extraordinary talents are purely natural abilities, abilities that have been refined through much learning and practice. Unlike the qualities attributed to the charismatic, these talents are not seen as a 'gift of grace' nor the result of divine inspiration. The virtuoso has no relationship with the supernatural.

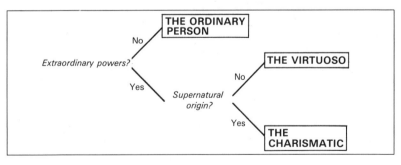

3:1 *Dimensional Logic for the Social Category "Charismatic"*

II. A Social Relationship

Charismatic Leadership

The existence of beliefs attributing charismatic qualities to an individual, by itself, does not establish a relationship of charismatic leadership between a collectivity and an individual. In order for this to exist, the charismatic person must establish a "rule over men" in "which the governed submit because of their belief in the extraordinary quality of the specific person" (Weber, 1946: 295). As we have just established, possession of an "extraordinary quality" sufficient to be seen as charismatic involves recognition of connection with the supernatural. Thus, it is only when leadership is based directly on the exceptional non-worldly powers attributed to an individual, that charismatic rule exists.

A second consideration concerns a distinction between two different kinds of charismatic rule. Building on Bierstedt's distinction between "leadership" and "authority" (Bierstedt, 1954: 71-72), Bendix (1960: 298-328) shows that Weber had two kinds of charismatic rule in mind. One is Weber's pure type of charismatic domination in which "the exercise of power is bound up with a concrete person and his distinctive qualities" (Bendix, 1960: 307). This Bendix labels *charismatic leadership*. It is a personal relationship between the leader and the led, based on their recognition of the leader's qualities as a unique individual. Thus the charisma is not transferable to anyone else.

In order to be transferred, charismatic rule must undergo "routinization" and be transformed into a "depersonalized" quality. This second type of charismatic relationship, is routinized charisma (charisma of an office), and adheres to any incumbent of a position of rule that is regarded as charismatic. Consequently, it "may be transmitted to the members of a family or become the attribute of an office or institution regardless of the persons involved" (Bendix, 1960: 308). Bendix labels this second type as *charismatic authority*. We will use Bendix's terminology from here on.[8]

Typology of Charismatic Leadership

By collapsing the two normative dimensions into one, adding two relational dimensions (whether rule over a collective has been instituted, and whether the rule has been routinized), and extending the hierarchical logic accordingly, a typology of four kinds of charismatic leadership is constructed: viz, groups with low potential for charismatic leadership, groups with high charismatic potential, groups in which charismatic leadership has been established, and groups in which charismatic authority is institutionalized (see Figure 3:2). Slightly modified in its application, this typology is the theoretical basis for my classification of the communes into four varieties of charismatic groups. Let us consider this classification and some corroborating data before describing the categories themselves.

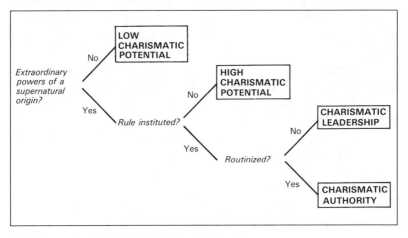

3:2 *Dimensional Logic for Charismatic Typology*

Using the qualitative measurement procedures described in Chapter One, 23 communes were classified as having *low charismatic potential*, since there was no evidence of a collectively held belief that anyone possessed charismatic qualities (see Table 3:3). While, in six groups, there were shared beliefs recognizing the need for a leader who held charismatic powers, these communes had yet to find such a person and institute a relationship of charismatic rule; they are groups with *high charismatic potential*. In 28 communes, however, charismatic rule had been established. Although charisma was personalized to a particular individual in all of these groups, only in six of them was the charismatic leader actually a permanent resident living with the group. In the other 22 communes, the charismatic leader was absent and lived in some other location. Accordingly, these communes have been labelled as *resident charismatic leadership* and *absentee charismatic leadership*, respectively. As we will see in later chapters, the presence or absence of the charismatic leader is strongly related to differences in the relational structures of these groups.

Although a number of the absentee charismatic communes were in the process of institutionalizing the charismatic leader's special knowledge and teachings into a body of formalized prescriptions and collective rituals, in none of them had routinization reached the point where the charisma had been depersonalized and thus could be held by any incumbent of the leadership position. Consequently, and regrettably, there are no instances of charismatic authority among the communes in this study.

Data providing some corroboration for this classification, and also offering empirical validation for the theoretical dimensions of the typology, are presented in Table 3:4.[9] Strong differences separate the two categories of charismatic leadership from their noncharismatic counterparts. Thus, of the 221 who were administered the Long Form Interview Schedule, 77% and 43% in the resident and absentee groups, respectively, both attributed charismatic powers and looked to the person they had named for leadership and guidance. This was all but nonexistent in the groups with high charismatic potential (6%) and the communes with low charismatic potential (3%). For these communes, the data suggest that leadership is based on the attribution of special but not supernatural powers.[10]

TABLE 3:3   CLASSIFICATION OF COMMUNES BY CHARISMATIC TYPE

CHARISMATIC TYPE	Number of Communes	Percentage
NONCHARISMATIC GROUPING		
Low charismatic potential	23	40.4%
High charismatic potential	6	10.5
Total	29	50.9%
CHARISMATIC GROUPING		
Charismatic leadership	28	49.1
Charismatic authority	0	0
Total	28	49.1%
TOTAL ALL COMMUNES*	57	100.0%

*Excludes three rehabilitation communes in which membership was not completely voluntary.

There is also evidence that the scope of leadership in the charismatic communes is perceived in much broader terms than in the noncharismatic groups, and includes both communal and personal matters. So that, while this is true for 71% and 40% of those who both attributed charismatic powers and sought leadership from the person they had named in the resident and absentee charismatic communes, respectively, this was much less likely in the other groups (17% and 16% in those with high and low charismatic potential). Indeed, the majority in the latter (83% and 68%, respectively) saw this person as having relevance only for personal concerns; they did not defer to this person over collective issues.

Overall, then, these data provide an independent source of validation for our qualitative charismatic classification of the communes, and in broad terms, support the normative and relational dimensions of the typology. In the following description of the four types of charismatic groups, we will ground the discussion with examples of specific communes.

TABLE 3:4   VALIDATION OF CHARISMATIC CLASSIFICATION

| | CHARISMATIC TYPE | | | | |
	Low charismatic potential	High charismatic potential	Absentee charismatic leadership	Resident charismatic leadership	TOTAL
No one has special powers/gifts	51.7%	31.3%	25.6%	3.3%	33.5%
Individual has special powers/ gifts only	6.7	31.3	5.8	0	7.2
Individual has special powers/ gifts AND leadership/ guidance	38.2	31.3	20.9	3.3	26.2
Individual has special powers/ gifts AND 1 or more super- natural powers	0	0	4.7	16.7	4.1
Individual has special powers/ gifts AND 1 or more super- natural powers AND leader- ship/guidance	3.4	6.2	43.0	76.7	29.0
TOTAL	100.0%	100.1%	100.0%	100.0%	100.0%
N* = ( )	(89)	(16)[1]	(86)	(30)	(221)

*N is the number of Long Form Interviews.
1. The N for this category is low because two of the six communes in this category are from Boston and the Long Form was not administered there.

Noncharismatic

i) Low Charismatic Potential   In virtually all social collectivities there are beliefs, variously held among members, about the exceptional powers or abilities that particular members are seen to have. However, as we established above, such beliefs, alone, are not sufficient to create a situation with high charismatic potential. There must also be the further recognition that the exceptional abilities have some kind of divine or supernatural basis. It is this criterion that distinguishes groups with low charismatic potential from those with high charismatic potential. The significance of these beliefs, as a necessary (but not sufficient) criterion for charisma, can be seen by considering Karp House. This commune is identical to Alabama Avenue (the first of the three charismatic groups described in Chapter One) in almost every respect, except that charismatic beliefs are missing.

Karp House

Like Alabama Avenue, Karp House is also a small, white christian commune in a transitional neighborhood, but it has a young family, the Lawsons, at its center. It had evolved from two households who had prayed and eaten together regularly. However, "leadership" in the earlier group was missing. The decision to live in a poor area is an important aspect of the group's commitment to "Christ and christianity along with a desire to help others." "We value human kindness, spiritual sensitivity and growth, simplicity and warmth. These values, in many different ways, find their base in the love of Christ," they explained.

There are two foundations to the commune. One is a belief in God and the pursuit of a simple, unostentatious, christian way of life: "We want to seek God here in our relations with all who come into the house; we are interested in living out the values of the kingdom of God."

> The other is a shared commitment to the group as a "family:" ... the idea of a household with a nuclear family at the center and the single people as satellites — I don't feel that we have set goals unless it's for everybody to feel that we have a good home situation for everyone ... where the members give support to each other on a daily basis (with) affirmation and faith in God.

As a family, the commune feels that age and family experience are important so that the older members, particularly the Lawsons, are seen as knowing what is best for the group. The youngest member expressed how he saw this with these words:

> I really like spending a lot of time with the (Lawsons') children, learning and giving what I can. And there's something about a marriage commitment as far as always being able to work things out. ... Bob and Mary (the Lawsons) ... have such a really good relationship. So I'm up for learning, as I've seen some pretty flaky marriage relationships. ... I trust Bob and Mary's leadership.

Despite the similarities between the two communes, especially their religious beliefs and commitments, leadership in Karp House, in contrast to Alabama Avenue, is based on beliefs about the Lawsons' greater wisdom as older members, and their greater experience in "family" matters. No one in this group is seen as being endowed with any exceptional abilities from the supernatural, spiritual or otherwise. Consequently, there is little potential for charismatic rule here.

The Co-Op

This is also true for the Co-Op, a second example of a commune with low charismatic potential. Like Workers of the World (the third charismatic commune described in Chapter One), the Co-Op is a commune with a strong political ideology and a commitment to political action. It aims, through a belief in Marxism and involvement in the Radical New Left, to achieve freedom from "oppression and exploitation of the individual by capitalism:"

> People are responsible for their actions, but many actions are forced by society. Every person has a right to food, shelter, and health. No one has the right to exploit another person — whether the exploitation is economic or social. Capitalism causes many of the problems we see in this country.

The commune was founded in 1971 and, despite a high degree of membership turnover, has retained its Marxist ideology and communalistic structure. At the time of the first wave of data collection in 1974, there were seven members, most of whom were doing academic work and shared a commitment to the maintenance of a mutually supportive household for their professional interests and political activities. They also shared a "fundamental distrust of individualistic, competitive, and capitalistic modes of interaction." One member explained the rationale for the group this way:

> The idea (is) people being able to live together — sharing our resources, each being productive and happy, developing our political consciousness about sexism, capitalism, and isolation, and (creating) a home to come to where you feel warm and accepted.

As a commune, the Co-Op has organized itself around the basic communist principle of: "From each according to his ability, to each according to his needs." Each member contributes toward communal expenses in proportion to his/her income and shares all resources and equipment "freely and openly." Also, so long as members are viewed as making a contribution, they have often been supported by the others while unemployed or doing work which does not bring in a regular income. Household chores and tasks are rotated, and there is a strong commitment to "break down oppressive behavior — especially traditional sex roles." There is no leader, and decisions are achieved through group consensus. A special effort is made to ensure all voices are heard and avoid the domination of any one member or clique.

ii) High Charismatic Potential   When a social collectivity believes that an individual or social position possesses charismatic qualities, but the belief is not institutionalized into a relationship of charismatic rule, a condition of high charismatic potential exists. Drawing on the distinction above, between charismatic leadership and charismatic authority, two kinds of high charismatic potential can be distinguished. The first exists when a particular individual is seen as possessing charismatic qualities, but is not regarded as a leader by those who hold this belief. Among the 57 communes in this research, there were no clear cases of such potentially charismatic individuals.

A different kind of charismatic potential exists when a group believes that their goals can be attained only when they are led by someone who possesses charismatic qualities, but as yet, no person is currently seen this way by them. The key difference between these two forms of charismatic potential, is whether the charismatic qualities are believed to be specific to a particular individual, and are therefore personal and not transferable to someone else, or adhere, instead, to any incumbent of a leadership position which, at present, is vacant.

Zephyr

Zephyr, a commune of three young, married couples, and a single person, is a good example of a group with potential for charismatic leadership. The commune has a Christian religious foundation that is seen as important by the members. One member told me the following in the course of a taped interview about the group:

> We have mumbled ever since the Fall about wanting to have regular worship services here in the house — but we have never been able to get it together. ... We've had a lot of trouble around this issue. ... Someone says like, 'why don't we do it?' (i.e., organize a service), and everybody goes 'um, um, and yeah'. Now, what to do next? ... I'll throw out suggestions, but I don't have the wildest idea how I could get people to do them. We don't have any charismatic figure. We don't have anybody. ... There isn't anybody who can kind of stand up to the others and say: 'We're going to do this'.

Charismatic Leadership

Charismatic leadership occurs when a group accords a particular individual control over its actions based on the belief in his or her possession of charismatic qualities. These charismatic powers are seen as being specific only to this person, and are not regarded by the group as adhering to any occupant of a leadership position. Charismatic leadership can be either *resident* (the charismatic leader actually lives with the group), or *absentee* (the leader resides elsewhere, but still has authority over the group's action).

iii) Resident Charismatic

Joy of God

The Joy of God is an example of a resident charismatic commune. It is one of a number of christian communal households that together form a larger religious community affiliated to a Catholic church. Founded in 1973, the commune has eight members in their early twenties, four of whom are women, with a couple at its center. The group feels a "deep commitment" to Jesus, their larger community, and "to administer to each other." Living together communally is an essential part of achieving their goal: "To function as the body of Christ and come to a deeper understanding of each other through Jesus Christ." Because they believe there are more opportunities in a commune to help one another and to serve other people,they feel the "House is a tool that has enabled us to come closer to God."

Just a few months before we started our fieldwork in 1974, the community had changed from a more democratic form of leadership to one of strong charismatic leadership under the authority of Dave, the group's Household Head. In speaking about this change, one member had this to say:

> Because we are completely committed to that (charismatic) authority, we do feel a new freedom. God is really leading us through our (Household) Heads. Submission. Without submission you can't really expect it to work in your life, because you haven't given anything. ... We realized: 'Okay, enough of this half-way authority submission; we have to do it all the way or it's not going to work'.

With the change in leadership came a change in the perception of Dave as their leader. He is now seen as the "means to achieve the Holy Promise: that if we live a truly christian way of life, we will be blessed and anointed by Christ." All of the others believe he possesses special gifts: "prophecy and vision — seeing where God is leading the House;" "gifts of healing which go right through people;" "words of knowledge, discernment of spirits, speaking in tongues;" and "faith, love, and understanding." While they also believe that everyone in the group possesses "some of these special gifts," which "come out of different people at different times," no one has them as much as Dave. "He has the Lord's anointing as Head of the House — a spiritual anointing."

iv) Absentee Charismatic

Love from Above

Love from Above is a commune with an absentee charismatic leader. The commune described here is one of eleven included in the Urban Communes Study from the Love from Above Organization (LAO). It is a highly centralized national federation of urban communal households founded by, and under the complete authority of, a Guru preaching an Eastern religion. He promises peace, love and perfect wisdom through the experience of God by total dedication to his teachings. The Guru's followers perceive him as a person who possesses exceptional spiritual powers: "(Guru) knows what each man needs on the spiritual path;" "He is in touch with the Soul, and experiences love, peace, and God directly;" "There is no end to his power;" the "world revolves around him;" "He is knowledge itself;" and they look to him for "personal" and "spiritual guidance."

> (Guru) has shown us the light of God. Something which, when I first saw it, just caused me to break out in a cold sweat. ... It was a really profound experience, and we're all having that. ... It's something that's very real.

There are two types of communal households. Novitiate houses of six or so members who want to follow and share their spiritual experience without giving up their normal life. Ashram households of 10 to 20 members, want to dedicate their whole energy and life to serving Guru by making a life-long pledge of celibacy, total compliance, and complete material sacrifice.

The Ashrams are more formally structured than the novitiate houses in terms of responsibility and a hierarchy of authority, with a strict daily schedule of spiritual practices, rituals, and collective activities. Within each city the Ashram is the headquarters in daily contact with the LAO. Directives flow from the Guru, through the LAO bureaucracy to the Ashrams, and then to the novitiate houses and other followers (see Figure 2:2, above).

Charismatic Authority

The second kind of charismatic rule is charismatic authority. This occurs when the control over a collectivity's actions is granted to the incumbent of a position of leadership on the basis of charismatic qualities believed to adhere to the position itself. Unlike charismatic leadership, the extraordinary powers are depersonalized, seen as belonging to the social position rather than as a personal quality the incumbent possesses. This depersonalization of charisma, via the process of routinization, also means that it is not the original charismatic leader who remains significant, but the legacy of the charismatic's teachings — the tools for achieving the charismatic promise. As noted above, none of the communes in the study were far enough along in the process of routinization to justify classification in this category, although three showed signs of moving in that direction.

III. A Social Form: A Relational Theory

The third concept of charisma in our scheme is the notion of charisma as a distinctive pattern of social organization. We have already encountered this concept in Weber's formulation of the principal characteristics of charismatic authority. In this theory, Weber identifies the properties he postulates that characterize a collectivity when pure or personalized charisma is present.

It will be recalled from Chapter Two that, at this level, Weber sees charisma as a communal form of social organization, distinguished by a lack of formal organization, division of labor, and regularized economic activity, with minimal hierarchy, and under the absolute domination of the charismatic leader. It will also be recalled that, not only is there little empirical support for this model from the communes' data, but there are also some important theoretical limitations with Weber's theory. This means that, while our normative and relational concepts of charisma are, in broad terms, compatible with Weber's ideas, it is at this structural level where the major difficulties with Weber occur. Consequently, the model of charisma's structural foundation that we briefly introduce here, and is the concern of Part Three of the book, has little in common with Weber's theory.

Inherent Instability

My thinking about the distinctive structural characteristics of charismatic social organization hinges on a postulate of the inherent instability of charismatic structures. This idea is not new; Weber recognized this and explained it in terms of the personal basis of the charismatic leader's legitimacy, in that authority over the group is always contingent upon the leader's ability to prove the continued possession of charisma:

> By its very nature, the existence of charismatic authority is specifically unstable. ... The charismatic holder is deserted by his following, however, (only) because pure charisma does not know any 'legitimacy' other than that flowing from personal strength, that is, one which is constantly being proved. ...
> The charismatic leader gains and maintains authority solely by proving his strength in life. If he wants to be a prophet, he must perform miracles; if he wants to be a war lord, he must

perform heroic deeds. Above all, however, his divine mission must 'prove' itself in that those who faithfully surrender to him must fare well. If they do not fare well, he is obviously not the master sent by the gods (Weber, 1968: 22-23; parenthesis in original).

Although the need for some form of demonstrable proof of the leader's continued possession of charisma may be one of the sources of instability, there are good reasons for doubting that it is a major factor. First, it assumes a fundamental skepticism of the charismatic leader by the followers. Such a view may be reasonable for new recruits who have not yet undergone a full conversion. But why should the followers be skeptical, acting more as Popperian scientists requiring repeated verification of the leader's charismatic powers? Does it not make more sense to start with the idea that the followers are, instead, optimistic and really do believe that the leader possesses the powers *they* have attributed to him?

But even if the followers are skeptical, there is the further difficulty of deciding when the leader's charismatic powers have deserted him. Unlike the Popperian scientist, the charismatic does not present her prophecy so that it can be refuted. That would be to invite failure and disbelief. Rather, the charismatic promise tends to be formulated in a way that it cannot fail. Furthermore, even if the failure of charismatic prophecy occurs, why should the charismatic leader not modify her prophecy so that belief in its efficacy remains intact (e.g., Lofland, 1966). It is this way with scientists who change their theories in their reluctance to accept the negative results of an empirical test (see Lakatos, 1970: 100-101).

Relational Properties

My postulate of the instability of charisma is based on an argument about the relational properties of charismatic structures. To achieve radical social change, a charismatic system must mobilize an enormous amount of social energy for the purpose of breaking with an established order. At the same time, it must support itself and ward off outside threats while constructing and institutionalizing a new social pattern. As an intense emotional bond that fuses the group into an undifferentiated whole, communion liberates the energy previously locked up as structure.

The importance of communion as a source of collective energy is something that Weber and other writers have neglected (see Schweitzer, 1974/5: 159-60).[11] Communion is the power plant in a charismatic structure. It generates the extraordinary intensity and quantity of energy needed for radical social metamorphosis. Collective energy is the material the group must generate, harness, and align toward collective ends if it is to accomplish the radical change in form desired. But, as the studies of collective behavior (Blumer, 1957; Turner and Killian, 1957; Smelser, 1962) and Zablocki's research on communes (1971; especially 1980: 146-186) have shown, collective energy is negatively correlated with social stability.

To maintain stability and increase the likelihood of survival under these conditions, a charismatic group must institute mechanisms of social control to regulate collective and individual behavior (see Figure 3:3). In addition to the institutionalization of the communion-generating activities, a clearly defined and well ordered power hierarchy operates not only to ensure each individual's accountability to the group, but also to maintain group stability by reinforcing the power of those in authority. Power, therefore, is patterned for containment and control; this property of strength is reflected in its geometry — a transitive hierarchy of densely interlocking relations.

Aside from the problem of generating and aligning an enormous quantity of energy, a charismatic system must solve even more basic problems if it is to persist as a collectivity and provide more than the occasional experience of fulfillment for its members. To do this, provision must be made to meet the material, emotional, and social needs of the members on a regularized, day-to-day basis. This will mean structure in the form of a differentiation of social positions and roles organized around the fulfillment of these needs. Such an order of regularized activities requires collective organization and control. This, too, leads to the expectation of a clearly articulated power structure in charismatic systems.

Given the above, we can postulate that two relational patterns will differentiate charismatic systems from noncharismatic forms of social organization. One is an interlocking pattern of highly charged bonds of fraternal love in which virtually every member is connected to everyone else. This is a reflection of the strong feelings of mutual affection and common identity produced by the experience of communion. The second is an interlocking, transitively-ordered, power hierarchy, aligned under the charismatic leader or, if absent, the leader's lieutenant. These patterns will vary directly with the intensity of charisma, being more apparent in collectivities where the charismatic leader is resident than where the leader is absent.

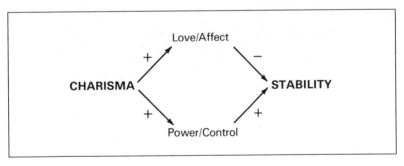

3:3 *Model Showing the Effect of Charisma on Social Structure*

Conclusion

For Weber, charismatic faith is a prerequisite for the success of charisma. Unless the group continues to acknowledge the leader's possession of exceptional powers, there is no basis for charismatic rule. Consequently, charisma, and the potential for radical change cease to exist. In this model, causal primacy is accorded to the normative level — that is, to charismatic beliefs alone.

In our model, however, it is the relational level that holds the key. To accomplish radical social transformation, charisma requires large quantities of collective energy. Aside from operating as the power plant that generates this energy, communion builds strong bonds of attachment and commitment among group members. But communion is highly unstable with a good likelihood of destabilizing, even fatal consequences for the group. Thus a well articulated power structure not only provides a means for controlling communion, but as a key element in the economic and routine organization that meets everyday sustenance needs, power also is an imperative for long-term survival.

NOTES

1. It is of interest to note that Weber himself was regarded this way:

   There, under the rose arbor, at a table heaped with books, sat Max Weber. ... What followed in the course of this first encounter with him was a wonderful and, for me, decisive revelation. For he began to block out a sociology of music for my benefit ... and I now drank in his words. ... I must have sat with him for more than two hours. ... When at last I took my leave ... I was literally drunk. I was at a turning point in my life. From that moment on, I had taken an oath of fealty to him; I had become his vassal. ... I want to say a few words about Max Weber's return to the lecture platform. ... It was one of the most magnificent addresses I have ever been privileged to hear. ... He spoke extemporaneously... and for more than two hours he held the audience spellbound. I should like to read ... (from) my diary. ... I wrote: '. . . When he ponders, his face contracts like the sky before a thunderstorm. It is a manly face; something elemental, at times actually titanic, emanates from him. He speaks freely in his resonant voice, using a magnificently controlled German, every word in its proper relation to the context. ... It was more of a political sermon than a learned discourse, coming straight from a great, overflowing heart and sustained by a breadth of knowledge and thought that again and again gave something new to us by the very context in which it was placed. ... For two hours a sold-out house listened in breathless suspense.' Those who have not heard him speak cannot imagine the power and expressiveness of his language. ... [His lectures on "Scholarship as a Profession" and "Politics as a Profession"] must be set among the classic examples of eloquence of the German mind and the German tongue. ... Max Weber was a daemonic personality. Even in routine matters there was something incalculable, explosive about him. ... He was utterly fearless and possessed 'civilian courage' ... to a degree that I have never before seen in any other German. ... He was also the charismatic man that he himself described. He had that exceptional gift of casting his spell upon everyone he encountered. No one who knew him escaped the spell. His disciples and his friends paid him homage. His adversaries paid him respect. ... I was, as far as I know, the last person to see him alive. ... On his deathbed he looked transfigured, ... noble as a Hohenstaufen emperor.

... [His wife] sent me a picture of him on his deathbed. It has hung above my desk for more than 40 years. ... Aside from [Chief Justice Harlan Stone], among thousands of encounters, I have never met another who could compare or in any way come up to Max Weber. (Quoted by Stark (1977: 688) from Karl Loewenstein's "personal recollections" (Loewenstein, 1966: 93-94, 96-99, 101-103) delivered at the Weber Centenary, June 3, 1964, University of Munich.)

2. When a careful reading of Weber is made, these same three aspects of charisma can be identified in his writings. Although, in Chapter Two, we found his model of charismatic social organization questionable on both theoretical and empirical grounds, his thoughts about charisma as a category and as a relationship are still useful, and so, where appropriate, will be incorporated into the concepts developed in this chapter.
3. From a psychoanalytic perspective, Schiffer (1973: 20-55) argues that eight "ingredients" are variously involved in the projection of charisma on to a leader; an element of foreignness, some subtle imperfection, a calling to public service, a romantically polarized aggression toward a human adversary, an aura of social status and wealth, a diffidence of sexuality, an element of hoax, and the attraction of a novel or innovative lifestyle.
4. Schweitzer's study, *The Age of Charisma,* is a notable recent exception (Schweitzer, 1984).
5. The difference in the greater incidence of attributions by noncharismatic members is due to the smaller average size of the noncharismatic communes. And although there is not room to present the data here, there also are few differences in the way in which attributions of these "characteristics" are interrelated when zero-order associations are examined by charismatic affiliation.

6. These results also call into question the notion that charisma is based solely upon the recognition of exceptional leadership talents.

7. Because a much greater proportion of the 116 charismatic than the 105 noncharismatic members belong to communes with religious ideologies (73% compared to 18%), it is important to establish that these differences are not simply a function of religion. Breaking both down by religion reveals some association of religion with mentions of supernatural qualities among the charismatic members: 66% of the 85 charismatic members in religious communes mentioned at least one supernatural quality, compared to 39% of the 31 who belong to nonreligious charismatic communes. Comparable figures for the noncharismatic members are: 5% of the 19 belonging to religious groups and 4% of the 86 residents in nonreligious communes.

   Additional analysis, to identify the source of this religious effect, was undertaken by partitioning the charismatic members in religious communes into those belonging to groups with an Eastern religious ideology (N = 58), and those in communes with a Christian ideology (N = 27). Of the former, 57% mentioned at least one supernatural quality, while 86% of those in Christian communes did so. Closer inspection revealed that 91% of the latter are members of communes with a charismatic leader who actually lives with the group. None of the Eastern religious charismatic communes have a resident charismatic leader; all of these groups acknowledge the authority of an absentee charismatic leader.

   If this was simply a religious effect, we would expect to see no difference between those in the Eastern religion and Christian religion categories. However, it is the presence of the charismatic leader in the Christian groups that accounts for the greater frequency of mentions of supernatural qualities in these communes, when compared to the Eastern religious charismatic groups. These results suggest that the greater frequency of mentions of supernatural qualities by those in the charismatic groups, while largely independent of religion, is associated with the actual presence of a charismatic leader.

8. Parsons (1947: 67) also recognizes this distinction when he says: "In the process of routinization the charismatic element does not disappear. It becomes, rather, dissociated from the person of the individual leader and embodied in an objective institutional structure ..."

9. These results were obtained by further analysis of the answers to the open-ended question asking whether there was someone in, or associated with, the commune who possessed "special spiritual (magical) powers or gifts" (See Table 3:2, above). Each respondent's answers were first coded hierarchically for the cumulative presence of the following three properties: mention of at least one "special" quality; that at least one of the "special" qualities given contained a supernatural dimension; and that the respondent "looked to" the person they had named for leadership and guidance in communal decisions and personal matters. The results were then aggregated and percentages derived for each type of charismatic group.

   The reader is reminded that this question was answered only by the five members of each commune who were administered the Long Form interview schedule. It is also important to reiterate that this interview schedule was not administered to the ten communes in Boston. Although necessitated by time and budget constraints, this omission is unfortunate. Given the results presented in Table 3:4, it would have been preferable to have been able to use this quantitatively more rigorous procedure to measure charismatic leadership in all communes.

10. Although, this result is as expected for low charismatic potential category, a greater attribution of supernatural qualities is predicted by the typology for groups with high charismatic potential. However, the interview question was phrased in terms of the "special" powers and gifts possessed by an *individual* (viz, "is there someone ... ?") rather than a social position. The qualitative data indicate that, while these communes expressed a desire for leadership by "someone" who possessed charismatic qualities (see the quote from a member of Zephyr, page 64) in none of these groups did the members actually have a particular individual in mind. These groups, then, have high charismatic potential by virtue of having attributed charisma to a vacant position of leadership for whom a specific person had yet to be found.

11. Zablocki (1971; 1980), Schweitzer (1974/5; 1984), and Roberts (1985 (a)) are exceptions.

PART THREE

SUBSTANTIATION

(Objects are) ... not fleeting and fugitive appearances because they are not only groups of sensations, but groups cemented by a constant bond. It is this bond, and this bond alone, which is the object in itself, and this bond is a relation ... .

Henri Poincaré, *La Valeur de la Science*, 1905.*

*Quoted in: *Imagery in Scientific Thought: Creating Twentieth Century Physics*, Miller (1984: 18).

Chapter Four

RELATIONS

Introduction

This chapter identifies the kinds of relations, in terms of content, that comprise charisma's structural base. The objective is to locate the subset of contents, from the larger pool of all bonds mapped in this study, that has the greatest ability to distinguish between the charismatic and noncharismatic communes. In order to be clear about the amount of discriminating power each content has in this analysis, each will be considered alone — that is, as a discrete dimension of social structure. Chapter Five will then examine how this subset of different contents are interrelated.

Theory

As a structure for radical social change, charisma must generate large quantities of collective energy. This is necessary if the charismatic group is to break with established order, provide for its members' basic everyday needs, fend off outside threats, and institutionalize a new utopia. Collective energy is supplied by communion. As an intense emotional bond, communion releases the energy locked up in established social patterns. In doing so, it mobilizes extraordinary levels of individual commitment and fuses members into an undifferentiated whole. However, communion is an extremely volatile bond, inherently unstable, with often fatal consequences for a group. By harnessing the liberated energy and regulating the process of communion, a strong power structure functions to maintain stability and ensure group survival.

At a relational level, then, charisma means the generation of a state of communion in which individuals are bonded by highly charged, interlocking relations of positive affect. Here is how a member of Love From Above, a charismatic commune, described this experience:

> When we get deeply into it, when we're deeply connected to it, it speaks for itself. It's such a powerful thing that it really gives us in and of itself the direction that we need to really see clearly. Having (the experience) is like looking through a window: ... you just see perfectly where you are and what your relationships really mean; ... what the significance of it is; and what we're really doing here. ... When we experience it, it lifts us totally above feelings, emotions, and things like that, to a place like, you might call it, a state of Grace. It's really intense and very high. ...

But the communion cannot be attained without complete unity among group members. Consequently, close, intimate relationships between pairs or among cliques are seen as undesirable; the charismatic group will take action to prevent or closely control such bonds. When asked if there were any cliques or subgroups in the house, a member of the Third Eye replied:

> We try to remove those as structurally as possible, but sometimes it does occur — like the painters or carpenters. If they're working off together all the time, sometimes they'll have a tendency to kinda form together and keep off in their thing. So what we usually do is see if it gets to be too heavy, and

even if they're a carpenter, we'll stick them in the restaurant, so they can get back into the (group) vibration as a whole. ... We try to have everybody work in the restaurant, at least sometime during the week, so that it gets to be a common work ground.

The priority of collective unity for communion also requires that there are few tensions and conflicts in the group. A member of the United Lotus brings this out in describing his feelings about the day-to-day experience:

I don't think I have been in any place where there is such a relaxed, joyish thing. And it's Yogi's (the leader) vibration. He planted the seed, and the thing that makes this place so unique is the fact that there is nobody who doesn't get along with everybody. It's a very relaxed feeling. People get along extremely well with one another. I've never been in a place where things work out so smoothly. There's very little tension here. It's amazing. It's beautiful. ...

Underlying these relational patterns, and functioning to direct, regulate, and control the charismatic structure, is the power of charismatic rule. This complete submission to the absolute authority of charismatic rule can be seen in the description of Guru, the leader of Love From Above commune:

We have just given up our lives to him. Just saying: 'I'm handing over the reins of my life ... to Guru, and this experience is enough of a guide to me to know what I want. Wherever I can go to serve him best in spreading that message, in doing whatever he would like me to do of service to him, is fine by me.' You do completely give up your will to run your life. You say: 'OK, he's shown me the purpose of my life, and I just want to get into that'. ... It's a big commitment.

If we postulate that these patterns are reflected in the nature and structure of the informal bonds among group members, it can be expected that:

Proposition 4:1 Relations of positive affect will be more salient in charismatic than in noncharismatic groups.

Because relations of tension and conflict are threatening to collective unity and, therefore, to the achievement of communion, it follows that:

Proposition 4:2 Relations involving negative affect will be less salient in charismatic groups than in noncharismatic situations.

And, because exclusive bonds of intimacy between pairs and cliques can threaten collective unity and jeopardize the authority of charismatic leadership and group stability, it is predicted that:

Proposition 4:3 Relations of dyadic intimacy will be less salient in charismatic than in noncharismatic groups.

Finally, given the volatility of communion and, therefore, the necessity of regulating relations among members to maintain group stability, it can be expected that:

Proposition 4:4 Power relations will be more salient in charismatic groups than in noncharismatic structures.

Let us now consider how consensus among members over the patterning of different relations in a group is related to charisma. Because ideological consensus and collective unity is a prerequisite to the attainment of communion, norms will be present defining the nature and form of relations of positive affect. And since ambiguity, tension, and the emergence of cliques are both threats to collective unity and to charismatic authority, it follows that the nature and boundaries of relations among group members will be clearly defined and backed by collective sanction. Given these conditions, it is expected that:

Proposition 4:5 A greater degree of consensus over relations of positive affect, and relations of power, will be present in charismatic groups compared to noncharismatic situations.

And that:

Proposition 4:6 There will be more consensus about relations of negative affect and those of dyadic intimacy in noncharismatic groups.

Finally, let us spell out how these different bonds will be patterned as dyadic relations among the members of a charismatic group. Because charismatic groups must both generate energy for change and yet also maintain stability, it is expected that:

Proposition 4:7 There will be greater proportions of affirmative dyads[1] of positive affect and power in charismatic compared to noncharismatic groups.

And, given the lower salience of dyadic intimacy and negative affect in charismatic structures, it is likely that:

Proposition 4:8 Greater proportions of prohibitive dyads[2] of negative affect and dyadic intimacy will be present in charismatic groups.

Analysis

Strategy

In this research, like most network studies, relations have been mapped dyadically across a number of different contents. Although we will be using our relational theory to guide analysis, it is necessary to explore other alternatives if we are to subject the theory to rigorous empirical scrutiny. For this reason, our analysis must consider all 13 of the contents mapped in the 46 communes.[3]

Each content will be considered separately as a discrete dimension of social structure. We start at the individual level of analysis, with the distribution of individual sociometric choices, and then move to the dyadic level to consider the relative incidence of different kinds of dyadic bonding. Our goal is to narrow the focus of analysis by addressing two questions: first, which of all the contents mapped are important to the communes? And, second, which kinds of dyadic bonding typifies the aggregated relational pattern for each content in the communes?

What ensues is based on the following logic. We begin with the fact that there are $N(N-1)$ different dyadic relations in a network for a given content — where N is the number of social actors. For each content we assume that there are only two levels of strength or intensity for a bond: a relation either exists or it does not. The incidence of sociometric choices, concerning the presence or absence of a tie, can be examined at different levels of analysis: viz, the individual level, the dyadic level, the triadic level, etc. Essentially, these are the marginals in relational data — the frequency distribution of sociometric choices for each category of a given content at a particular level of analysis. We can take the total number of all possible sociometric choices, the marginal distributions for the individual and dyadic levels, and the areas of their intersection (see Figure 4:1) and compute the following aggregated network-level measures: *relational salience, normative consensus,* and *dyadic connectedness.* When calculated for each content, these measures enable us to verify our propositions by providing information about: which contents are important to the network; whether norms exist among network members for ties of different contents; and the degree of interlinkage among actors for each content. Because the analysis requires, first, that individual choices be aggregated for each group and then averaged by charismatic type, it will be important to watch for communes that are consistently deviant from overall trends.

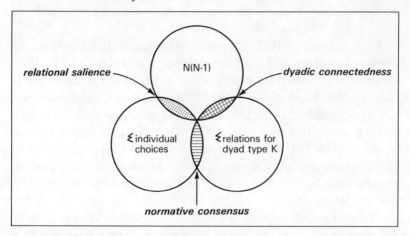

4:1 *Three Measures of Dyadic Density*

Relational Salience

Relational salience provides an initial measure of the relative prominence of different contents in a network. It is defined as the sum of all choices made for a given content, as a proportion of the total number of all possible choices. When the results for different contents are compared, a measure of the relative salience of each content for a group is obtained. The measure assumes that a response by an actor, whether positive or negative, indicates the potential importance of a content. "No response" is thus taken to mean that a content is less fundamental to a network. Computed for each content, and compared against all others, this procedure, when used in conjunction with substantive theory and ethnographic evidence, offers a simple, systematic way of differentiating potentially important contents from those that may be less salient.[4]

When all 46 communes are considered together, Figure 4:2 shows that positive affect and power are the contents with the greatest salience, while those of dyadic intimacy (*sexual* and *sleeping together*) and negative affect are the lowest. Although this general pattern does not change much when the communes are divided into charismatic and noncharismatic groupings, the differences, with the exception of *power,* tend to run in the expected direction. For the 21 charismatic communes, relations of positive affect generally have a higher salience, especially *loving* (.886 compared to .742), reflecting the importance of communion in these groups. And, as expected, bonds of negative affect and dyadic intimacy tend to be less salient. While there are more sociometric choices for *power* in the 25 noncharismatic groups (.839 compared to .730), we will see below, that this is largely due to an ideological bias against the acknowledgment of power in some of the charismatic communes. In sum, although the differences tend to run in the predicted direction, they are not strong enough to clearly distinguish between the two kinds of groups.

	CHARISMATIC (21)*	NON CHARISMATIC (25)*	Total (46)*
1.00			
.900	Loving		
		Power	
.800	—Improving—		Loving —Power—
			Improving
	Power	Loving Improving	
.700		—Exciting—	
			Exciting
	Exciting		
.600			
		Awkward	
.500		Fajob	Awkward
		Tense	
.400	Awkward		—Fajob— Tense
	Tense		
.300	—Fajob[1]—	Signif.	
			Signif.
.200	Signif.[2]	Sexual	
	Jealous Hateful Exploitive Sleep	Exploitive Hateful Jealous Sleep	Sexual Exploitive Hateful Jealous Sleep
.100	—Sexual—		
0			

Mean Relational Salience

*N = ( ).
1. Fajob = ego knows alter's father's job; used as a measure of the depth of the relationship between ego and alter.
2. Signif. = alter mentioned as one of the five "most significant" persons to ego.

4:2 *Relational Salience of Contents by Charismatic Grouping*

Dyadic Bonding

Leaving aside the question of whether a relation is directed or undirected,[5] there are three types of dyadic bonding of sociological importance derived from the measurement procedures employed in this research. The first is an *affirmative dyad* — a reciprocated relation where both *i* and *j* agree about the presence of a given content between them. Because they both independently agree about the nature of the tie between them, there is greater validity in the inference that the relation does actually exist. Moreover, when the proportion of affirmative dyads in a network is high, this suggests the presence of a norm allowing or prescribing such a relational pattern among network members.

The second is a *prohibitive dyad*. This is a reciprocated relation in which both *i* and *j* agree that a given content is *not* present between them and, at higher proportions, suggests the likelihood of a norm prohibiting this kind of tie. Because both *i* and *j* independently agree that a relation does not exist, this is a more valid way of determining those areas in the social structure where particular kinds of relations actually do not exist, than by merely taking situations of "no choice" or "no answer" — a procedure that is often followed by network researchers.

The third combination of *i* and *j*'s relational choices is that of dissension; that is, *i* says the relation exists and *j* says it does not. While affirmative and prohibitive dyads indicate the boundaries of social structure, dyads of *dissent* locate potential areas of ambiguity, confusion, or conflict. These dyads are indicators of role conflict or sociological ambivalence (Merton, 1976). When aggregated for the whole network, this bonding pattern may also locate those areas in a social structure with a high potential for change.

Normative Consensus

Taking the number of dyads that the members of a group agree about as a proportion of the total number of choices made for a given content, provides a measure of the presence of norms allowing or requiring certain kinds of relations among members. In Table 4:1, the differences in normative consensus between the charismatic and noncharismatic groups are clearest for the affirmative dyads. As an expected reflection of greater ideological unity and communion, there is more consensus in the charismatic communes about the contents of positive affect. This is especially true for *loving* bonds (.611 compared to .337) over which the charismatic groups have as much as 45% more consensus. By contrast, 13% of the dyads reported by noncharismatic members are agreements that *loving* is not an element in the relation between the pair of individuals involved.

Aside from slightly more agreement among charismatic members that their relations are not *tense* and not *awkward*, there is little difference between the two kinds of groups for the contents of negative affect.[6] And, while there is evidence that bonds of dyadic intimacy are more acceptable in the noncharismatic communes, there is also more consensus about power in these groups. However, as we will see in a moment, this result for *power* is due to an ideological bias against the acknowledgment of relations of inequality in some charismatic groups.

Dyadic Connectedness

Dyadic connectedness is a crude measure of the degree of interlinkage for a particular kind of dyadic bonding among group members. It is obtained by taking the number dyads of a given type (for example, affirmative dyads) as a proportion of the total number of relations possible in a group. Computing dyadic connectedness for the three kinds of dyadic bonding and comparing their relative preponderance across different contents, provides some initial data on the patterning of relations.[7]

In Table 4:2, data on the dyadic connectedness of affirmative and prohibitive dyads are presented. There is little for the prohibitive dyads to distinguish between the charismatic and

TABLE 4:1 NORMATIVE CONSENSUS OF CONTENTS BY CHARISMATIC GROUPING

CHARISMATIC GROUPING	Proportion affirmative ("yes") dyads			Proportion prohibitive ("no") dyads		
CONTENTS	Charismatic (21)*	Noncharismatic (25)	Total (46)	Charismatic (21)	Noncharismatic (25)	Total (46)
Positive Affect						
Loving	.611	.337	.462	.025	.126	.080
Improving	.542	.411	.470	.041	.061	.052
Exciting	.244	.172	.205	.125	.128	.127
Negative Affect						
Awkward	.064	.029	.045	.337	.225	.276
Tense	.009	.025	.018	.456	.358	.403
Jealous	.006	.009	.008	.666	.712	.691
Hateful	.057	.007	.030	.683	.693	.688
Exploitative	.009	.002	.005	.713	.676	.693
Dyadic Intimacy						
Fajob[1]	.270	.498	.394	—	—	—
Sexual	.029	.083	.059	.778	.676	.727
Sleep together	.057	.078	.069	.774	.793	.784
Dominance						
Power	.259	.295	.278	—	—	—

*N = ( )

— These data were not gathered in the appropriate form for this analysis.

1. Fajob = ego knows alter's father's job.

noncharismatic groups. Of greater interest are the results for the affirmative dyads. While the overall pattern for both kinds of communes is much the same, it is clear, as expected, that bonds of positive affect (with the exception of *exciting*) occur in greater proportion in the charismatic than in the noncharismatic communes (.580 compared to .327 for *loving*, and .540 against .393 for *improving*). In addition, there is also evidence of more dyadic intimacy among the members of the noncharismatic groups.

For the contents of negative affect and power, however, measurement problems have had an impact. For negative affect, the underreporting of tension and conflict is reflected in the very low proportions and minor differences between the two kinds of communes. For power, the problem is more complicated and requires that we make a momentary digression.

Two measures of "power" are given in Table 4:2: one using a "strict" criterion (of acknowledged dominance, where actor *i* claims *power* and *j* defers)[8] and the other a "relaxed" criterion (which also includes relations of uncontested dominance — where *i* claims *power* and *j* responds with "no answer", and uncontested deference — where *i* gives "no answer" and *j* defers to *i*). When the strict definition of acknowledged dominance is relaxed to also include ties of uncontested dominance and uncontested deference, there is a 40% increase in the mean level of dyadic connectedness (from .229 to .361), overall, in the 46 communes.

What this means can be seen in Figure 4:3. The sociograms in the top half of the page are images of power constructed from a strict operational definition in four charismatic communes. While this definition illuminates the structure of power for communes "A" and "B", the lower incidence of relations and lack of structure exhibited by communes "C" and "D" raise the question of its validity for all groups.

An examination of the ethnographic data reveals strong evidence of ideological contamination in the measurement of certain relational contents, particularly power and negative

TABLE 4:2 DYADIC CONNECTEDNESS OF CONTENTS BY CHARISMATIC GROUPING

CHARISMATIC GROUPING	Proportion affirmative ("yes") dyads			Proportion prohibitive ("no") dyads		
CONTENTS	Charismatic (21)*	Noncharismatic (25)	Total (46)	Charismatic (21)	Noncharismatic (25)	Total (46)
Positive Affect						
Loving	.580	.327	.442	.018	.106	.066
Improving	.540	.393	.460	.040	.059	.051
Exciting	.169	.176	.173	.139	.105	.120
Negative Affect						
Awkward	.016	.028	.023	.338	.220	.274
Tense	.009	.024	.017	.432	.345	.385
Jealous	.006	.010	.008	.631	.688	.662
Hateful	.011	.006	.008	.657	.668	.663
Exploitative	.009	.002	.005	.668	.650	.658
Dyadic Intimacy						
Fajob[1]	.100	.260	.187	—	—	—
Alter signif[2]	.114	.168	.143	—	—	—
Sexual	.028	.080	.056	.730	.653	.688
Sleep together	.054	.072	.064	.732	.771	.753
Dominance						
Power (strict)	.202	.253	.229	—	—	—
Power (relaxed)	.331	.380	.361	—	—	—

*N = ( )
— These data were not gathered in the appropriate form for this analysis.
1. Fajob = ego knows alter's father's job.
2. Alter signif = alter mentioned as one of the five "most significant" persons to ego.

91

affect. For power, especially, ideology operates to suppress accurate reporting from members in some charismatic communes. In these groups, a common unity and equality is extolled; differences of power and status are deemed an undesirable trait. As exemplars, the leaders are unwilling to acknowledge their authority over other members, even though obedience and deference is clearly apparent to an observer.

The effect of such ideological contamination shows up in the images for communes "C" and "D" at the bottom of Figure 4:3, which indicates deference relations (broken lines), almost exclusively centered on the sociometric (and actual) leader. So that while the members report that their leader holds the "greater" *power*, the leader responds to our sociometric instrument with "no answer", "equality", or "not relevant".

Using sociological criteria as a guide, a variety of other operational definitions of power were explored. Eventually I located one that made both sociological sense and was corroborated, in broad terms, by other material collected on power from each commune. This is the "relaxed" operational definition. The great improvement in measurement can be seen in the images constructed from it at bottom of Figure 4:3.

Despite its greater validity, however, Table 4:2 shows that this relaxed definition still reveals more *power* dyads in the noncharismatic than in the charismatic communes (.380 versus .331). But while these results appear to offer little support for my thesis of the importance of power in charismatic systems, there are two additional steps that must be taken in the analysis of relational data in order to minimize the risk of spuriously accepting or rejecting a hypothesis.

The first of these is to examine individual communes for deviant cases that may have an exaggerating, depressing, or cancelling-out effect on the aggregated differences between the charismatic and noncharismatic groupings. The second is the important question of structural differences.

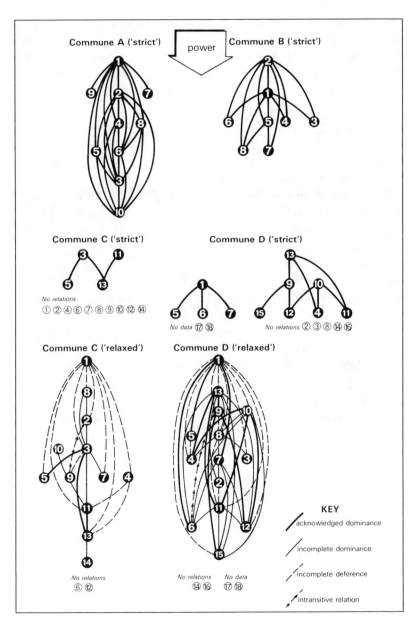

4:3 *"Strict" and "Relaxed" Operational Definitions of Power For Selected Communes*

These differences can be evident at higher levels of structure, even when dyadic patterns for different groups show little variation. It is only when further analysis is undertaken in these terms, that the importance of power, as one of the cornerstones of charisma's structural foundation, is revealed.

Deviant Cases

When the communes are examined individually, there are two subsets of charismatic and noncharismatic groups that tend to stand out as deviant cases. The first set are four charismatic communes which, upon closer inspection, share an important distinguishing characteristic: namely, that the charismatic leader is physically resident in the group. All of the other 17 charismatic groups have acknowledged the authority of a charismatic leader who lives in some other geographical location — in most cases, in a different state. It will be recalled from Chapter Three, that we have labelled these two sets of communes as resident charismatic and absentee charismatic, respectively.

The other subset of deviant cases are five noncharismatic groups that were classified in Chapter Three as groups with high charismatic potential. These communes share a collective belief that the group's goals can only be achieved with the aid of someone possessing exceptional, supernatural abilities, but who at present, even if known to them, has no relationship of leadership or authority over the group. In the analysis that follows, the remaining 20 noncharismatic communes have been placed in the low charismatic potential category.

In Table 4:3, the results of an analysis of selected contents for the four types of communes are presented. Of the two categories of deviant cases, the groups with resident charismatic leaders are quite different from the other communes. Thus, except for the measure of dyadic intimacy (*fajob*), the resident charismatic groups consistently have the highest measures for relational salience, normative consensus, and dyadic connectedness for *loving*, *improving*, and *power* contents. Even when compared to the absentee charismatic communes, there are substantial differences of 34% and 47% for normative consensus, and 38% and 47% difference for dyadic connectedness for *loving* and *improving* bonds in favor of the resident charismatic groups. This is even stronger for *power*, with the latter having more than 70% greater consensus and 60% greater interlinkage among members for both measures. Such large differences for *power* are partly due to the ideological bias mentioned above, which is present in 11 of the absentee charismatic groups with an Eastern religious ideology. But we will also see in Chapter Six, that a strong structural difference still remains when the suppressor effect of ideology is removed.

While not as strong, the data in Table 4:3 show that there is a distinctive relational profile for the communes with high charismatic potential. Not only are there consistent differences for normative consensus and dyadic connectedness across the four contents between the high and low charismatic potential categories, but for *loving* and *improving* contents the former are closer to the absentee charismatic groups.

Overall, then, there is evidence that these four kinds of groups tend to have different relational structures. Although, the small number of resident charismatic communes prevents a more conclusive inference, these results are broadly consistent with the thesis that resident charismatic leadership is a catalyst that facilitates high levels of communion, and establishes a dense structure of power relations. In Chapter Six we will see that there are strong differences among the four kinds of communes in the geometric patterning of these bonds.

Summary

In this first stage of analysis, we have been quite successful in achieving our primary objective: identifying the kinds of relational contents that distinguish between the charismatic

TABLE 4:3   MEASURES OF DYADIC DENSITY (SELECTED CONTENTS) BY CHARISMATIC TYPE

	Resident charismatic (4)*	Absentee charismatic (17)	High charismatic potential (5)	Low charismatic potential (20)	TOTAL (46)
DYADIC DENSITY					
Relational Salience					
Loving	.974	865	.834	.718	.808
Improving	.964	754	.782	.707	.755
Fajob[1]	.495	246	.584	.454	.395
Power	.776	719	.945	.811	.789
Normative Consensus					
Loving	.848	556	.517	.292	.462
Improving	.870	464	.505	.387	.470
Fajob	.494	217	.575	.478	.394
Power	.625	172	.368	.277	.278
Dyadic Connectedness					
Loving	.845	520	.511	.281	.442
Improving	.867	461	.494	.369	.460
Fajob	.245	073	.388	.228	.187
Power (strict)	.486	135	.348	.229	.229
Power (relaxed)	.645	267	.410	.374	.361

*N = ( )
1. Fajob = ego knows alter's father's job.

and noncharismatic communes. There is good evidence that bonds of positive affect, especially *loving* and *improving* contents, are more salient, buttressed by group norms, and more densely patterned among members in the charismatic communes. This is consistent with the thesis of the importance of communion in charismatic structures. And, as expected, there is also less dyadic intimacy in these groups. Partly because of underreporting and ideological biases encountered in mapping these relations, little was found for contents of negative affect and power.

A second purpose of the analysis was to identify how these relations are patterned as dyads. Of the three major forms of dyadic bonding, it is clear that affirmative dyads (i.e., where both social actors agree about the presence of a bond between them) offer the greatest discriminating power between charismatic and noncharismatic groups. This holds across all contents for the measures of normative consensus and dyadic connectedness.

The analysis of deviant cases revealed that communes with resident charismatic leadership and those with high charismatic potential have distinctive relational structures. High incidences of *power, loving,* and *improving* contents, across the three levels of measurement, are found to separate the resident charismatic groups from the others. Although not as strong, there is also evidence that communes with high charismatic potential have relational patterns more akin to the charismatic groups than to those with little potential for charisma. However, because there are few cases in the two deviant categories, caution must be exercised in interpreting these results.

In the next chapter, our relational model of charisma's structural foundation becomes more complicated. The focus of analysis changes from uniplex relations, in which each content is viewed as a discrete dimension of social structure, to multiplex relations in which the interrelation among different contents is examined. In pursuing this question, we will endeavor to shed more light, not only on which kinds of relations are interrelated, but also how and why they combine in a particular way in charismatic groups. This analysis will involve a closer examination of the meaning and significance, in both phenomenological and structural terms, of the contents themselves.

NOTES

1. An affirmative dyad is when a pair of social actors, i and j, both agree a given relation exists between them (see Appendix A, pages 315–318).
2. A prohibitive dyad is when i and j both agree a given relation is not present between them.
3. There are a number of important differences in the numbers of communes that Zablocki (1980) and I use in our respective analyses. In the larger Urban Communes Project, data were systematically gathered from 60 communes. In my research, however, I exclude three communes in which membership was not totally voluntary, while Zablocki has included these in his analysis. After examining the available ethnographic materials and consulting with fieldworkers, I decided to treat the five residential households of the Spectra organization in Boston as distinct communal groups, in the same way that we had been counting, as separate, the Ashrams and Novitiate households of the Love From Above organization. Zablocki, however, treats the five Spectra Boston households as one commune. A third difference is that I decided to lower the criterion for including groups in my relational analysis from the 85% (that Zablocki used) to a 75% criterion of complete enumeration of the potential relations in a group. This was done to obtain the largest N possible in each of my charismatic and noncharismatic subcategories. These changes resulted in the addition of six more groups in my relational analysis (N = 46) when compared to Zablocki's (N = 40). Spot checks throughout all phases of the analysis reported in this study indicate that the differences between the two samples do not lead to significantly different results.
4. This procedure is likely to be more effective in large networks where, because of the large number of potential relations involved, members are more likely to give "no response" when mapping the relations in a network. In small networks, however, "no response" is less probable, so that the total number of choices made by network members is likely to be very close to

the total number of all possible relations. This means that a slight adjustment must be made to the computation. Thus, for those networks in which this occurs, taking the total number of positive choices (those that affirm a tie exists) as a proportion of the total number of all possible relations, and comparing the results across all contents, will provide a measure of relational salience. Depending upon theoretical expectations and observational evidence, one can just as easily use the number of negative choices (responses asserting that a tie is not present) as the numerator.

5. See Appendix A (pages 315 to 327), for this distinction and its sociological implications.

6. It should be noted here that ethnographic evidence from observations, fieldnotes, and taped interviews indicates that while tension and conflict tend to be underreported in the noncharismatic communes, these relations tend to be filtered out of the responses of the charismatic members by an ideological bias.

7. The major computational difference between normative consensus and dyadic connectedness, is that different denominators are used. In the latter, the denominator is the total number of all possible dyads for a network: for the former it is the total number of relational choices actually made by network members for a given content.

8. Because this definition requires that both *i* and *j* independently agree about which of them has *power,* it has the advantage of excluding potentially spurious responses that may reflect the personal view or intentions of either social actor. However, while such a strict criterion makes sense at a dyadic level, it can result in relational configurations of questionable validity at the group level when sociograms are constructed. This was sometimes the case in this study, where it was found that the sociograms did not correspond with the ethnographic evidence on the structure of power in a number of the communes. Closer examination indicated that an ideological dictum proclaiming equality among all members of these groups, was being adhered to — especially by leaders. When the "strict" criterion of acknowledged dominance was relaxed to also include uncontested dominance (where *i* claims *power* and *j* gives "no answer") and uncontested deferences (*i* defers *power* to *j,* and *j* gives "no answer"), the images of power structure were more congruent with the ethnographic evidence. For further discussion of these different operational definitions of power, see Chapter Eight (pages 199–205) and Appendix A (pages 315–327).

Chapter Five

INTERRELATIONS

Introduction

We have argued that communion is one of the two structural foundations of charisma. Communion generates the large amounts of collective energy required by the charismatic group to achieve a radical transformation. However, communion is inherently unstable and unless counterbalanced by a strong power structure, it can result in the destruction of the group altogether. To substantiate these ideas, we need to show how communion is produced in charismatic structures, and why it is inherently unstable. To accomplish this, the nature and form of communion must be examined in greater depth.

To answer these questions, our analysis focuses on three clusters of relational contents. First, the three contents of positive affect (loving, improving, and exciting), to provide relational indicators of communion. Second, the contents of love, intimacy, and brotherhood, to establish the fraternal (nonromantic) basis of love as communion. And finally, the contents

101

of love and power, to verify our hypothesis of the coexistence of communion and power in charismatic systems. We begin this task by constructing a set of tools that will enable us to conduct the kind of analysis these questions require.

Interrelations Among Contents

Social structure is more than social ties among social actors along discrete relational dimensions. Also involved is the interrelation of different contents, which, as a form of bonding among the contents themselves, exists independently of the connections among individuals. This idea of structure as the interrelation among different kinds social relations, is the notion of multiplexity (Gluckman, 1955).[1]

A study of the interrelation among relations requires that two basic questions about social structure be addressed: first, which kinds of social relations are interrelated? And, second, how are they interrelated? Let us start by considering the different ways by which relations can be interrelated.

Multiplex Strategy

One approach to the interrelation among contents is to think in terms of the different relations that logically can connect a set of elements. Each logical relation can then be viewed in terms of its sociological significance.

Logically speaking, there are three basic ways by which two elements, A and B, can be related to each other to produce an output: an *OR* function in which the presence of either element generates output; an *AND* function in which both elements are necessary to produce the result; and a *NOT* function in which the absence of one element produces the other (see Figure 5:1).[2] These different logical relations are usually referred to as union, intersection, and complementation, respectively. A fourth "conditional" function can be derived to capture contingency: for example, the likelihood of intersection between A and B *GIVEN* the presence of one of the two elements.

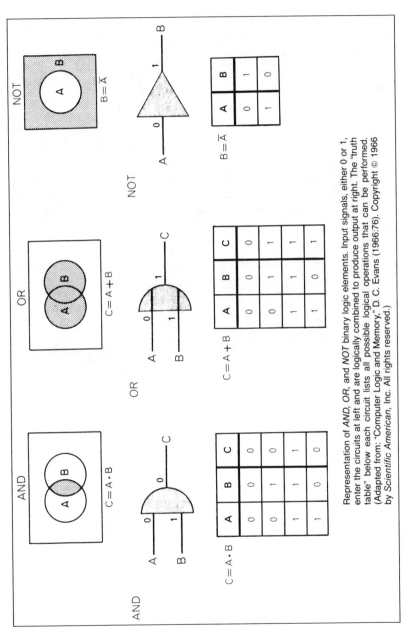

5:1 *Logical Relations Between Elements "A" and "B"*

In Table 5:1 these four different logical relations are considered in terms of their potential sociological significance. When relational contents are interrelated by *OR* logic, it is likely that they serve similar or comparable sociological functions. The *OR* logical operator means that either A or B is involved in an equivalent capacity. *AND* logic, however, requires that both contents must be present: whenever content A is present, so is B — they are correlated or are coexistent; neither can be manifest without the other. The *NOT* logical operator implies mutual exclusivity: when one element is absent (A), the other must be present (B). This can establish the boundaries of social structure in a negative sense: knowing what does not exist implies what can or may exist. Finally, conditional logic may be indicative of various kinds of social exchange, bonds involving contingency, or relations that are linked sequentially by cause and consequence.[3]

TABLE 5:1   SOCIOLOGICAL INTERPRETATION OF BONDING LOGIC FOR MULTIPLEX CONTENTS

LOGICAL BOND	RELATION	SOCIOLOGICAL INTERPRETATION	EXAMPLE (A = love, B = sex)
OR	union ($A \cup B$)	equivalent	intimacy
AND	intersection ($A \cap B$)	corequisites	modern marriage
NOT	complementation ($\overline{B}$) ($\overline{A}$)	mutually exclusive	friendship prostitution
CONDITIONAL	contingency ($A \vert \cap B/B$)	dependent, sequential	traditional (arranged) marriage
	($B \cap A/A$)		romance

By identifying the logic by which different contents are interrelated, and the type of dyadic bonding that results, it is possible to specify multiplex sociometric images for a given social structure. Table 5:2 presents the patterns of multiplex bonding for the three clusters of contents expected to differentiate charismatic from noncharismatic systems. All contents are interrelated by *AND* logic and assume that there are only two states for each relational content: the content is present ($+$) or not present ($-$) from the viewpoint of each individual. It is expected that the charismatic communes will be distinguished, both by the kinds of contents involved, and also by the bonding pattern typifying dyads for the group as a whole.

TABLE 5:2   EXPECTED PATTERNS OF MULTIPLEX BONDING FOR CHARISMATIC GROUPING

MULTIPLEX CONTENTS	*Charismatic*	*Noncharismatic*
Elements of Communion L = Loving I = Improving E = Exciting	$\begin{pmatrix} L & I \\ + & + \\ & AND \\ + & + \end{pmatrix} \begin{pmatrix} L & E \\ + & + \\ & AND \\ + & + \end{pmatrix}$	$\begin{pmatrix} L & I \\ + & - \\ & AND \\ + & + \end{pmatrix} \begin{pmatrix} L & E \\ + & - \\ & AND \\ + & - \end{pmatrix}$
Loving and Dyadic Intimacy L = Loving F = Fraternal S = Sexual Fj = Fajob	$\begin{pmatrix} L & F \\ + & + \\ & AND \\ + & + \end{pmatrix} \begin{pmatrix} L & S \\ + & - \\ & AND \\ + & - \end{pmatrix}$ $\begin{pmatrix} L & Fj \\ + & - \\ & AND \\ + & - \end{pmatrix}$	$\begin{pmatrix} L & F \\ + & - \\ & AND \\ + & - \end{pmatrix} \begin{pmatrix} L & S \\ + & + \\ & AND \\ + & + \end{pmatrix}$ $\begin{pmatrix} L & Fj \\ + & + \\ & AND \\ + & + \end{pmatrix}$
Loving and Power L = Loving P = Power	$\begin{pmatrix} L & P \\ + & + \\ & AND \\ + & + \end{pmatrix}$	$\begin{pmatrix} L & P \\ + & - \\ & AND \\ + & - \end{pmatrix} OR \begin{pmatrix} L & P \\ - & + \\ & AND \\ - & + \end{pmatrix}$

KEY

Relations	Contents	
	A	B
i⟶j	+	−
j⟶i	+	−

} A B
  + −
  + −

+ = relation present
− = relation absent

Each image matrix specifies the logical element joining the two contents and the pattern of interrelation between individuals in a typical dyad. For example, the image matrix for *loving AND improving* contents for charismatic groups, represents a dyad in which i and j agree that both contents are involved in their relation. The corresponding image matrix for noncharismatic structures means that both individuals agree that their relation involves *loving* but not *improving*. The rationale for the image matrices for the three multiplex clusters shown in Table 5:2 will be presented as we consider each cluster.

Two statistical tools will be used to assess the correspondence between the expected multiplex images specified in Table 5:2, and the patterns observed in the communes.[4] Dyadic connectedness (as defined above, pages 83 to 88) provides a measure of the incidence of multiplex contents and conditional probability measures the degree of intersection among contents. Let us now lay the theoretical foundation for the multiplex analyses we will undertake in this chapter.

Concept of Communion

In his book, *The Ritual Process,* Victor Turner distinguishes between two social forms: one is a "structured, differentiated, and often hierarchical system of politico-legal-economic positions," and the other an "unstructured" and "relatively undifferentiated ... communion of equal individuals" (Turner, 1969:96). He labels the latter state "communitas." For Turner, communitas has an "existential quality," involving the "whole man in his relation to other whole men," whereas structure has a "cognitive quality... it is essentially a set of classifications, a model for thinking about culture and nature and ordering one's public life." Thus, "communitas emerges where social structure is not" (Turner, 1969: 126-127).

In a similar way, Herman Schmalenbach (1961) differentiates states of structure from those of nonstructure. In distinguishing "community" from "communion," he argues that
community (as social structure) "is that association which
flourishes on the basis of a "natural, intrinsic solidarity." It
encompasses "everything that is mutually inherited, to
which one has been born or raised"; it is something that is
"given" and "self-evident;" it simply exists and is taken for
granted by its members. Because it is "ordinarily" experienced by the individual as an "unconscious" form of association, community is something that only becomes conscious to
its members by "contrast" or when "disturbances" occur:

> The reality and basis of community do not consist in feel-
> ing. ... The essence of community is association constituted
> in the unconscious. Community ... precedes emotional recog-
> nition of it by its members. Feelings are simply subsequent
> forms of experience at the level of consciousness. They are
> products of community. ... feelings associated with commu-
> nity or directed toward it ... presuppose something that
> already exists.

On the other hand, because it is based solely on the conscious
experience of shared feelings, communion has a "radically
different" nature:

> Emotional experiences are the very stuff of the relationship.
> They are in fact their basis. Jubilant followers who swarm
> around a leader chosen in an inspired flood of passion do not
> intend ... to be bound up with him and one another on the
> basis of the characteristics they naturally have in common.
> They are bound together by the feeling actually experienced.
> Indeed, each one is *en rapport.*
> ... The stuff of which it (communion) is made — the basis of
> its sustenance — is actually the cognitive recognition of feel-
> ing. (Schmalenbach, 1961:335-336.)

During communion, the group acts as a powerful reflector
in which each round of interaction is self reinforcing, building
quickly by a process of emotional contagion to higher and

higher levels of intensity. Fusing everyone into a single, undif-ferentiated form, communion is like a reaction chamber of free flowing, spontaneous interaction. It is a state in which powerful potentialities for change are liberated: it "breaks through the interstices of structure", "transgresses or dis-solves" the norms that govern structured and institutional-ized relationships (Turner, 1969:128-129). In the process of "stripping" roles and "levelling" statuses, it converts in-dividuals into homogeneous wholes and floods them with "affect". Unimpeded by social roles and positions, the emotional energy moves rapidly, without restriction or resistence, through the open interlocking channels of all rela-tions in the group. Thus, as a reaction chamber, communion generates highly concentrated quantities of energy experi-enced as a collective euphoria. It is because the collective energy can be converted into extraordinary levels of commit-ment and purposeful activity (which can be aligned for radi-cal social transformation), that communion is crucial for the charismatic group.

De-individuation

But the *de*-structuring of an established order and the cre-ation and institutionalization of new social patterns does not occur in a single instant. Although such revolutionary change is quick when compared to gradual social evolution, radical social transformation requires the repeated generation and application of large concentrations of collective energy. Conse-quently, in order that an ever-ready supply of collective energy is available for immediate mobilization, communion must be made to occur on a predictable, routine basis (Zablocki, 1971). This means that communion is always present as a latent potential in the social structure of a charismatic system. This requires, in turn, that individuals are receptive to commu-nion when collective energy is needed by the group.

For this to be possible, the individual must become an instrument of the group, be completely responsive to the needs of the collective. Individual aspirations must be in harmony with the goals of the collective, and always take second place. This is most likely when a member's individuality has been stripped away and replaced by a new identity embracing an unquestioning loyalty and complete identification with the collective (Coser, 1976).

Ego-loss

There are two processes involved in stripping and replacing an individual's identity: ego-loss and ego-merging (Kanter, 1972). Ego-loss is accomplished through what Kanter terms "de-individuating mechanisms" (1972:110-111). These are designed to break down the individual's concept of self by de-emphasizing the uniqueness and importance of individual identity. A member of the United Lotus explained the "problem" with individuality this way:

> The biggest problem is getting hung up on your own trip... because the more you're into your own thing the less you are able to help the community work smoothly. The more you give to the community, the more it grows. Everybody gets closer together.

To facilitate ego-loss, many charismatic communes have established formalized socialization procedures such as a novitiateship or a period of trial membership (see Table 2:2 above). These often involve: the renouncement of the new member's previous economic and social independence; a pledge of personal and material commitment to the group — or, in the case of Love from Above, a signed legal contract; special dietary and/or dress habits to be followed by all members; "new" first and second names, especially in many of the Eastern religious communes; and encounter group games and rituals.

Some idea of how these mechanisms are designed to systematically strip away the individual's sense of self can be seen in the following description of two "games" in which a fieldworker participated during an orientation session for prospective members to Utopia House:

> Slim stood up and said that the first game we're going to do is mimicking. He said to choose partners — "somebody you don't know." The first thing that we were told to do was act out whatever our partner said exactly, with the same facial expression, the same hand gestures, in every way possible. The first question that we were told to do was: "What turns you on about the person you are facing?" And we started to proceed and talk about what we liked about the person across from us. ... After two minutes were up, the other side reciprocated. Then everybody moved down one place. ... We were then asked to tell our most vivid sexual fantasy. Once again, I was to initiate it, and I started, he mimicking me the whole time. After two minutes, that was over and we reversed. He did the same with me mimicking him.
>
> The next game was called "on the spot." A person was put "on the spot" and other people would direct questions to him or her about anything. Jose was the first person put "on the spot" and people were asking him about everything; about his sex life, about what he didn't like about himself, about the fact that he was overweight, his age, what he wanted most out of life, what was hindering him from doing that, what was wrong with him, what he despises about himself, what he would do to change his life. This went on to a point where it was clearly uncomfortable; there were very complex questions being asked and people were dealing with subconscious motivations. ...

Ego-merging

The second process, ego-merging, involves replacing the individual's identity with the identity of the group. In many of the charismatic communes, ego-merging is facilitated by a tightly scheduled routine of activities that the individual must follow each day. Among other things, these include: group chores and work, collective activities such as meals and meetings, special collective practices and rituals, and proselytizing for new recruits (see Table 2:1 above).

During communion, differences in rank, position, and personal characteristics cease to exist and are replaced by a profound experience of collective unity. An example of this phenomenon was witnessed by a fieldworker visiting a religious meeting in which one of the charismatic communes was participating:

> There was a real diversity of (white) people and yet they were sharing something — sharing the joy, praising the Lord, having the Lord come into their hearts, and having the Spirit enter them. As I looked around the room, I saw people having their arms outstretched and feeling a real joy; shouting, praising the Lord. It struck me that they were engaged in behavior which, in most other circumstances, would be considered abnormal ... that the decorum and adult demeanor of having control and so forth was put aside ... certainly (they were) letting down a whole lot of barriers and restrictions which they would ordinarily place upon themselves in terms of their behavior. (My additions.)

For the individual, communion is experienced as a state of total union with the group:

> Just a sharing of that experience is something that everyone can relate to. It's not a conscious reasoning or logic. It's something that you feel inside — really deep inside. From that place, it's like a practical zero. The value of zero is that you're not thinking or having a feeling about something. You're just knowing something: that *THIS* is true. It's that deep an experience and comes from knowing that there's total cooperation. You arrive at a common consciousness.

I. Communion: Relational Elements

Theory

Under charismatic conditions, there are three relational elements of communion. The first, the base upon which the others rest, is a powerful cohesion that fuses individual members into a collective unity. This is experienced in an intense bond of brotherhood and love. A member of the Joy of God describes the new sense of "oneness" that followed their leader's decision to have all property, finances, and resources, owned by individuals, vested solely in the group:

> That's the reality that, oh, in the last six months, that we have begun to see, where we really are a family now. And we truly do love one another and would do anything for one another. There's just nothing that we wouldn't do; there's not even a doubt that passes.

The second element of communion is a strong feeling of optimism about the future. This follows from the belief in the efficacy of charismatic leadership as the means to achieve the desired utopia. Grounded in the shared charismatic experience, this optimism touches all aspects of daily life and is reflected in the relations among members. As Lofland (1966) found in his study of a "doomsday cult", this optimism can remain even after the failure of prophecy or a group-threatening crisis. Undaunted by the fact that one of their houses had only just burned down the night before we arrived to spend a day with them, a member of Alabama Avenue told me:

> Well, we're expecting God to do a lot. ... I believe that God will be adding more people — especially men. God, at this point, seems to be saying to us, that we're to obtain property, where the two houses burned, and to build on that property. ... We're expecting God to move on this neighborhood. ...

After pointing out that there were no "romantic involvements" between the men and the women in the commune, she went on to share her expectations about their future relationships:

> ... I believe all of our relationships will be deepened, and I think this time next year you're going to find us much, much closer to each other, and much, much more personally involved with each other in a lot more intimate ways; really much deeper inside each other, into our own real selves.

The third element of communion is an exuberant bond of euphoria. Because the euphoria is a consequence of the catalytic effect of nonroutinized charismatic leadership, and reflects the group's awe and excitement over the direct experience of the energizing power of the charismatic leader, this element will be less likely under conditions of absentee charismatic leadership. In talking about how the group felt when, three months earlier, they had made the decision to live together, a member of a resident charismatic commune recalls that:

> ... there was a feeling of expectancy and excitement. ... We were really excited about what God was going to do — because God has given words, you know, prophecies. ... We were excited ... about being involved in the community, and excited about being involved with each other in this closer way than we ever had been involved in other than our natural families.

Analysis

The expected patterns of interrelations among these elements of unity, optimism, and euphoria are specified in the image matrix in Table 5:2 above (see page 105). The three elements of communion are represented by the contents of *loving, improving,* and *exciting,* respectively.

Table 5:3 gives the densities (dyadic connectedness) and conditional probabilities for multiplex combinations of the three contents for the dichotomous and four-way charismatic classifications of the communes. Reflecting the unity of brotherhood and an optimism for the future, it is expected that the contents of *loving* and *improving* would coexist in charismatic groups generally, while *loving* will also coexist with *exciting* when the catalytic power of resident charismatic leadership is present.

Overall, the data provide broad support for these ideas. The charismatic communes are clearly differentiated from the noncharismatic groups, both by the higher density and by the higher conditional probability for the dual bond of *loving AND improving.* Not only do 41% of all relations in the charismatic groups, compared to 18%, involve these two contents, but there is a higher likelihood of the coexistence of the other if either content is present. Also expected are the low densities of *loving AND exciting* bonds that can be seen in both kinds of groups. Finally, the higher conditional probability of *exciting GIVEN loving* in the noncharismatic groups (.432 compared to .252) is consistent with the more romantic and personally intimate nature of love in these communes.

Even more interesting are the data for the four-way charismatic classification. Here we can see the consequences of the catalytic effect of direct charismatic leadership in the resident charismatic groups. Although there are only four cases, these groups stand out strongly with consistently higher densities and conditional probabilities for the three contents. Even though the mean density of *loving AND improving*, at .742, is more than double its incidence in either the absentee or the high charismatic potential groups, it is the addition of *exciting* that gives the communes their distinctive quality. Thus, as many as 36% of the relations in these groups are charged with the triple contents of *loving AND improving AND exciting*. And there is a 41% probability of *improving AND exciting* coexisting together with *loving* whenever the latter bond is present.

Equally intriguing are the data for the groups with high charismatic potential. As we saw in the last chapter, these communes have relational structures more similar to the resident charismatic communes than either of the other categories. And while they have more than twice the density found in the groups with low charismatic potential for the dual bond of *loving AND improving*, it is the *exciting* content that makes the difference. Just over a quarter of all relations are *loving AND exciting* contents, and nearly a fifth involve all three contents. This compares with densities of 10% and 12% respectively, for both the absentee charismatic and low charismatic potential groups. With a very high conditional probability of .982 for *loving AND exciting GIVEN exciting*, it is clear too, that, as in the resident charismatic communes, excitement is contingent upon the presence of love.

TABLE 5:3 MULTIPLEX STRUCTURES OF COMMUNION CONTENTS BY CHARISMATIC GROUPING AND CHARISMATIC TYPE

DYADIC CONNECTEDNESS	CHARISMATIC GROUPING			CHARISMATIC TYPE			
	Charismatic (21)*	Noncharismatic (25)	TOTAL (46)	Resident Charismatic (4)	Absentee Charismatic (17)	High Charismatic Potential (5)	Low Charismatic Potential (20)
Duplex Bonding							
Loving AND Improving	.410	.176	.282	.742	.332	.364	.151
Loving AND Exciting	.157	.150	.153	.386	.104	.261	.122
Triplex Bonding							
Loving AND Improving AND Exciting	.130	.099	.113	.355	.076	.179	.069
CONDITIONAL PROBABILITIES							
Duplex Bonding							
Improving GIVEN Loving (I·L/L)	.689	.532	.604	.889	.642	.556	.493
Loving GIVEN Improving (L·I/I)	.700	.448	.562	.870	.656	.553	.422
Exciting GIVEN Loving (E·L/L)	.252	.432	.351	.448	.209	.491	.417
Loving GIVEN Exciting (L·E/E)	.805	.710	.753	.942	.773	.982	.642
Triplex Bonding							
Improving AND Exciting GIVEN Loving (I·E·L/L)	.192	.259	.228	.413	.139	.249	.261

*N = ( )

115

The major difference between the groups with absentee charismatic leadership and the others is, as expected, the greater density of *loving AND improving* relations, and the low densities of multiplex bonds involving excitement. Reflecting the union of brotherhood and optimism, this pattern sets them apart from the communes with low charismatic potential on one side, and those with resident charismatic leadership and high charismatic potential on the other.

II. Love: Fraternal Union

Theory

Love has distinctive meaning and function in charismatic structures. It is based on the equality and unity of members as a brotherhood: Group members think of one another as fellow kinsmen — as "sisters", "brothers", "father", "mother", "daughter", "son" etc. — invoking the power of the familial incest taboo as a way of regulating intimacy. For example, a member of a large charismatic commune wanted to make it quite clear that while:

> ... there are both brothers and sisters living here in this house; there are no sexual relationships or anything like that. We all live in separate parts of the house and we serve together, we eat together, and so on; but we just live on that relationship of brother and sister. Every once in a while you may develop a close relationship with someone, but it's always put in its proper perspective. ...

Love is a universal bond; it embraces all members. It is not personalized or particularized — not reserved for certain unique qualities or held just for a specific individual:

> ... We're so little concerned about getting into each other in a heavy way because, for us, love is not gazing into each other's eyes, but gazing in the same direction. That's the kind of love relationship that I feel with other people in the house; not the kind in which you get all attached to each other and have to go through pangs of disengagement. ...

Intimate relationships can deflect individual loyalties and commitment to the group, thereby reducing participation. And, as exclusive cliques, intimate relationships constitute a threat to collective unity and charismatic leadership. Consequently, dyadic intimacy must be carefully controlled.

This is accomplished in a variety of different ways. In a third of the charismatic communes, celibacy is normatively mandated; men and women sleep in separate rooms or, in some groups, even in different houses. In others, intimate and sexual relationships are depersonalized by group marriage or promiscuous pairing in which all members have complete sexual access to one another. Even where marriage is allowed, a number of mechanisms are used to reduce what one commune called the "emotionality and exclusivity of marriage." For example, in the Third Eye, where marriage is seen as the "highest level of spiritual fulfillment," permission to marry must be obtained from the charismatic leader, who has sometimes "suggested" or "arranged" marriages between members. And, even though unmarrieds are required to practice celibacy, sexual relations between the married couple must only take place once a month.

Dyadic intimacy is also controlled in other ways in the charismatic communes. A good example is sleeping arrangements. More than 75% of those in charismatic groups share bedrooms — generally with two or three other members. In some communes we observed as many as five and six people to a room. In the noncharismatic groups, however, everyone has a private bedroom, although couples are an exception. Some charismatic groups use membership turnover as a way of breaking up relationships which are seen as becoming too close — as the leader from one of the Love from Above communes recounted:

> In another house, one sister was sleeping with a brother for a long time. I knew about it but chose not to confront them about it. It eventually came up as a result of some other problem and it was arranged for her to take a vacation. But I found out that she went somewhere else entirely with him for a

month. When she came back I just sat down and talked to her about the whole thing. … She was very upset about this, and the upshot of this was that she ended up being transferred to another community.

Analysis

The results of the multiplex analysis presented in Table 5:4 provide systematic evidence of the fraternal, non-intimate nature of love in the charismatic communes. On average, while 23% of all relations in the charismatic groups are affirmed dyads in which *loving* and *fraternal* contents coexist, this is true for only 6% of the relations in the noncharismatic groups. Furthermore, the conditional probabilities show that the co-presence of these contents is much more likely in the former than in the latter, when either content is present. Reflecting the more personally intimate meaning of love, 10% of the dyads in the noncharismatic groups involve love and sexuality.[5] When the two charismatic groups which practice "free love" and "open sex" are removed,[6] only 2% of the relations in the charismatic communes involve this kind of love. And, when these dyads are examined on a case-by-case basis, most are married couples.

A similar pattern is apparent for *loving AND fajob*, indicative, again, of the low incidence of relations of personal intimacy in the charismatic groups. It is clear that love has only a low likelihood of also involving either dimension of personal intimacy. Some idea of what these differences actually mean, as relational patterns, is conveyed by the sociograms for three charismatic and three noncharismatic communes in Figure 5:2.

The results for the four-way charismatic breakdown in Table 5:4 are not much different from those we have just described — with the notable exception of the resident charismatic groups. These communes have nearly twice the density of *loving AND fraternal* bonds when compared to the absentee charismatic groups (.351 versus .192). This result is in line with our expectation that the relational patterns we have

TABLE 5:4 MULTIPLEX PROFILE OF LOVE BY CHARISMATIC GROUPING AND BY CHARISMATIC TYPE

	CHARISMATIC GROUPING			CHARISMATIC TYPE			
DYADIC CONNECTEDNESS	Charismatic (21)*	Noncharismatic (25)	TOTAL (46)	Resident Charismatic (4)	Absentee Charismatic (17)	High Charismatic Potential (5)	Low Charismatic Potential (20)
Duplex Bonding							
Loving AND Fraternal	.232	.059	.138[+]	.351	.192	.222	.029
Loving AND Sexual	.044	.101	.075	.048	.044	.106	.100
Loving AND Fajob	.084	.146	.117	.220	.042	.165	.141
CONDITIONAL PROBABILITIES							
Duplex Bonding							
Fraternal GIVEN Loving (L•Fr/L)	.378	.108	.231[+]	.386	.375	.222	.086
Loving GIVEN Fraternal (L•Fr/Fr)	.511	.192	.338[+]	.657	.477	.200	.190
Sexual GIVEN Loving (L•S/L)	.098	.354	.237	.055	.108	.225	.386
Loving GIVEN Sexual (L•S/S)	.526	.681	.610	.750	.479	.527	.719
Fajob GIVEN Loving (L•Fj/L)	.127	.518	.340	.266	.095	.473	.530
Loving GIVEN Fajob (L•Fj/Fj)	.535	.544	.540	.914	.408	.651	.524

*N = ( )

[+] Excludes 11 Boston groups that were not asked the "fraternal" question (five of which are absentee charismatic, two high charismatic potential, and four low charismatic potential). Zablocki's figures for the Boston communes (1980:173, Table 4-5) are incorrect; he has inadvertently included these groups in his calculations.

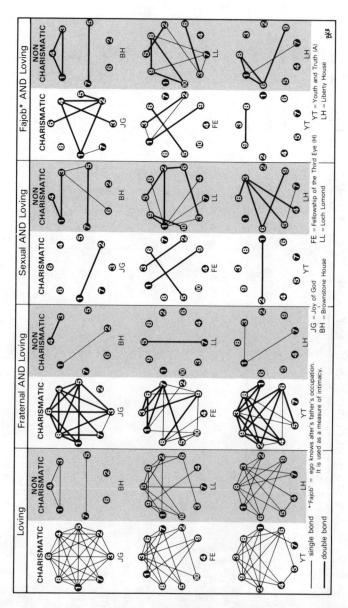

5:2 *Multiplex Sociograms Showing Relational Correlates of Love in Selected Charismatic and Noncharismatic Communes*

postulated should vary directly with the intensity of charisma: that is, they should be more evident when the charismatic leader is present than when absent. The higher incidence of *loving AND fajob* dyads in these groups is consistent with a pattern we observed in our fieldwork, in which one or two members, other than the charismatic leader, took on the role of counselor and confidante to help with personal worries and problems some members faced from time to time. This pattern can be seen in Figure 5:2 for the Joy of God.

III. Power and Communion

Theory

There are two arguments for the third set of multiplex images in Table 5:2 (page 105, above) that show the expected interrelation of love and power. The first is structural and is derived from our theory of the mechanics of radical social change. To achieve a total transformation of social order, a charismatic group must generate extraordinary amounts of collective energy. This is accomplished by communion. But communion is a highly volatile and inherently unstable bond that, if not carefully regulated, will jeopardize group survival. Under these conditions, power operates as a control mechanism containing, harnessing, and aligning the liberated energy toward collective ends. Consequently, for successful transformation and group stability, power must be an ever-present coexistent with communion.

The second argument is social-psychological. At this level, power is awarded to those members who have a greater knowledge and experience of charismatic means. This knowledge is valued because it is seen as a prerequisite to individual fulfillment. Coexistent with power, therefore, is gratitude expressed as love. These patterns can be seen in the way a member of the United Lotus describes the relational ambience in his group:

> The basis of the Community is Yogi (the leader). He is like the Spiritual Father of this place. And we are all here because, basically, we want to follow his teachings, and just try to learn the things he has to give us. ... All kinds of personality things, or any unique things between people are really secondary. ... This is his home, and we are just here to learn from him. ... There are not any, what you'd call, 'intimate relationships', where people are extremely close, because it just doesn't seem to be here; although people are very loving to each other. ... The thing that makes it so unique here is Yogi's vibration. He's so loving. There's an aweful amount of love here; an incredible amount of love here if you are open to it. Sometimes you're not, but it is always here.

By contrast, power in noncharismatic groups reflects inter-member rivalry and domination. This, Heider (1958) has argued, reduces the likelihood of a bond of love also existing between the individuals involved. Accordingly, the group is differentiated into a system of "ranked cliques" with bonds of positive affect connecting individuals sharing the same stratum, and power between those from different strata (Davis and Leinhardt, 1972).

Analysis

In Table 5:5 data are presented for the density, the mean number of relations for each member averaged by commune, and the conditional probabilities for the dual bond of *loving AND power*. Considering the dichotomous charismatic breakdown first, it can be seen that there are consistent differences across each of these measures that tend to support our argument. Although the difference in density is small (.105 compared to .062), more than 80% of the members in the charismatic groups are connected to one another by a bond in which power and love coexist. Essentially, this means that virtually all members are tied into the group by at least one relation that, while it embraces the individual with the love of brotherhood, simultaneously maintains alignment and control. This

TABLE 5:5 MULTIPLEX STRUCTURE OF LOVE AND POWER BY CHARISMATIC GROUPING AND BY CHARISMATIC TYPE

Loving AND Power[1]	CHARISMATIC GROUPING			CHARISMATIC TYPE			
	Charismatic (21)*	Noncharismatic (25)	TOTAL (46)	Resident Charismatic (4)	Absentee Charismatic (17)	High Charismatic Potential (5)	Low Charismatic Potential (20)
Dyadic connectedness	.105	.062	.082	.277	.065	.110	.050
Mn. # rels. per member	.823	.358	.572	1.883	.577	.620	.293
Pr. of power GIVEN loving (P•L/L)	.167	.201	.185	.327	.129	.251	.188
Pr. of loving GIVEN power (P•L/P)	.518	.295	.397	.864	.436	.457	.255

*N=( )
1. Relaxed definition of power.

123

is true for only 36% of those in the noncharismatic communes. We also find that there is a fifty percent likelihood of the coexistence of love and power occurring, whenever a power relation exists between a pair of members in the charismatic groups.

Considerable variation is apparent when the four-way charismatic classification is considered. Once again, the resident charismatic groups and those with high charismatic potential stand out from the other categories. For the former, more than a quarter of all possible relations involve love and power as coexistents. The members in these groups average nearly two of these bonds each. Moreover, there is an 86% likelihood that love will be present whenever a relation of power exists between a pair of members.

These attributes are a strong contrast to the absentee charismatic groups. The latter average a very low density of .065, and have a little more than half of their members tied into the group by this dual bond. Furthermore, the probability that love will coexist with power has all but halved to 44%. However, what is particularly noteworthy is that, in virtually every respect, the groups with high charismatic potential are closer to the absentee charismatic communes than they are to those with low charismatic potential. Indeed, with the lowest density, fewest mean number of bonds per member, and only a 26% probability of love coexisting with power, the groups with low charismatic potential are quite different. Overall then, these results provide a reasonable level of support for our primary theoretical expectation that power and love are coexistent relations in charismatic groups.

Summary

In Chapter Four, we narrowed our focus to a subset of relational contents that were able to differentiate charismatic from noncharismatic groups: viz, positive affect and power. Building on this foundation, this chapter has been concerned with how these contents are interrelated in charismatic groups.

Three sets of theoretically significant multiplex bonds have been examined. Viewing the contents of positive affect as measures of three distinct elements of communion, we found that *loving* (unity) and *improving* (optimism) tend to coexist in charismatic groups, while being differentiated in noncharismatic communes. Reflecting the catalytic effect of direct charismatic leadership, the relational structures in the resident charismatic groups also evidence a euphoric element *(exciting)* that tends to coexist with unity and optimism.

In examining the interrelation of love and dyadic intimacy, it is clear that the former has a distinctly fraternal meaning of a strong, unifying bond of collective affection in charismatic groups. But sexual and personal intimacy characterize love in noncharismatic groups.

Finally, consistent with our argument of the regulation of communion by power, we found that love and power coexist in charismatic groups while existing as separate relational dimensions under noncharismatic conditions. Throughout the analysis we have continued to find strong evidence that groups with resident charismatic leaders and those with high charismatic potential, stand out from the other categories with quite distinctive relational patterns.

NOTES

1. In contrast with the previous networks research, where multiplexity has meant either the multiple roles (Nadel, 1957; Boissevain, 1973) or the diversity of relations that enmesh the individual (Mitchell, 1969; Fischer, et al, 1977), I am using the concept in a different way. In this study, multiplexity refers to the kind and degree of interrelatedness among relational contents that typifies a particular structure — in this case, a charismatic structure. Consequently, my approach has more affinity to Harrison White and his collaborators' "block models" of "multiple networks" (see White, et al., 1976).

   My thinking on multiplexity has benefitted from David Bohm's discussion of the concept (Bohm, 1980:166-171). As a physicist, Bohm uses the concept of "multiplex" to capture the "enfolding of an unlimited set of Euclidean systems of orders and measures into each other". He derives his notion of multi-plex from the root "plex", which means to fold. "Simplex" thus means "onefold", and here is equivalent to Gluckman's sociolog-ical concept of "uniplex" relations, as social ties that involve only one content. "Complex", according to Bohm, means many sepa-rate objects folded together — that is "joined to each other". It is this meaning of multiplex, of many relational contents enfolded into each other, that I am using in this book.

2. By combining the *AND* and *NOT,* and the *OR* and *NOT* relations, two further logical functions can be derived: a *"NAND"* relation in which the output C is produced by the absence of A *AND* B; and a *"NOR"* relation in which C is the result of the absence of A *OR* B (Evans, 1966). These are the logical obverse of the *AND* and *OR* functions, respectively (compare Figure 5:1 with Figure 5:N1).

3. Other sociological interpretations are possible of the ways by which social relations may be interrelated. A more definitive interpretation of the meaning of the alternative logical combina-tions for a particular social pattern will require specifying addi-tional substantive parameters.

4. Two computer programs were developed by the Urban Com-munes Project to enable the kind of multiplex analysis under-taken in this chapter. The first program, *DAMP* — *D*efine *A*djacency *M*atrix *P*rogram (Messeri, 1975(a)), is used to define a particular subset of contents, the type/s of dyadic bonding, and enumerate the bonding logic of multiplex forms to construct sociomatrices for input into other programs for structural analy-sis. The second program, *STAM* — *ST*atistical *A*nalysis of *M*atrices (Messeri, 1975(b)), performs basic statistical analyses on the sociomatrices from *DAMP.* It provides estimates of den-sity, in-degrees and out-degrees, identifies disjointed subsets and sociometric levels of hierarchy, performs simple matrix addi-tion, and computes the ratio of relations between matrices of dif-ferent relations.

5. While I have kept the operational criterion for a *loving* rela-tion strict by requiring that both *i* and *j* answer "yes", I have relaxed the criterion for a *sexual* relation to include responses of "sometimes". See "The Relationship Question-naire", Appendix B.

6. These groups are Spectra (A) and Utopia House, and had dual bonds of *loving AND sexual* content in 23% and 25% of all dyads, respectively.

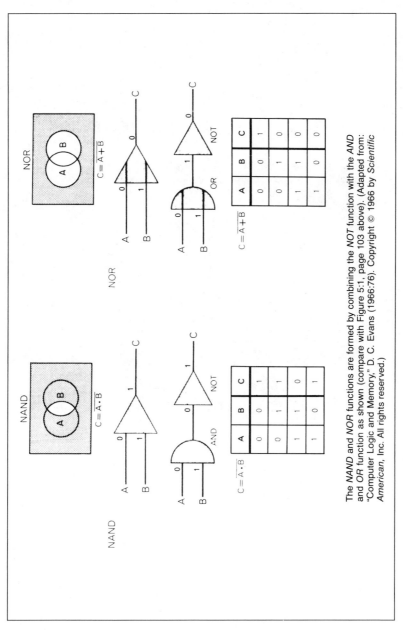

The *NAND* and *NOR* functions are formed by combining the *NOT* function with the *AND* and *OR* function as shown (compare with Figure 5:1, page 103 above). (Adapted from: "Computer Logic and Memory," D. C. Evans (1966:76). Copyright © 1966 by *Scientific American*, Inc. All rights reserved.)

5:N1 *"NAND" and "NOR" Logical Functions*

Chapter Six

FORM

Introduction

Social structure is multi-faceted and multi-dimensional, and must be researched from a number of vantage points to reveal underlying patterns and regularities. In studying charisma's structural foundation, we have attempted to accomplish this by successively narrowing the focus to fewer contents, while simultaneously examining, in greater depth, the patterning and interrelation of the remaining relational dimensions. In identifying the relations that form charisma's structural base and specifying how they are interrelated, the analysis has, so far, only considered dyads, the most elemental relational unit.

Although we have found distinctive patterns of dyadic bonding in the charismatic communes, the question remains as to how the dyads are structured for the group as a whole. Two groups, for example, with similar types and distributions of dyads, can have completely different relational patterns when global images are constructed for each group: one in

129

which every member is connected to at least one other person; and the other involving two or more separate cliques with high proportions of intraclique relations but with few interclique ties. To detect such differences, and to accurately construct images of global structure, requires a shift to higher structural levels and measurement units.

In this chapter, therefore, we will move to a higher level of analysis and address the question of the global organization of charisma. Our goal is to assess the degree of correspondence between images of communion and power, constructed from aggregations of mappings of dyads, and the global patterns we have postulated for charisma's structural foundation. Since there are a number of alternative approaches available, we must chose a method for analyzing global structure that is both congruent with our theory, and also appropriate given our relational measurement procedures.

Global Structure

Broadly speaking, three approaches have been developed for the analysis of relational mappings of global structure: viz, methods of analysis that focus on structural proximity, those that emphasize structural connectedness, and others that stress structural equivalence.

Structural Proximity

The first approach, structural proximity, views social structure as a multi-dimensional space of intersecting vectors of social proximity (MacFarland and Brown, 1973). This approach is based on the assumption of social distance — the idea that social phenomena can be described by a set of ordinal dimensions, along which social units are classified according to the amount of social space between each pair. Using Smallest Space Analysis (a technique that provides a graphic n-dimensional representation of the multi-dimensional solution), Laumann has pioneered the use of this method in his innovative studies of urban social networks and community elite structure (Laumann, 1973; Laumann and Pappi, 1976).

Structural Connectedness

Structural connectedness borrows its focus and many of its basic concepts from graph theory. Here structure is viewed geometrically, as particular configurations are formed by the relations among actors in a network. Examples of such geometric patterns are triads, tetrads, and higher order sub-network configurations; e.g., cliques, paths, chains, lattices, etc. (Harray, et al., 1965; Friedell, 1968; Alba and Kadushin, 1976; Holland and Leinhardt, 1976). Although, like structural proximity, this approach requires analysis of the actual relations that directly or indirectly connect social actors to one another, here there is no assumption of metric ordinality underlying a network's organization. Instead, geometric units and imagery are used to model the arrangement of relations among network members.

Structural Equivalence

The third approach is structural equivalence. It views social structure as divided into sets of actors which are distinguished from one another by the structural properties of the positions that the actors in each set occupy (White, et al., 1976; Burt, 1977). In block modeling, for example, the members of a "block" are distinct because they share the same relational property; this differentiates them from other "blocks" in a network. In this approach, the criterion for separating one set of actors from another does not necessarily mean that those actors belonging to the same set are actually connected to one another by social ties. All that is required is that they hold some relational property in common (Arabie, Boorman, and Levitt, 1978) — for example: two sets of actors who have no social ties, either with those in their own set or with those in the other set, but each set shares a different belief about a third party. A major difference between this approach and the other two, then, is that those in a structurally distinct set are not necessarily directly connected by social ties.

Which of the three approaches is selected by a researcher is important. Not only are these approaches based on very different substantive assumptions about underlying principles of social structure, but each may provide a different image of structure.[1] Fundamentally, however, selection of the appropriate method of analysis should be guided by the kind of structure postulated in a researcher's theory, and also by the kind of relational data gathered in a study (Granovetter, 1980). Because I have postulated differences in the geometric patterning of the actual relations that connect members, Holland and Leinhardt's (1976) triadic is the procedure we will use.

I. Structure of Communion

Theory

We have seen that communion is an intense emotional bonding in which individuals are fused into an undifferentiated unity — "oneness," as some members of the charismatic communes label it. There are two ways communion is generated. One, a circular, cumulative, pairwise process, starts between a particular pair of individuals and then radiates with increasing intensity throughout all relations in a group. In his study of the Bruderhof, a religious commune, Benjamin Zablocki describes this process as it unfolds the day after consensus had been achieved at a meeting resolving a crisis:

> The next day at work, the Brothers and Sister greet each other with fresh remembrances of their common euphoria. Each member throws himself into his work with new vigor. Individuals are moved to spontaneous acts of kindness toward one

another. These acts become contagious. Perhaps the children's reaction to their parents' reaction to them the night before has set the stage for a new wave of joy breaking out in the school. This in turn reinforces the joy of the grownups. ... Any interaction at any time, any task, any activity can be the starting point for a wave of joy. (Zablocki, 1971: 189-190.)

This process has been called circular reaction in studies of collective behavior (Blumer, 1946).

Communion can also be generated by a carefully orchestrated ritual aimed at facilitating and fusing individual energies into a "spontaneous" alignment of collective union (Turner, 1969). This occurred when one of our field-workers was attending a prayer meeting of the larger religious community in which the Dove, a charismatic commune, was participating.

What I was struck by was a feeling of community and a feeling of belongingness. People were happy: "Praise the Lord!;" "hallelujah!;" "thank you, Jesus Christ!" They smile a lot and it's a joyous occasion.

It was quite a thing to hear the resounding chorus of the five or six hundred people who were there: singing, praising the Lord, smiling and touching one another, and some doing a little dance as they're standing by their seats. ... It's a very moving, very eerie experience. Certain words get chanted or sung over and over again. It develops a certain kind of rhythm, a certain cadence. It starts very slowly, not very loudly — maybe 10 or 15 people with their arms outstretched and gradually increases. It begins to build up and it begins to increase in speed. People are opening up: having their arms stretched out, opening up towards Jesus, and chanting over and over again. It gets louder and you see more hands go up; you see more hands go up over on one side and then on the other. And finally it reaches a crescendo and then just stops.[2]

If we postulate that relations in charismatic groups will contain both residual elements of previous instances of communion, and also reflect a continual readiness and receptivity to future occurrences, then we can expect that:

Proposition 6:1 The structure of relations of positive affect in charismatic groups will be interlocking with each member connected to virtually everyone else.

Furthermore, given that the charismatic leader is a catalyst and facilitates higher levels of communion when present, it is expected that:

Proposition 6:2 The structure of positive affect bonds will be more interlocking when the charismatic leader is present than when (s)he is absent.

But in groups with low charismatic potential, where there exists a greater diversity of purpose among individual members, and where ties based on interpersonal attraction are more likely, we can expect that:

Proposition 6:3 Positive affect relations will be disjointed involving partially connected cliques, exclusive dyads, and isolated individuals.

Finally, because they share unrealized personal aspirations and the belief that these can only be attained through unity and collective effort, but lack the catalyst of charisma, it is expected that:

Proposition 6:4 Members of groups with high charismatic potential will be linked by bonds of positive affect, although less densely interlocked than in charismatic groups.

Verification: Triadic Analysis

To verify these propositions requires using a method that can separate interlocking structures, in which more-or-less everyone is connected, from more disjointed patterns involving cliques, exclusive dyads, and isolates. Also, the procedure must be as free as possible from researcher and structural bias to ensure that verification is impartial and systematic. And because virtually any relational pattern can be viewed as structurally meaningful, it is important to have some basis for assessing the extent to which a given pattern is more than the product of chance.

A method that meets these requirements has been created by Holland and Leinhardt (1970; 1976). This method, triadic analysis, was developed for analyzing the structural properties of small to medium-sized groups. Triadic analysis subdivides the relational structure into triads and then, through a census of all possible triads, measures the distribution of 16 different triadic configurations (see Figure 6:1).

The 16 triad types are distinguished from one another by their composition in terms of three kinds of dyads: *M*utual dyads, in which a symmetric relation connects two social actors: *A*symmetric dyads, involving an ordered or directed relation between the two; and *N*ull dyads, in which there is no relation connecting a pair. This *MAN* classification scheme means that each triad type can be uniquely identified and labelled. Thus, for example, the 012 triad, shown in Figure 6:1, has no Mutual relations, one Asymmetric relation, and two Null relations.[3]

It will be recalled from Chapter Four, that an *affirmed* dyad (where both individuals agree a given relation connects them) is the type of dyadic bonding that offered the greatest discrimination between the charismatic and noncharismatic communes. In Holland and Leinhardt's *MAN* scheme, this is the same as a mutual relation. Consequently, only four of the 16 triadic configurations are relevant for verifying our propositions: the 003 of three unconnected individuals; the 102, labelled as the isolated pair; the 201, three individuals partially connected by only two bonds; and the 300, in which all relations exist among the three individuals.[4]

Triadic analysis provides two procedures for verifying the propositions. The first is to compare the proportion of all possible triads for a group that are structured as 102 triads against the proportion for 300 triads. As a single, mutual bond connecting only two of the three members of each triad, the 102 triad is an indicator of the degree to which the relations in a group are structured as isolated dyads. On the other hand, the 300 triad is a completed triad of three mutual dyads. This triad provides a measure of the extent to which the global organization of relations is an interlocking pattern of bonding connecting virtually everyone.[5]

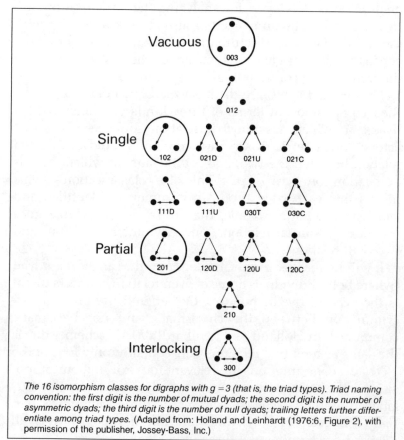

The 16 isomorphism classes for digraphs with g = 3 (that is, the triad types). Triad naming convention: the first digit is the number of mutual dyads; the second digit is the number of asymmetric dyads; the third digit is the number of null dyads; trailing letters further differentiate among triad types. (Adapted from: Holland and Leinhardt (1976:6, Figure 2), with permission of the publisher, Jossey-Bass, Inc.)

6:1 *Holland and Leinhardts' 16 Triad Types Showing Subset for Analysis of Undirected Relations*

But even if differences were found, there is still the question of whether a given frequency of triads is due to chance. In the second phase of triadic analysis, an assessment can be made of whether this is statistically likely. This is done by comparing the frequency of observed triad counts with their expected frequency. The result of this comparison is numerically summarized as a test statistic *tau* (τ). The expected frequencies for each of the 16 triad types were generated by Holland and Leinhardt by estimating triad distributions from random simulations of relational patterns.[6]

Analysis

The results of the triadic analysis are presented in Table 6:1. The analysis has been undertaken separately on the uniplex contents of *loving, improving,* and *exciting,* and on the dual bonds of *loving AND improving,* and *loving AND exciting.* The table presents the mean distribution of the four symmetrical triad types across the four-way charismatic classification. It also lists the mean τ statistic for the triad incidences that are statistically significant (i.e., pr. $\leq$ .005). The sign of the statistic indicates direction: a positive τ means that more triads of a given type occurred than expected by chance, and a negative τ indicates fewer.

Considering the distribution of triads first, there are two points that emerge from the data in Table 6:1. The first, is the strong contrast between the resident charismatic and the low charismatic potential communes.[7] While the former evidence an interlocking structuring of positive affect, the pattern in the latter is composed primarily of exclusive dyads. Thus, in the resident charismatic groups more than 90% of all triads for *loving,* and *improving,* and 80% for the dual bond of *loving AND improving,* are structured as 201 or 300 triads; in the groups with low charismatic potential, at least 30% of all triads are patterned as 102 triads for these relations. The resident charismatic groups also have an element of collective emotional intensity to their affective bonds — more than 30% of the triads for *exciting,* and those for *loving AND exciting,* are patterned as 201 or 300 triads.[8] Overall, these results, are quite consistent with our expectation that positive affect is structured as communion in resident charismatic groups,[9] while it is particularized as pair bonds in groups with low charismatic potential.

TABLE 6:1   TRIADIC ANALYSIS[1] OF COMMUNION (UNIPLEX AND MULTIPLEX CONTENTS) BY CHARISMATIC TYPE

Mean Proportions of Triad Incidence[2]

UNIPLEX CONTENTS CHARISMATIC TYPE	Loving				Improving				Exciting			
	Resident Charis-matic (4)*	Absentee Charis-matic (17)	High Char-ismatic Potential (5)	Low Char-ismatic Potential (20)	Resident Charis-matic	Absentee Charis-matic	High Char-ismatic Potential	Low Char-ismatic Potential	Resident Charis-matic	Absentee Charis-matic	High Char-ismatic Potential	Low Char-ismatic Potential
Symmetrical Triad Type												
003	.013	$.189^{2\ .194ii}$	.192	.386	0	$.216^{2\ .063i}$	$.257^{1.774i}$	.286	.242	.735	.454	.643
102	.080	.306	.360	.418	.080	.369	.285	.400	.414	.208	.372	.300
201	.283	$.268^{-1.868i}$	.159	.153	.254	$.227^{-3.262iii}$	.192	.224	$.212^{-1.868i}$	.049	.092	.047
300	.625	$.237^{3.030iii}$	.290	.042	.666	$.189^{4.326iiii}$	.266	.090	$.132^{3.047iii}$	.008	.081	.009
Total	1.001	1.000	1.001	.999	1.000	1.001	1.000	1.000	1.000	1.000	1.000	1.000

MULTIPLEX CONTENTS

Symmetrical Triad Type		Loving AND Improving			Loving AND Exciting			
003	.015	$.360^{2.042'}$	.415	.626	.272	.748	.459	.686
102	.180	.373	.270	.302	.405	.200	.377	.266
201	.370	.181	.124	.059	.217	.046	.085	.045
300	.436	$.087^{2.858''}$	.191	.014	$.107^{2.599''}$	.006	.079	.003
Total	1.001	1.001	1.000	1.001	1.001	1.000	1.000	1.000

1. The pr. values for τ scores reported in this book were taken from: Table A, "Proportions Under the Normal Curve," Runyon and Haber (1967:250–251).
2. Mean τ scores (small figures) given only when statistically significant. Symbols denote the following pr. values:
   ' .05
   '' .01
   ''''' .001
   ''''' .00005

*N = ( ). The number of communes in these categories remains the same for all contents analyzed here.

The second point to emerge from Table 6:1, is the structural similarity of the absentee charismatic and high charismatic potential groups. Both types of groups are more like each other than they are to the resident charismatic and low charismatic potential categories, respectively. Although there is some collective structuring of positive affect (see the 300 triads for *loving*, and *improving*, especially), most is channelled to the interpersonal level (102 triads). However, there also is some evidence of an important difference between these groups. While not as clear as expected, perhaps, greater emotional intensity shows up in the bonds of the groups with high charismatic potential (e.g., *exciting* relations). On balance, though, the structuring of positive affect in these groups is quite similar.

Some idea of what the triad distributions mean in terms of global organization in the four types of communes can be seen in the sociograms of Figure 6:2. The more densely interlocking structure of positive affect is clearly apparent for the example of the resident charismatic group — including the more emotionally intense multiplex patterns, and is consistent with the pattern we would expect for communion. The absentee charismatic example reveals a less densely interlocking pattern — still largely collective in structure — with much less multiplex emotional intensity. And while there is structural similarity between the former and the high charismatic potential example, the difference of a greater emotional intensity *(loving AND exciting)* in the latter is clearly apparent. Finally, the pattern of cliques, exclusive dyads, and isolates shows through for the groups with low charismatic potential.

When the *tau* statistics in Table 6:1 are examined, however, it would seem that, with the apparent exception of the absentee charismatic communes, the triadic patterns for virtually all relations appear to be accounted for by random factors alone. Furthermore, when the absentee charismatic groups are controlled on size, by removing the five largest groups which fall outside the size range of the other communes, the mean τ scores drop below 1.61 (where $pr. = .05$), which means the results are no longer "statistically" significant.

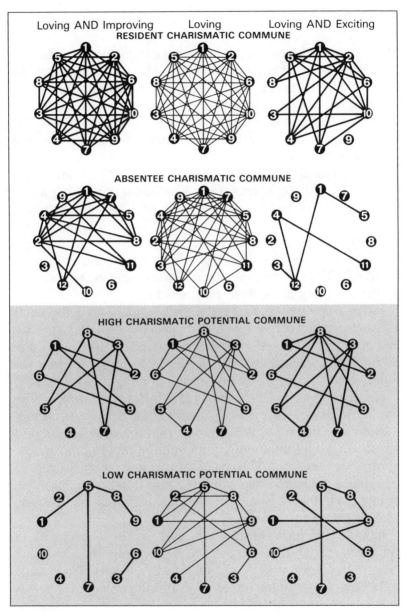

6:2 *An Example of Communion Structure in a Commune from Each Charismatic Type*

Validity of tau

This raises the question of the validity of *tau* in this analysis. This is an important issue because if the use of this statistic is considered appropriate, then the structural differences we have found can be explained by random factors, alone. On the other hand, if there are reasonable grounds for doubting the validity of the T statistic here, then it would be wiser to disregard it.

In her critical evaluation of T, Hallinan (1974: 31-36) argues that the statistic contains three weaknesses: first, as a test statistic, T does not measure the strength of a relationship; second, testing the significance of T is extremely difficult when the size of a group is small; and, third, T is based on a random model which is not "totally suitable for sentiment choices." Of the three, the second has the greatest applicability here, although the third may also hold.

Hallinan points out that the appropriateness of using *tau* as a test of significance is dependent upon the statistic's approximation to the normal distribution. Because the maximum number of values that T can assume is one more than the number of possible triads in a group, large groups with many triads have many possible values, while small groups with few triads have many fewer values. Thus, with a much narrower range of values, it is possible that the distribution of T for small groups may not be adequately represented by the normal distribution. This means that there is an increased possibility of error in accepting the null hypothesis for small groups. Whether T is appropriate in this case depends upon what is meant by "small".

In both Hallinan's discussion, and in the earlier work of Holland and Leinhardt, there is agreement that a "small group" has fewer than eight members. However, in a more recent discussion, Holland and Leinhardt (1976: 181) suggest that a group's size should be "at least" ten to have confidence that T approximates a normal distribution. Because 35 of our 46 communes have fewer than 10 members (26 have less than

8), and because 9 of the 11 groups with 10 or more members are in the absentee charismatic category, it is reasonable to suspect the validity of the T statistic in this case. Therefore, in accepting the structural differences among the four kinds of communes as sociologically significant (something that is corroborated by the ethnographic evidence), we will leave aside the question of statistical significance.

II. Structure of Power

In Chapter Four we found that power is important in the social structure of both charismatic and noncharismatic communes. The question to be addressed now concerns the extent to which there are differences between these groups in the global organization of power relations.

Theory

We have argued that in order to achieve a radical transformation of social structure, charismatic groups must generate large amounts of collective energy. This is accomplished by fusing individuals together in an intense communion to release the energy locked up as existing structure. As a highly charged emotional bond, communion is extremely volatile and has a destabilizing effect on a group. A strong, clearly articulated power structure counterbalances this pressure by enabling a charismatic system to harness and align the energy for the achievement of collective ends. If we postulate that this pattern will be reflected in the geometry of power relations, we can expect that:

Proposition 6:5 Power relations in charismatic groups will form a single, highly interlocking, transitively-ordered structure aligned under the charismatic leader.

Because the charismatic leader is a catalyst facilitating even higher levels of communion, in order to counterbalance the increased destabilizing pressure on the group, it is likely that:

Proposition 6:6 The properties specified for power in Proposition 6:5, will be more evident when the charismatic leader is resident than when absent.

And, because stability can be increased when the catalytic effect of resident charismatic leadership is reduced by routinization, we can also expect that:

Proposition 6:7 The power structure of absentee charismatic groups will contain more elements of formal organization than that of resident charismatic groups.

But, while groups with high charismatic potential are energized around shared unfulfilled needs, they lack the collective means for alignment and control. Accordingly, it is expected that:

Proposition 6:8 The power structure in groups with high charismatic potential will be less hierarchical and more disjointed with leader rivalry and intransitivity.

And finally, because social energy is channelled primarily into highly particularized interpersonal bonds, we would predict that:

Proposition 6:9 The structure of power relationships in groups with low charismatic potential will manifest little collective organization, with cliques, dominance chains, and isolates.

Analysis

Despite the problem that *undirected* (symmetric) and *directed* (asymmetric) relations are confounded together by Holland and Leinhardt in the dyad classification that underlies their *MAN* scheme,[10] the technique can be modified to analyze ordered or directed relations such as power. In Figure 6:3 the seven asymmetric triads relevant to the analysis of directed relational structures have been labeled: the remaining nine triad types are inappropriate for our purposes because they each have at least one nondirectional relation.[11]

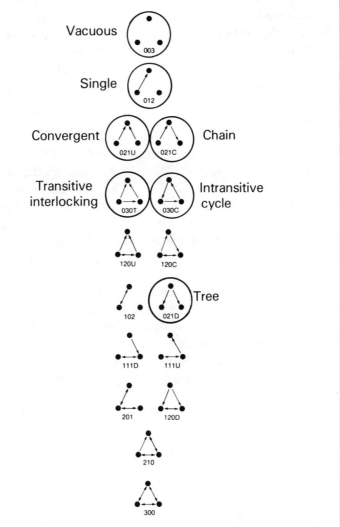

The 16 isomorphism classes for digraphs with g = 3 (that is, the triad types). Triad naming convention: the first digit is the number of mutual dyads; the second digit is the number of asymmetric dyads; the third digit is the number of null dyads; trailing letters further differentiate among triad types. (Adapted from: Holland and Leinhardt (1976:6, Figure 2), with permission of the publisher, Jossey-Bass, Inc.)

6:3 *Holland and Leinhardts' 16 Triad Types Showing Subset for Analysis of Directed Relations*

To operationalize the concepts contained in the propositions above, we will use the 030T triad to measure the degree
of interlock, and the 030C triad to capture intransitivity.[12] The
extent to which a power structure is disjointed, or composed
of isolated positions is measured by the incidence of the 012,
the 021U, and the 003 triads. A high high incidence of the
021D, and 021C triads will be used as an indicator of formal
elements of organization.

Propositions 6:5 through 6:9 predict that the power structures of the charismatic communes will be more centralized
around a single dominant leader than those of the noncharismatic groups. We can define a leader, in graph-theoretic
terms, as any individual who is not subordinate to any other
member, and who dominates at least one person in the commune.[13] Sole leadership means that only one member holds
this position, while multiple leadership means more than one
person is dominant.

Although there is not the space for tabular presentation
here, the data show that centralized leadership is more likely
when the charismatic leader is physically present in the
group.[14] Thus, while all four of the resident charismatic
groups have sole leadership, multiple leadership is found in
70% of the absentee charismatic communes. Other evidence
from the latter indicates that this reflects more formalized
positions of leadership, specialized by function and scope of
authority, assigned by the absentee charismatic leader (see
the example in Figure 2:2, page 39). Multiple sociometric leadership also is the predominant form in the noncharismatic
groups, although here it more typically reflects competition
for leadership and rivalry.

A similar pattern is present when the degree of sociometric
dominance is considered. Taking the most dominant sociometric leader in each commune[15] and computing the proportion of direct *power* relations they hold over other members, shows that the groups with resident charismatic leaders
stand out with virtually every member (.95) under the direct
power of the charismatic leader. The highest figure for the

other communes is .66 for the groups with high charismatic potential.

TABLE 6:2   TRIADIC ANALYSIS OF ("RELAXED") POWER BY CHARISMATIC TYPE

	Mean Proportions of Triad Incidence[1] CHARISMATIC TYPE			
	Resident Charismatic (4)*	Absentee Charismatic (17)	High Charismatic Potential (5)	Low Charismatic Potential (20)
Asymmetrical Triad Type				
003	$.085^{1.709\prime}$	.423	.238	.293
012	.162	.388	.357	.382
021D	$.314^{3.724\prime\prime\prime\prime}$	$.078^{2.469\prime\prime}$	$.194^{2.990\prime\prime\prime\prime}$	.088
021U	.084	.037	.095	.093
021C	$.068^{-2.952\prime\prime}$	$.038^{-2.002\prime}$	$.040^{-1.828\prime}$	.062
030T	$.288^{2.509\prime\prime}$	$.033^{1.943\prime}$	.071	.069
030C	$0^{-2.028\prime}$	.004	.006	.013
Total	1.001	1.001	1.001	1.000

1. Mean T score (small figures) given only when statistically significant. Symbols denote the following *pr.* values:
    '   .05
    ''   .01
    '''   .001
    ''''   .0001
*N = ( ).

Moving on to the triadic analysis, Table 6:2 gives the mean distribution of the seven asymmetric triads broken down by charismatic type. As before, the mean *tau (T)* statistic is provided when "statistically" significant.

With the notable exception of the resident charismatic groups, at first glance the triad distributions appear to indicate more structural similarity than difference when divided by charismatic type. However, this is due to the relatively high incidence (greater than 50%) of the vacuous 003 triad and the 012 triad of exclusive dyads. While this pattern would seem to suggest highly fragmented and disjointed power structures, quite large structural differences can result from very small changes in the relative incidence of triad types. This is something we will see in a moment from the hierarchical sociograms in Figure 6:4, when some examples are considered. There is evidence, too, that a less rigorous ("unrestricted") operational definition of *power* reveals not only more densely connected power structures, but also stronger differences in triadic structure generally consistent with our theoretical expectations (see Chapter Eight).

Of the three triads that have two asymmetric relations (the 021D, the 021U, and the 021C), differences are apparent among groups only for the 021D see Table 6:2. While both the absentee charismatic and groups with low charismatic potential have less than 10% of any of their 021 triads structured this way, the 021D triad is present for nearly 20% of the triads in the communes with high charismatic potential and more than 30% in the resident charismatic groups. The τ statistics indicate these distributions appear to be statistically significant — that they are not due to chance. Furthermore, it is possible that fewer chains (021C triad) have occurred than expected by chance in all but the groups with low charismatic potential.

Providing good support for our expectation, the data show a dense (29%) pattern of interlocking transitive triads (030T triad) for the resident charismatic communes. This is in strong contrast to the relatively low incidence of this triad in the other categories — each with fewer than 8%. Moreover, not only is this significant at the .01 level for the resident charismatic communes, but even the seemingly low proportion (3%) of this triad in the absentee charismatic groups is apparently more than expected by chance. However, given the problem mentioned above, of the size bias of the *tau* statistic, it may be unwise to use it as the basis for inferences about structural differences among the groups.

Finally, while it is clear that there are relatively few incidences of intransitivity (030C triad) the very small differences that are present run in the expected direction. Thus, little or no intransitivity is present in the charismatic groups, with the highest level occurring in the groups with low charismatic potential.

By way of summarizing the findings, a visual image of the differences is presented in Figures 6:4(a) and 6:4(b). For the resident charismatic groups (Figure 6:4(a)), at least, the sociograms confirm what has emerged from the analysis: these groups have highly ordered power structures. They have greater consensus over power relations; there is a higher density and greater connectivity of power; there is complete transitivity; and they have clearly delineated, multi-leveled hierarchies (four or more levels), aligned under the charismatic leader who, with the exception of one group, holds direct power over everyone else. In addition, most (87%) of the structure is comprised of acknowledged dominance relations, indicating a high degree of consensus about the structure of power in these groups.

Two kinds of power structures are evident among the absentee charismatic groups. One tends to have more levels, fewer positions at any particular level, and is dominated by a single leader (appointed by the absentee charismatic leader). The other kind, has multiple leaders and is structured as a single, multi-leveled power hierarchy. For these groups, there is another level of power above the appointed leaders for which systematic data, unfortunately, were not collected — that occupied by the absentee charismatic leader. From the sporadic data that is available, though, it appears that the absentee charismatic leader occupies a strong position of power which is generally acknowledged by everyone.

The images for the communes with high charismatic potential (Figure 6:4(b)) reflect the greater incidence of the 021D triad (the tree) identified by triadic analysis. And it is apparent that the structures tend to have few levels with almost as many sociometric leaders as subordinates. They also tend to have less structural coherence — they are more disjointed, evidencing cliques and isolated individuals.

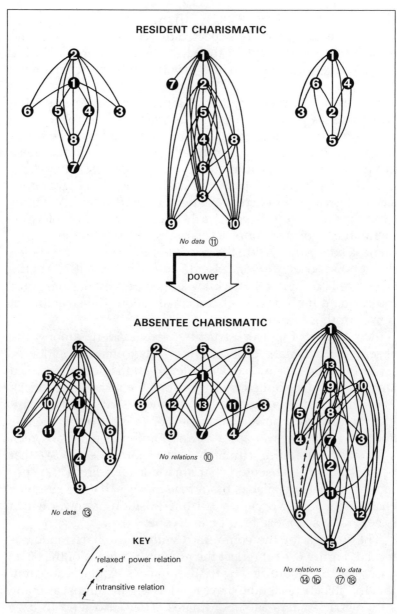

6:4(a) *Selected Examples of ("Relaxed") Power Structure in Resident and Absentee Charismatic Communes*

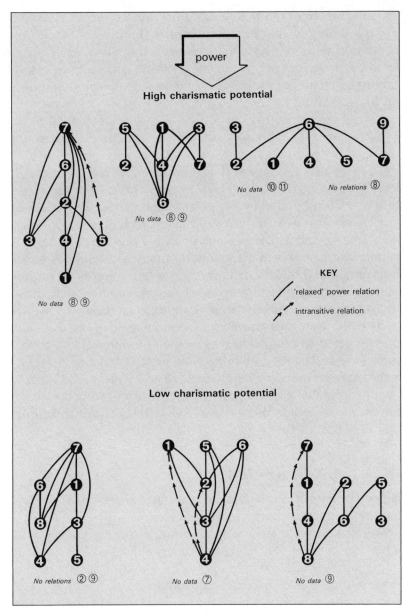

6:4(b) *Selected Examples of ("Relaxed") Power Structure in High, and Low Charismatic Potential Communes*

This pattern of multiple leadership can also be seen for the groups with low charismatic potential (Figure 6:4(b)). When compared with the charismatic groups, there is much less collective structuring of power. The patterns appear to be elaborations of chains of dyadic dominance — patterns that reflect an interpersonal rather than a collective order of power.

Let us conclude this section on a more speculative note. What is striking about these power structures, especially those in the resident and absentee charismatic communes, is the degree of coherence and order that is present at the group level (e.g., Figure 6:4(a)). This is something that, in broad terms, is corroborated by the ethnographic evidence. Taken at face value, these patterns would seem to be more appropriately interpreted as the product of global processes of organization than simply a function of micro-level processes of interpersonal interaction. This interpretation raises an important, intriguing question when it is remembered that these images are constructed from mappings of dyads in which each dyad was measured as a separate entity, as if it was unconnected to other relations in the commune. How, therefore, can such coherent images of global structure be constructed from mappings of discrete dyads, unless information about the global organization of the group is somehow contained in the dyads themselves? We will take up this important question in Part Four.

III. Validity of Results

It is clear from the analysis, so far, that charisma is associated with relational structures that have a strong, elaborated power structure, interlocking relations of positive affect, and a high probability that bonds of fraternal love will be present when a power relation exists between a pair of members. But there are still two important questions to be resolved concerning the validity of these findings. The first concerns the extent to which such global organization is emergent and cannot be explained by properties of the lower order elements from which social structure is constructed. The second concerns the degree to which factors other than charisma are more strongly associated with the relational patterns we have identified.

Emergent Structure and Structural Bias

Once the distinctive global characteristics of a network have been identified, it is important to establish whether these can be considered as indicators of the network's emergent structure, or are merely aggregated attributes of the network's components. This is a very difficult problem because, at present, global images of structure cannot be based on relational measurement at the group level. Rather, they must be constructed by aggregating mappings of dyads into larger relational units such as triads, cliques, or blocks. As a consequence, it is necessary to assess the extent to which a given global pattern is a reflection of the actual nature of a network's holistic organization, instead of being an artifact of the method of analysis used.

Two issues must be resolved for inference of emergent structure to be valid: a substantive issue concerning the appropriate level of analysis at which emergent structure can be inferred for a given social phenomenon (Wallace, 1975; 1983); and a methodological issue of spurious inference due to structural bias in the analytic techniques employed (Hallinan, 1974).

Some resolution of these issues can be achieved by multilevel analysis (Falter, 1978). Essentially, this procedure enables the researcher to control for the effects of lower levels of structure and, thereby, empirically demonstrate the existence of a structural residual that cannot be explained by attributes of more elemental units.

For the analysis that follows, we will focus on the five relational contents that have consistently distinguished the charismatic from the noncharismatic groups; the contents of *loving, improving,* and *power,* and the dual bonds of *loving AND improving,* and *loving AND power.* Because there are too few cases in the resident charismatic and high charismatic potential categories (N = 4 and 5, respectively) for multivariate analysis, we will work with the dichotomous charismatic — noncharismatic classification.

Although the quantitative relational analysis has been carefully cross-validated against ethnographic data, it is still necessary to ensure that the findings are not merely a result of structural biases in triadic analysis (Hallinan, 1974). Both because the *tau* statistic is biased against smaller sized groups (especially where N<7), and because, with fewer members, a higher density of dyads is more likely in the small communes, it is important to examine the effect of group size on the relational patterns observed.

This precaution is also important for another reason. In triadic analysis, triads are constructed by aggregating dyads. This means that differences in the incidence of dyads may explain the differences observed in triadic patterns. To control for such structural spuriousness, it is therefore imperative to check that the charismatic-noncharismatic triadic differences are independent of differences in the incidence of dyads.

These two sources of structural bias are examined in Table 6:3. While the results of the analysis of size reveal, that if anything, differences in the density of both dyads and triads (across all contents), tend to be suppressed by the differences in group size, quite a strong positive relationship is present between size and the magnitude of the T statistic. Although the latter shows an increased probability that the structure of the charismatic groups is due to chance, there are still statistically significant differences between the charismatic and noncharismatic communes.

For dyads, a positive relationship between the incidence of dyads and the incidence of triads exists for both categories. However, small but consistent differences still remain between the two when sub-samples with similar densities of dyads are compared. These results also show that the differences in dyad density tend to reduce the size of the mean T statistics — especially for the charismatic groups.

TABLE 6:3   TRIADIC ANALYSIS[1] (SELECTED TRIADS) OF COMMUNION CONTENTS AND POWER CONTROLLING FOR COMMUNE SIZE AND FOR DYADIC CONNECTEDNESS

CHARISMATIC GROUPING	Matched by Size[2]		Matched by Dyadic Connectedness (d.c.)		Control Sample		
	Charismatic (11)[3]	Non-charismatic (23)	Charismatic	Non-charismatic	Charismatic (17)	Non-charismatic (23)	Total (40)*
Mean size	8.6	6.6	n.a.	n.a.	10.6	6.6	8.3
CONTENT							
Loving							
mean d.c.	.584	.304	.468	.406	.558	.304	.412
mean propn. 300 triad	.306$^{1.639\prime}$	.506	.166$^{4.143\prime\prime\prime\prime}$ (9)	.085 (15)	.275$^{3.299\prime\prime\prime}$	.056	.149$^{1.789\prime}$
Improving							
mean d.c.	.623	.366	.416	.451	.561	.366	.449
mean propn. 300 triad	.381$^{1.662\prime}$	.104	.128$^{4.928\prime\prime\prime\prime}$ (9)	.116 (12)	.316$^{4.394\prime\prime\prime\prime}$	.104	.194$^{2.220\prime}$
Loving AND Improving							
mean d.c.	.466	.161	.321	.236	.418	.161	.271
mean propn. 300 triad	.202	.021	.080$^{4.258\prime\prime\prime\prime}$ (13)	.032 (15)	.166$^{3.515\prime\prime\prime}$	.021	.083$^{1.684\prime}$

(Continued)

155

TABLE 6:3   TRIADIC ANALYSIS[1] — (Continued)

CHARISMATIC GROUPING	Matched by Size[2]		Matched by Dyadic Connectedness (d.c.)		Control Sample		
	Charismatic (11)[3]	Non-charismatic (23)	Charismatic (11)	Non-charismatic (16)	Charismatic (17)	Non-charismatic (23)	Total (40)*
Power							
mean d.c.	.361	.378	.305	.332	.336	.378	.360
mean propn. 030T triad	.127 [1.902ʺ]	.072	.046 [2.531ʺ]	.035	.100 [2.668ʺ]	.072	.084
mean propn. 021D triad	.108	.100	.087 [3.476ʺʺ]	.085	.108 [2.910ʺʺ]	.100	.104 [1.708,]
Loving AND Power							
mean d.c.	.119	.057	n.a.	n.a.	.105	.057	.077
mean pr. loving AND power/power	.536	.277	n.a.	n.a.	.543	.277	.390

1. Mean T scores (small figures) given only when statistically significant. Symbols denote the following pr. values:

   ' .05
   '' .01
   ''' .001
   ''''' .00005

2. This is the adjusted size and excludes members who did not fill out the Relationship Questionnaire.

3. This excludes six charismatic communes with size >12.

*N = ( ).

Overall though, of the two sources of structural bias, the positive relationship of group size to the T statistic is more serious. This finding has both a methodological and a social-theoretic interpretation. Methodologically, our results could be seen as evidence of the bias of the statistic against the smaller groups. But even if this is true, it does not account for the statistically significant T that distinguishes the charismatic groups when the two sub-samples are matched on size. A more compelling interpretation is that through the dual structures of communion and power, charisma is a strong cohesive force that permits larger social collectivities.

Alternative Explanations[16]

Given the characteristics of the charismatic communes identified in Chapter Two, there are five social factors which may offer an alternative way of explaining the structural differences; degree of ideological consensus, level of religiosity, extent of authority, degree of institutionalization, and for the charismatic communes, affiliation to a larger organization (federation status).

Starting with ideological consensus, Table 6:4 shows a structural residual in the charismatic groups that is independent of this variable. Thus, while the analysis of sub-samples shows higher incidences of both dyads and triads in the charismatic groups, it also is apparent that greater ideological consensus is associated with more structure. But even so, the mean T for the charismatic communes in the "low" category still signals the presence of triadic structure that cannot be explained by chance.

With little overlap between the charismatic and noncharismatic communes on religious affiliation, analysis was undertaken at both the group and individual levels of analysis.[17] Grouping the communes by the intensity with which

TABLE 6:4 TRIADIC ANALYSIS[1] (SELECTED TRIADS) OF COMMUNION CONTENTS AND POWER BY SUBSAMPLES OF CHARISMATIC GROUPING MATCHED ON SELECTED VARIABLES

CHARIS-MATIC GROUPING	"LOW" IDEOLOGICAL CONSENSUS			RELIGIOSITY			DEGREE OF AUTHORITY			"SOME" OR "FEW" RULES		
	Charis-matic (8)*	Non-charis-matic (15)	Total (23)	Charis-matic (7)	Non-charis-matic (8)	Total (15)	Charis-matic (5)	Non-charis-matic (9)	Total (14)	Charis-matic (8)	Non-charis-matic (21)	Total (29)
Control Variable	n.a.	n.a.	n.a.	$.486^{2}$	.456	.470	1.60^{3}	1.33	1.43	n.a.	n.a.	n.a.
CONTENT												
Loving												
mean d.c.[4]	.515	.309	.380	.544	.404	.469	.424	.340	.370	.545	.321	.383
mean propn. 300 triad	$.211^{2.273'}$	.060	.112	$.284^{3.809''''}$	$.105^{1.603'}$	$.188^{2.632''}$	$.141^{2.124'}$	.057	.087	$.268^{2.241''}$	.062	.119
Improving												
mean d.c.	.474	.353	.395	.494	.428	.459	.504	.350	.405	.536	.385	.429
mean propn. 300 triad	$.193^{2.537''}$	.092	.127	$.249^{6.143''''}$	.112	$.176^{3.025''}$	$.285^{3.225''}$	.089	$.159^{1.659'}$	$.265^{2.457''}$	.109	.152
Loving AND Improving												
mean d.c.	.334	.180	.233	.389	.265	.323	.321	.189	.236	.401	.162	.228
mean propn. 300 triad	$.081^{2.266''}$	.028	.046	$.165^{4.856'''''}$	.036	$.096^{2.618'}$	$.097^{2.005'}$	.017	.046	$.151^{2.197''}$	.023	.058

158

Power

mean d.c.	.240	.401	.345	.349	.433	.394	.352	.417	.394	.308	.376	.356
mean propn. 030T triad	$.040^{1.738'}$	.097	.077	$.110^{3.125''}$	.118	$.114^{1.773'}$	$.107^{1.838'}$	.098	.101	$.101^{2.489''}$	.074	.061
mean propn. 021D triad	.053	.097	.082	$.095^{3.301'''}$	.135	$.116^{1.938'}$	.097	.116	.109	.071	.086	.082

Loving AND Power

mean d.c.	.063	.058	.060	.108	.146	.128	.069	.078	.075	.099	.056	.068
mean pr. loving AND power/power	.450	.245	.316	.541	.311	.418	.388	.361	.371	.481	.268	.322

*N = ( ).
1. Mean τ scores (small figures) given only when statistically significant. Symbols denote the following pr. values:
   '   .05
   ''   .01
   '''   .001
   '''' .0001
   ''''' .00005
2. Mean religious attitude score.
3. Mean Gutman "authority scale" score.
4. d.c. = dyadic connectedness.

(selected) religious attitudes are held (Table 6:4) still results in unexplained structural differences. Moreover, for the charismatic communes (Table 6:5), triadic structure is independent of the intensity of religion; both categories of religious intensity have comparable densities of dyads and triads, and the T statistics have similar significant values. While there is no single, conclusive piece of evidence, that the association between charisma and relational structure is independent of religion, a consistent pattern of results points in this direction.

Similar results can be seen for formal organization (Table 6:4). Matching communes with comparable levels of authority still leaves the charismatic groups with higher densities of dyads and a triadic structure that cannot be explained by chance. And while authority is positively associated with triadic structure, when the charismatic communes are considered alone (Table 6:5), the T statistics, although reduced in magnitude, remain statistically significant — clear evidence of an independent charismatic effect.

Continuing evidence of this charismatic effect is evident when the degree of institutionalization is considered (Table 6:4). Again, comparing sub-samples with similar extents of rules, the charismatic groups have higher densities of dyads and more triadic structure than the noncharismatic sub-sample. And, although formalization of normative patterns is associated with the presence of these relational properties, there also is evidence of an independent association of structure with charisma (Table 6:5).

Finally, comparing the Love from Above communes with the rest of the charismatic communes (Table 6:5), reveals almost identical relational patterns for both sets of groups. Because the former, as affiliates of a larger nation-wide federation, share a common culture and organization, these results suggest that the structural properties we have identified are not specific to particular organizational cultures, but are more general characteristics of charismatic groups.

TABLE 6:5 TRIADIC ANALYSIS[1] (SELECTED TRIADS) OF COMMUNION CONTENTS AND POWER FOR CHARISMATIC COMMUNES CONTROLLED BY SELECTED VARIABLES

CONTROLLED BY	IDEOLOGICAL CONSENSUS			RELIGIOSITY			DEGREE OF AUTHORITY		
Control Variable	Consensus (9)*	<Consensus (8)	Total (17)	High (9)	Low (7)	Total (16)	High (9)	Low (8)	Total (17)
Control Variable	n.a.	n.a.	n.a.	1.492^2	.486	1.052	4.67^3	1.75	3.29
CONTENT									
Loving									
mean d.c.[4]	.596	.515	.558	.553	.544	.549	.620	.488	.558
mean propn. 300 triad	$.332^{4.211\prime\prime\prime\prime}$	$.211^{2.273r}$	$.275^{3.299\prime\prime\prime}$	$.259^{3.114\prime\prime\prime}$	$.284^{3.809\prime\prime\prime\prime}$	$.270^{3.418\prime\prime\prime}$	$.349^{4.293\prime\prime\prime}$	$.192^{2.176r}$	$.275^{3.299\prime\prime\prime}$
Improving									
mean d.c.	.639	.474	.561	.632	.494	.572	.626	.439	.561
mean propn. 300 triad	$.425^{6.783\prime\prime\prime\prime}$	$.193^{2.551r}$	$.316^{4.394\prime\prime\prime\prime}$	$.395^{3.823\prime\prime\prime}$	$.249^{6.143\prime\prime\prime\prime}$	$.331^{4.906\prime\prime\prime\prime}$	$.386^{6.302\prime\prime\prime\prime}$	$.237^{2.568r}$	$.316^{4.394\prime\prime\prime\prime}$
Loving AND Improving									
mean d.c.	.494	.334	.418	.454	.389	.425	.493	.335	.418
mean propn. 300 triad	$.243^{4.625\prime\prime\prime\prime}$	$.081^{2.266r}$	$.166^{3.515\prime\prime\prime}$	$.182^{2.758r}$	$.165^{4.856\prime\prime\prime\prime}$	$.174^{3.676\prime\prime\prime}$	$.234^{5.054\prime\prime\prime\prime}$	$.091^{1.762r}$	$.166^{3.515\prime\prime\prime}$
Power									
mean d.c.	.422	.240	.336	.343	.349	.346	.396	.270	.336
mean propn. 030T triad	$.154^{3.494\prime\prime\prime}$	$.040^{1.738r}$	$.100^{2.668r}$	$.103^{2.461r}$	$.110^{3.125\prime\prime\prime}$	$.106^{2.751r}$	$.123^{3.306\prime\prime\prime}$	$.075^{1.647r}$	$.100^{2.668r}$
mean propn. 021D triad	$.156^{4.624\prime\prime\prime\prime}$	.053	$.108^{2.910r}$	$.127^{2.911r}$	$.095^{3.305\prime\prime\prime}$	$.113^{3.084\prime\prime\prime}$	$.140^{4.760r}$	.072	$.106^{2.910r}$
Loving AND Power									
mean d.c.	.141	.063	.105	.106	.108	.107	.144	.141	.105
mean pr. loving AND power/ power	.626	.450	.543	.525	.541	.532	.675	.394	.543

(Continued)

TABLE 6:5 TRIADIC ANALYSIS[1] — (Continued)

CONTROLLED BY	EXPLICIT RULES			FEDERATION STATUS		
	Many (8)	Few (9)	Total (17)	L.A.O.+ (6)	Other Charismatic (11)	Total (17)
CONTENT						
Loving						
mean d.c.[4]	.554	.561	.558	.578	.546	.558
300 triad mean propn.	$.272^{4.595'''''}$	$.278^{2.147''}$	$.275^{3.299'''}$	$.251^{3.545'''}$	$.288^{3.165'''}$	$.275^{3.299'''}$
Improving						
mean d.c.	.608	.520	.561	.583	.549	.561
300 triad mean propn.	$.391^{7.704'''''}$	$.249^{2.305''}$	$.316^{4.394'''''}$	$.320^{5.724'''''}$	$.314^{3.668'''}$	$.316^{4.394'''''}$
Loving AND Improving						
mean d.c.	.450	.390	.418	.437	.408	.418
300 triad mean propn.	$.198^{5.156'''''}$	$.138^{2.056''}$	$.166^{3.515'''}$	$.140^{4.297'''''}$	$.181^{3.088'''}$	$.166^{3.515'''}$
Power						
mean d.c.	.384	.294	.336	.223	.398	.336
030T triad mean propn.	$.111^{3.014'''}$	$.091^{2.360''}$	$.100^{2.666''}$	.029	$.139^{3.308'''}$	$.100^{2.668''}$
021D triad mean propn.	$.155^{4.957'''''}$	.066	$.108^{2.910''}$	$.064^{3.095'''}$	$.131^{2.809''}$	$.108^{2.910''}$
Loving AND Power						
mean d.c.	.144	.096	.105	.075	.121	.105
mean pr. loving AND power/ power	.583	.507	.543	.540	.545	.543

*N = ( ).

+ Communes affiliated with the Love from Above Organization.

1. The mean *T* scores are given only when statistically significant. See Table 6:4 for significance levels.
2. Mean religious attitude score.
3. Mean Guttman "authority scale" score.
4. d.c. = dyadic connectedness

162

Summary

Overall then, there is reasonable evidence of an association between charisma and the structural properties postulated by our relational theory. Reflecting the latent presence of communion, we have seen that relations involving positive affect tend to have an interlocking structure in charismatic groups, which is intensified when the charismatic leader is present. And we have found also that these groups are distinguished by a strong, well ordered structure of power relations. Again, as expected, this pattern is intensified for the groups with resident charismatic leaders. Finally, there is consistent evidence of a relationship between charisma and these relational structures that is both independent of structural bias in the methods of analysis used, and also independent of other measures of social organization.

In the next chapter, the last in this third part of the book, we take the final step in verifying our theory: testing the thesis that, to remain stable and survive, a charismatic system must counterbalance the high level of collective energy generated by communion with a strong, well ordered power structure. To validate this expectation, we need to show that these relational patterns have direct consequences for the stability of a charismatic group. This means our analysis will add yet another dimension of complexity by examining the effect of power and communion on group survival over time.

NOTES

1. While some researchers have reported similar results when using different relational methods on the same data (e.g., Rogers and Kincaid, 1981), it is important to achieve greater understanding of the conditions under which different methods produce convergent and divergent images of structure (see Schwartz, 1977).

2. The fieldworker noticed that "signals were given from one or two of the co-directors, so that after... the chanting began, it was one of the co-directors who first put his hand up and then other people began doing that. ... The whole thing started at the behest of one of the co-directors."

3. See pages 311 to 315 in Appendix A for a fuller description of the *MAN* scheme.

4. It is strongly recommended that the reader consult pages 311 to 327 of Appendix A for an understanding of some basic problems with the *MAN* scheme, and to see why I have employed a different classification of dyads.

5. A potential limitation of this analysis, involves the attempt to make inferences about the global organization of relations from triad distributions. It is generally assumed that patterns derived from aggregations of subunits such as triads are not equivalent to the actual structure of the system as a whole. Moreover, as in most network studies, relations in the communes have been measured dyadically, so that it is possible that differences in triadic organization may merely reflect variation at the dyadic level. One solution to this problem is multilevel analysis — to demonstrate the existence of a structural residual that cannot be explained when the effects of lower structural levels are controlled. This procedure has been employed in this study and will be described later.

   However, even this solution does not solve the problem of basing inferences about global structure on measurement of dyads. In Part Four of this book, this issue is confronted directly, where it is found that dyadic mappings (like the method used in this study) may indeed contain information about global structure.

6. Despite the convenience of Holland and Leinhardts' procedure for our purposes, verification of the propositions will not be a straightforward matter. One problem is the influence of group size on the *tau* statistic. Holland and Leinhardt (1976: 36) point out that the test statistic, T, may increase with the size of the group, and that its distribution should be plotted against group size when comparisons among groups of widely varying sizes are made. With a big difference in the size of the charismatic (Mean $N = 12$) and noncharismatic (Mean $N = 7$) communes, this precaution has been followed in the analysis reported here.

   A second, more basic problem, is that the T statistic is computed from the relative distribution of relations across the triad types, and, consequently, is dependent upon the incidence of ties for a given triad type. However, our theory is not concerned with just the incidence of the 300 triad, but with the degree to which these fully connected triads are interconnected with one another. Unfortunately, triadic analysis does not measure the degree of overlap among triads. Despite the potential for subjective bias, this has been assessed by a visual inspection of sociograms.

7. A triadic analysis of the charismatic-noncharismatic grouping of the communes also reveals similar structural differences. This can be seen, in part, in Table 6:4, below. Space does not permit a full presentation of these results. The interested reader should consult Bradley, 1980, Chapters Six and Seven.

8. While there is evidence that relations involving the *exciting* content tend to be dyadically exclusive in these groups, closer inspection reveals that this is due primarily to the much higher proportion of members who are married couples (relative to the other communes).

9. Although there is not room to present them in tabular form, there are some results for multiplex relations of *loving AND improving AND exciting*. With the exception of the resident charismatic groups, the mean proportion of the incidence of the 003 triad type is around .750, with most of the remaining .250 structured as 102 triads. While the greatest proportion of triads (about .450) in the resident charismatic groups are of the 102 type, just over 25% are 201 or 300 triads. This suggests a reasonable degree of interlockingness and is compatible with the postulate of an emotionally charged residual of the communion in these groups.

10. It is recommended that the reader consult Appendix A (pages 311 to 327) for this distinction and its implications for analysis of relational data.

11. It should be noted here, that an analysis of "mutual" power relations (mutual claims of dominance, mutual claims of deference, and mutual claims of equality) reveals no evidence of structural differences among our charismatic categories.

12. Intransitivity is when *i* has *power* over *j*, and *j power* over *k*, and *k* has *power* over *i*, so that power flows in a continuous cycle.

13. The use of such a weak definition of leadership here is necessary to take into account leaders whose power flows indirectly through chains of relations.

14. An exception is the Tower, where there is evidence that the charismatic leader is losing charisma and being relegated to a more subordinate position.

15. This is the leader/s holding the greatest number of direct or indirect *power* relations over the other members.

16. Less direct analytic procedures had to be employed because there is little overlap between the charismatic and noncharismatic communes on the test variable and many of the control variables. This involved a comparison of sub-samples matched by category for the factor under consideration. Consequently, many of the comparisons between the charismatic and noncharismatic groups had to be restricted to a particular category or subset of categories within the control variable. This can restrict the extent to which results can be generalized to the whole sample of communes. This problem was partially resolved by checking for a lack of covariation between the control variable and relational structure when charisma was held constant.

17. The results of an analysis at the group level (not presented here; see Bradley, 1980: Chapter Seven) comparing small sub-samples of charismatic (N = 4) and noncharismatic Christian communes (N = 4), and also charismatic (N = 4) and noncharismatic (N = 19) sub-samples of nonreligious groups, show evidence of a consistent association between charisma and relational structure that is independent of religion. (This is corroborated by the results of Carlton-Ford's (1986) analysis (using more formal statistical methods) of the commune data.) However, because these results are based on such a small number of cases, they must be treated with caution.

Chapter Seven

STABILITY

Introduction

We have just seen in Chapter Six that relations of positive affect and power have a distinctive global form in charismatic groups. As vestiges of communion, bonds of positive affect are highly interlocking connecting virtually everybody to everyone else. Structured to contain and align the energy released by communion, power relations are patterned for strength as an interlocking, transitive hierarchy, tying all members into a single structure.

Building on this foundation, we are now in a position to validate the last general proposition of our theory: the prediction that, to remain stable and survive, a charismatic system must counterbalance the energy released by communion with a strong power structure. While, using cross-sectional data, we have established an association between these two relational forms and charisma, empirical demonstration of a longitudinal consequence provides "the only fully appropriate "test" of a causal proposition's validity" (Lieberson, 1985: 180). Accordingly, we will endeavor to show that there also is reasonable evidence of a *causal* relationship between the inter-relation of these structures and group stability. To do this we must examine the effect of communion and power on group survival, overtime (Lieberson, 1985: 179-183).

Theory

Instability of Communion

As an unconditional union among equal and total beings, communion is a generic bond — a product of "men in their wholeness wholly attending". It is a relation that eclipses or suspends the culturally-prescribed segmentalized order of positions and roles that normally holds individuals. It is a relation that releases affect — energy that was otherwise com-mitted and used, that is now suddenly available. To "stand outside" social structure is to "exist" wholly, to experience the undivided totality of the *e'lan vital*; it is to be in "ecstasy" (Turner, 1969: 128 and 138).

Communion is a precariously fragile bond, intensely emo-tional and occurring only momentarily as single or discrete acts. Communions "can shake us to the very root, destroy us, or even drive us to distraction or madness, but they do not endure", warns Schmalenbach (1961: 340). After observing how communion is used by the Bruderhof (a third generation religious, charismatic commune) for periodic rejuvenation, Benjamin Zablocki concludes that:

> The periods in which euphoria is absent are perhaps less potentially destructive for a community than are the times when euphoria itself gets out of hand. Collective behavior is dangerous stuff. Observers of the phenomenon know how volatile it can be — how rapidly a boisterous dance can turn into an ugly melee, or a holiday crowd into an angry mob. One of the problems is unpredictability. Another is the apparent wave nature of collective behavior emotions, their tendency to oscillate between extremes. In communities these extremes have often become the extremes of love and hatred, of creation and destruction. (Zablocki, 1971: 191-192.)

Aside from the unpredictable oscillation between these extremes, there is also the problem of the fleeting, fickle nature of the states of "emotional seizure":

> In magic and religious charisma, 'acute ecstacies are transitory in their nature ...' (Weber, 1968: 535). In political charisma, moreover, the emotions of the demonstrators in the street may be fickle and peter out after the meeting has ended. Or the enthusiasm tends to disappear if the demagogue worships mainly his vanity or is engaged in self-glorification for its own sake. The result of these emotional fluctuations is a temporary charisma. (Schweitzer, 1974/5: 158)

To be more than a moment of collective euphoria, communion must be a part of a more permanent social form. It is only momentary social arrangements that can dispense with institutionalized order:

> ... Spontaneous communitas is richly charged with affects, mainly pleasurable ones. ... Communitas has something "magical" about it. Subjectively there is in it the feeling of endless power. But this power untransformed cannot readily be applied to the organizational details of social existence.
> ... (Consequently,) communitas cannot stand alone if the material and organizational needs of human beings are to be adequately met. (Turner, 1969: 129 and 139; my addition.)

Yet even when communion occurs in a more durable structure, there is no guarantee that group stability can be maintained. This is because higher intensities of communion unlock increasingly more of the energy tied up as social structure resulting in increased pressures toward instability. This means that an even greater degree of social organization and control will be necessary to counteract the rise in pressure if stability is to be preserved.[1]

Regulating Communion

By harnessing the experience of communion, a group can make it more predictable and also reduce the likelihood of its destructive consequences. This can be achieved by institutionalizing the conditions and activities that trigger communion. This gives the group greater control over the experience and its consequences.

To successfully institutionalize communion, Zablocki (1971: 164-192) argues that the group must meet a number of requirements. First, it must have some ability to trigger the experience with a consistently high degree of regularity and intensity for communion to be useful. This is achieved by ritualizing those activities with the greatest potential for triggering communion, and by fostering the individual's ability for full participation as well. For the latter, the group must ensure that communion is perceived as an intense, positive experience that can be transformed into an enthusiastic, unconditional commitment for the group. This involves surrounding the experience with an interpretive framework that sees communion as something positive and not frightening. Finally, in order to rely on communion as an effective means for generating energy and to use it constructively, the group must be able to handle its basic unpredictability. This means creating a collective receptivity to communion and a capacity to use it whenever it occurs.

But the institutionalization of communion will necessitate social organization in another way. To be able to deliberately trigger the experience, some differentiation among individuals must be present, with those who are seen as "knowing" most about it (the charismatic leader and/or the lieutenants) acting as facilitators guiding, monitoring, and regulating the experience. This is crystallized as a hierarchical alignment within the group. It provides the means for controlling the experience by increasing the likelihood that communion does not get out of hand, resulting in negative rather than positive consequences for the group.

Another way stability can be fostered is routinization. By routinizing the charismatic leader's teachings into a package of ready-made rituals, the intensity of communion can be reduced. Because the leader is a catalyst inspiring extraordinarily high states of communion, absence of the catalyst will lower the intensity of the experience and, therefore, reduce the amount of energy liberated. However, while routinization may decrease the risk of instability from collective cataclysm, it can mean increased difficulties in establishing a new order. Without the catalyst, the group may be unable to generate and align enough energy to achieve social transformation. Under these conditions, disaffection and disillusionment may follow leading to the demise of the group altogether.

From the above reasoning, we can derive the following propositions. Because the intense emotion of communion melts down social structure, converting it into highly volatile collective energy, it is expected that:

Proposition 7:1 The higher the state of communion, the lower will be the stability of a group.

Under charismatic conditions, where communion is used to generate the extraordinary level of collective energy required for radical social transformation, we should find that:

Proposition 7:2 Higher states of communion will reduce the stability of charismatic groups.

And, as a catalyst facilitating even more extraordinary states of communion, that:

Proposition 7:3 Instability is more likely under conditions of resident charismatic leadership than absentee charismatic leadership.

However, as a mechanism to align and control the energy liberated by communion:

Proposition 7:4 A strong (interlocking, transitively-ordered) power structure increases group stability by counterbalancing the destabilizing pressure from communion.

Or alternatively, since the charismatic leader is an energy-facilitating catalyst:

Proposition 7:5 Stability can also be improved by reducing the catalytic effect of the charismatic leader through routinization.

Finally, while relations in groups with high charismatic potential are charged with unrealized aspirations and an anticipation of charisma, because the order of actualized charisma is absent, it is expected that:

Proposition 7:6 Groups with high charismatic potential will be highly volatile and unstable.[2]

I. Charismatic Stability

Using commune survival as a measure of group stability, we will start by examining the survival rates of our four charismatic categories over the four years during which the communes were followed (see Figure 7:1). Taking our two larger categories first, it would seem that the communes with low charismatic potential enjoy a higher rate of survival when compared to the absentee charismatic groups. Looking more closely, however, we can see that this difference is due to the greater rate of dissolution of the latter in the first study year (31.8% versus 13.0%), and that their durability gradually improves overtime to all but close the gap (45.5% compared to 52.5%) by the end of the fourth year. Such a change suggests that this improvement may be related to group age.[3]

This same pattern of high initial dissolution and then improved stability can be seen for the resident charismatic groups, pointing, again, to the possibility of an "age" effect.[4] Although we must be cautious (since N = 6), it does seem that despite the presence of much higher levels of communion (established above in Chapters Five and Six), these communes are, on average, more durable than their absentee charismatic counterparts. Though riding the roller coaster of communion seems to make them the most volatile of the four categories of groups. But it is the unfulfilled "need" for charisma — the limbo of frustration, anticipation, and exasperation — that, as expected, creates the most unstable situation. So that while survival rates for the other categories were around fifty percent by the end of the fourth study year, only one of the six groups with high charismatic potential had endured to this point.

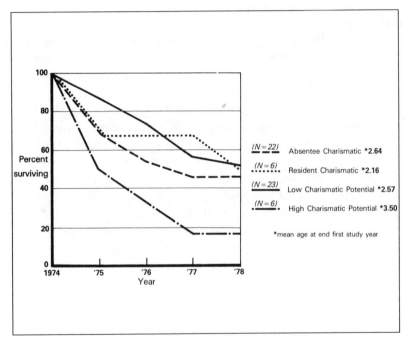

7:1 *Survival Status of Communes from 1974 Through 1978, by Charismatic Type*

Confirmation of the presence of a strong but converse "age" effect can be seen in Figure 7:2. Dividing the charismatic and noncharismatic groups into cohorts of "young" (less than 2 years old) and "old" (founded 2 or more years before the study) reveals an extremely interesting and surprising set of findings. The young charismatic groups

($N = 17$) are highly unstable in the first year, with a dissolution rate of almost fifty percent — a level comparable to the groups with high charismatic potential. Beyond the first year, though, there is quite an improvement stabilizing at forty percent across the last two years.

The major surprise comes with the pattern for the older charismatic groups; they are the most stable of all categories and consistently maintain a twenty percent survival advantage over their noncharismatic counterparts. Not only does this finding call into question the idea (promulgated by Weber and others) that charisma is quintessentially an unstable social form, but it suggests an even more intriguing possibility: that charisma can provide a more efficient means of group survival than that provided by some noncharismatic systems. However, to reach the threshold of this region of collective effectiveness, these data suggest that a charismatic group has to pass an early critical period during which survival hangs in balance. If our theory is correct, gaining control of the energy released by communion is the key to stability, and it is mastering this problem that gives the group real access to charisma's awesome power and efficiency.

A second surprise is that the young noncharismatic communes are, on average, more stable than the old — the converse to the pattern for the charismatic groups. What is interesting is the striking difference in survival rates in the first year — especially when compared with those for the charismatic groups. Thus, we see that the old charismatic and young noncharismatic groups enjoy high and remarkably similar survival rates (91% and 88%), while their counterparts suffer greater losses (69% and 53%, respectively). Although these are quite different patterns, our theory suggests that energy might be the common factor: the charismatic groups are unstable in the short run because they must learn to successfully manage the high levels of energy liberated by communion; the noncharismatic groups are unstable in the long run because they lack an effective means for the regeneration of energy — energy that, overtime, has either been depleted by deflecting it from the group, or is locked into closed, rigid, routines of mechanical behavior.

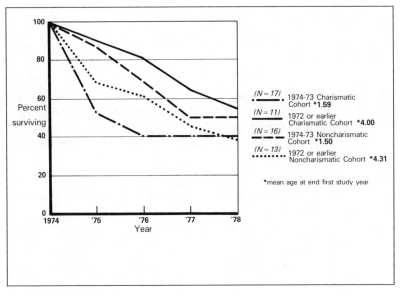

7:2 *Survival Status of Charismatic and Noncharismatic Communes from 1974 Through 1978, by Cohort*

II. Communion, Power, and Stability

Dyadic Effects Systematic evidence of a relationship between group stability and relational affect has been uncovered by Benjamin Zablocki in his analysis of the Urban Communes Data (Zablocki, 1980).[5] Labeling this the "cathexis effect", he finds that the proportion of mutual "loving" dyads in a commune is positively associated with two indicators of group instability — membership turnover[6] and group dissolution: the higher the proportion of "loving" dyads, the higher the level of membership turnover, and the greater likelihood of commune disintegration (see Zablocki, 1980, Figure 4-5:165).[7]

My own analysis of these data, in relation to charisma, is presented in Figure 7:3; I have included *power* dyads as well. Starting with *loving* dyads, we can see graphic confirmation of our earlier findings: that the charismatic groups tend to generate more love than the noncharismatic communes. More importantly here, we can see that while Zablocki's "cathexis effect" on group dissolution still holds when the communes are grouped by charismatic type, there is also evidence of a differential tolerance for energy as well. Thus, there is only 1 noncharismatic group that has more than 61% of *loving* dyads, and it does not survive. On the other hand, 10 charismatic groups have more than 60% of all possible dyads energized with love, and 6 of them are still in existence twelve months later.[8] To avoid the "cathexis effect" and survive these otherwise fatal levels of energy, our theory predicts a relationship between power and stability in the charismatic communes as well.

Based on the "relaxed" operational definition of *power* dyads[9] (Figure 7:3), we can see that there is some support for this expectation. Four of the five nonsurviving charismatic communes are in the lowest two *power* categories. Given our thesis that power is needed to control energy, this finding is consistent with the greater instability we have just found for groups in the higher *loving* categories. On the other hand, the increased likelihood of dissolution among the high *power* noncharismatic groups suggests that here power may be a suffocating force — particularly if coexistent with little love.

To validate our theory, however, we must go further and demonstrate the existence of a direct relationship between love and power, and the stability of charismatic groups. Moreover, because we have argued that it is *how* these relations are globally structured that explains stability, we must also move our level of analysis from the dyadic level to a higher order of structure. To do this, as we did in Chapter Six, we will use Holland and Leinhardts' (1976) triadic analysis.

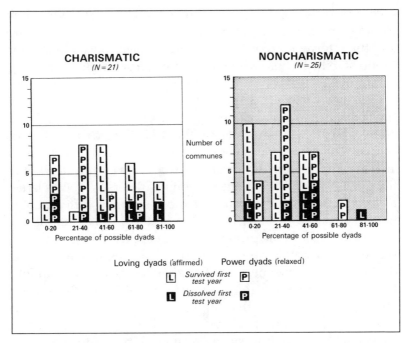

7:3 *Dyadic Structure (Wave One) of Love and Power for Charismatic and Noncharismatic Communes by Survival Status (Wave Two)*

A final point, before moving on, concerns a change in the operational definition of power. As we will see in Part Four, my most recent work has shown that it is possible to relax the operational definition even further to include an additional set of responses to the *power* item of the "Relationships Questionnaire". This increases the structural coherence of images of communal power structure. Because an analysis (not presented here) undertaken with the "relaxed" definition shows that it does not have the same explanatory utility, I have conducted the analysis which follows with this new "unrestricted" operational definition.[10]

Triadic Effects Before grouping the communes by charismatic type, let us consider the relationship between triadic structure[11] and overall commune survival (twelve months later) for each of the two test years. Figure 7:4 substantiates what our findings implied at the dyadic level: that both the structuring and the interrelation of love and power have consequences for group stability. Thus, while the triadic structure for surviving communes is almost the same for both test years, it is different for nonsurvivors, especially in the first test period. In the survivors love is segmented as a special, exclusive bond among particular pairs of members (102 triad) rather than shared, collectively, as a communion (300 triad), and there is also greater collective control (030T *power* triad). Indeed, it is the greater intensity of communion (.370 versus .136) relative to lower collective control, that most strongly differentiates nonsurvivors from survivors in the first test year. Channeling energy away from the group into exclusive dyads, but within a framework of collective regulation, would seem to reduce the destabilizing consequences of higher levels of communion. But the pattern for communes disintegrating in the second test period suggests that high levels of such dyadically-discrete energy can also have destabilizing consequences — especially if a group lacks the relational means for collective control (030T *power* triad).

This relationship between energy and power, and stability becomes even clearer when the communes are divided into charismatic types (see Figures 7:5 and 7:6): distinctive triadic structures associated with stability are revealed. Starting with our bifurcated classification (Figure 7:5), we can see, over both test years, that whether love is segmented as discrete dyads or diffused as communion, energy must be counter-balanced by power for a group to still be in existence twelve months later. The importance of this can be seen most clearly in those groups in which this structural balance is absent (eg., charismatic nonsurvivors in Year One and noncharismatic nonsurvivors in Year Two). However, the charismatic groups are not only infused with much more communion, but also seem able to maintain stability with less (relative) collective control than the noncharismatic communes. Compare, for example, charismatic survivors to noncharismatic nonsurvivors in the first test year. Although both have about the same mean proportion of *loving* 300 triads (.245 and .242, respectively), the much higher proportion of 030T *power* triads in the latter (.395 versus .226) is still not enough to ensure stability.[12]

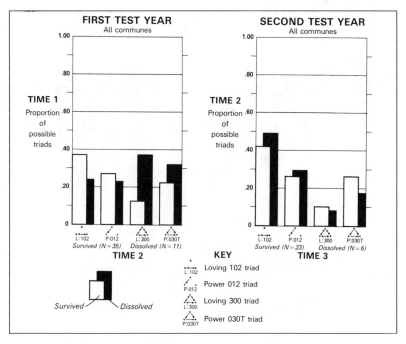

7:4 *Triadic Structure of Love and Power for All Communes by Survival Status, First and Second Test Years*

Although, with fewer cases, we must be cautious when dividing the communes into their four charismatic subtypes, even greater differences in triadic structure associated with stability are revealed (see Figure 7:6).[13] As expected, the three resident charismatic survivors counterbalance high communion (.561 for the *loving* 300 triad) with high collective control (.464 for the *power* 030T triad).[14] And while there is only one resident charismatic nonsurvivor, the structural imbalance that proceeded its demise (high (.817) communion and

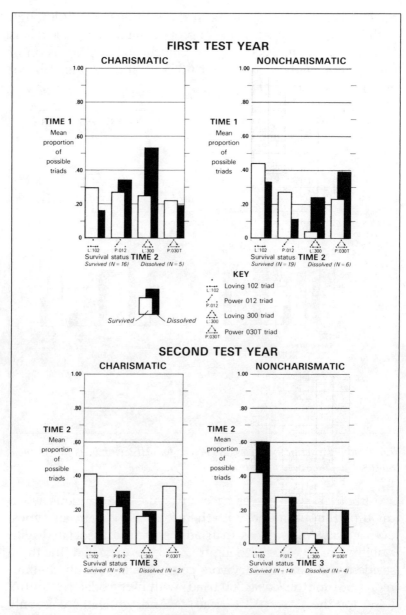

7:5 *Triadic Structure of Love and Power for Charismatic and Noncharismatic Communes by Survival Status, First and Second Test Years*

low (.500) control) can be seen in the four absentee charismatic nonsurvivors too. Moreover, a comparison of the latter with their more stable counterparts shows that a balance between love and power at the dyadic level also may have enhanced survival.

Throughout the analysis in the earlier chapters, we have noted that the groups with high charismatic potential have relational structures that, in many respects, are quite similar to the resident charismatic communes. However, Figure 7:6 shows that there is a price to be paid for such structural similarity: dissolution. On the other hand, the two survivors have much more in common with the groups with low charismatic potential — although for the latter there is little, structurally, separating stable from unstable groups.

Overall then, in the first part of this chapter, we found that once past an initial period of high instability, a charismatic group has better likelihood of survival than a noncharismatic one. And now we have just seen that stability is related to the structuring and control of energy: that counterbalancing communion with collective power increases the likelihood of survival.

III. Relational Change and Stability

But while these results are consistent with our theory, more is required to validate our proposition of a *causal* relationship between energy and power, and stability. Causality is the process by which a change in a given variable, X, produces a change in another variable, Y (Stinchcombe, 1968:31). Empirically, evidence of a causal relationship is "only" established by *longitudinal data measuring the change in X and the change in Y* (Lieberson, 1985:180). Yet so far, with our panel data, we have shown only that there is a relationship between the value of X at one point in time (ie., levels of communion and power at Time One) and the value of Y at a subsequent time (survival status one year later). Consequently, we must show as well that the changes in communion and power over time are associated with a subsequent change in group survival (Lieberson, 1985:174-217). This can be done by determining how far change in triadic structure between the two waves of data collection *(panel effects)*, and change in survival status twelve months later, is consistent with the effects of relational changes on stability predicted by our theory.

Panel Effects Starting with the surviving charismatic groups, Figure 7:7 shows that the pattern of change is consistent with our expectations. These groups have reduced the proportion of *loving* 300 triads from the level at Time 1 by an average of .167 (a mean reduction of 52% from .320 at Time 1). Theoretically, this change should reduce the energy generated by communion thereby reducing the destabilizing pressure. At the same time, there has been an increase in the proportion of 030T *power* triads by an average of .089 (an increase of 35% over the .258 for Time 1). Since we have argued that collective power acts to counterbalance the destabilizing energy liberated by communion, theoretically, this change too should enhance the prospects for survival.

Although there are only two charismatic nonsurvivors, the relational change in these groups also seems compatible with our theory. While there is a .078 decrease in communion, this is only half the reduction made by the charismatic survivors. More significant, however, is the change in control. In contrast to the survivors, these groups reduced 030T *power* triads by 46%. It is likely, therefore, that the proportion remaining at Time 2 (.139) was not sufficient to contain the communion generated (.188) — despite an increase in interpersonal power (012 triad). But with just two cases, these results must be treated with caution.

For noncharismatic groups, while most of the relational change concerns power, the seemingly small (.050) increase of dyadic love in the nonsurvivors may well have been fatal. With a mean proportion of .550 for 102 *loving* triads at Time 1, these communes already had nearly 25% more than the survivors; by Time 2 this had grown to a 43% difference (.600

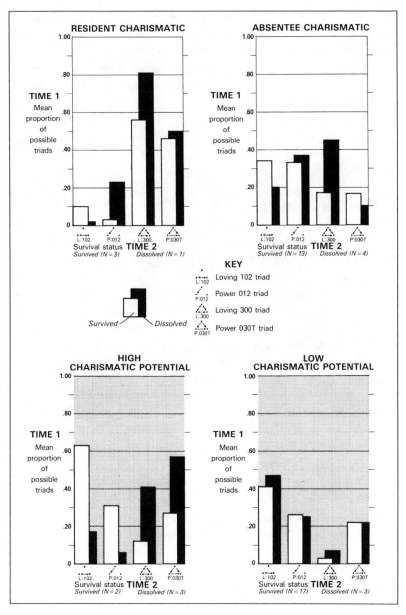

7:6 *Triadic Structure of Love and Power by Charismatic Type, by Survival Status, First Test Year*

versus .419, respectively). At such a high level, the slight increase in power (.038 for 030T triads) may not have been enough collective control to maintain stability.

These results do offer a reasonable degree of support for the theory. Despite the limitations of our test, the data are quite consistent with our expectations and there is little contradictory evidence. But even with this consistency, there is the question of whether confounding factors are also involved — particularly those bearing directly on the meaning of time and change in longitudinal data.

Confounding Effects Of the possibilities, two factors are especially important since, theoretically, each could generate patterns that, in the aggregate, would parallel our results. The first is an *aging effect* — that as groups age, social differentiation progressively converts the free energy available into structure. In old groups, for example, this would mean a low level of communion and a high degree of structural elaboration; in young groups, the opposite. The second is a *period effect* — that groups founded in different historical contexts institutionalize energy as structure to a varying degree. For example, those of one period may lock most of it into formalized patterns of organization, leaving little available for other social forms; those of another, may do the converse. The overall picture created by either effect could mirror the interrelation between communion and power we found above.

Since both factors involve time, dividing the communes into the "young" and "old" categories employed earlier (see page 175) provides a means of testing for these effects. Evidence of an aging effect is that relational patterns evolve with changes in commune age; they are not bound in time by historical circumstance. On the other hand, relational patterns distinctive to groups founded at a particular time, persisting despite changes in age, indicate a period effect.

Figure 7:8 presents the triadic structure of the charismatic and noncharismatic survivors at Time 1 and Time 2, grouped by age cohort.[15] Starting with charismatic survivors, while there is no evidence of a period effect, there appears to be some consonance with an aging effect; relations in the young groups move over time toward the structure of the old (see the changes in triadic structure shown in Figure 7:9 below). Furthermore, except for the old at Time 1, this becomes even clearer when the mean age of each category is considered: there is a relatively smooth evolution in triadic structure from the young in the first test year (mean age, 1.6 years), to that for these same groups a year later (2.7 years), to the pattern for the old in Year Two (5.5 years). It is clear that if based solely on these data, it would not possible to differentiate these aging "effects" from relational changes postulated to enhance the stability of charismatic systems. Fortunately, as we will see in a moment, a comparison with the noncharismatic groups offers some insight about what may be happening here.

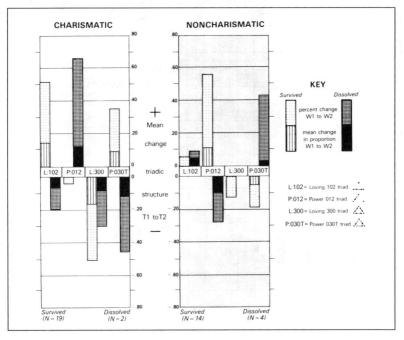

7:7 *Change in Triadic Structure (T1 to T2) of Love and Power for Charismatic and Noncharismatic Communes by Survival Status*

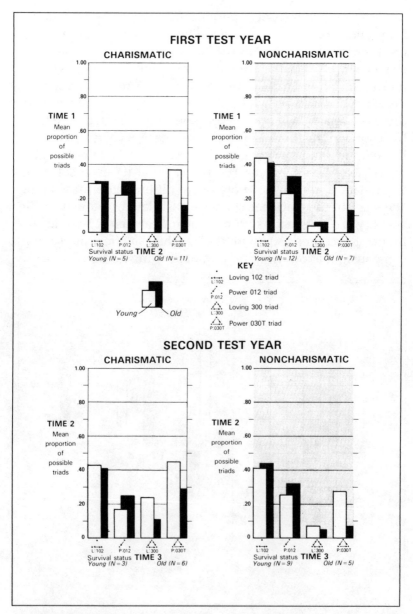

7:8 *Triadic Structure of Love and Power for Surviving Charismatic and Noncharismatic Communes by Age, First and Second Test Years*

But first, for the noncharismatic communes themselves, Figure 7:8 shows no indication of an aging effect; the triadic structure for both age cohorts holds across both waves, and there is little evidence of an age-related trend. On the other hand, a period effect seems present for power: in the young groups, both collective and interpersonal forms of power are important across the two waves; in the old, collective control is down around the same low level as communion (these patterns tend to be consistent with changes shown in Figure 7:9). Indeed, it is the lack of collective organization in the old cohort, for both *loving* and *power*, that is most striking. Even if these groups were founded with such a proclivity, it is unlikely that such a low and diminishing level of structural integration will be sufficient for survival in the long run.

Returning to the question of whether something other than an "aging effect" is propelling relational changes in the charismatic groups, comparing them with the noncharismatic groups shows a marked convergence in structure over-time. Structurally, both the direction of this convergence and it's consequence is revealing. First, while the noncharismatic groups remain relatively constant, relations in the charismatic groups move strongly toward the noncharismatic pattern (see both Figures 7:8 and 7:9). Thus, by Time 2 the relational structure of the old charismatic groups has devolved so far as to be almost indistinguishable from that of the young noncharismatic groups (Figure 7:8). Second, as we found above, it is the old charismatic and young noncharismatic cohorts that have the best chances for survival overtime. These findings suggest a structural uniformity that is independent of group culture: that this combination of communion and control is more stable and more durable than other patterns.

But this stability has a price. By lowering the level of communion and increasing the level of collective control (Figure 7:9), the old charismatic groups have severely curtailed their prospects for social transformation. These changes, then, are not just the result of an aging process. More likely, they are a manifestation of the fundamental paradox the charismatic group faces. Radical change demands the conversion of structure into energy. Yet, the greater the energy liberated the more survival is in jeopardy. On the other hand, stability requires the institutionalization of energy into structure. But, the more energy is locked up as structure, the more change is in question. Time brings direct experience of the risks and costs of radical change, which in turn brings pressure for security and survival. These forces may thus co-opt energy meant for change and thereby cause structural devolution of the charismatic group.

Examining the degree of relational change between the two waves in more detail (see Figure 7:9), we can see that the pattern for both cohorts of charismatic survivors is broadly consistent with our expectations for stable groups. For example, communion has declined in the young and old charismatic survivors (from .444 to .236, and .258 to .112, respectively). At the same time, there has been an increase in dyads of exclusive love — almost to the same degree. This is similar to a pattern we noted earlier and points, again, to some kind of reciprocal relationship between collective and interpersonal levels in the structuring of energy. Furthermore, in the older charismatic survivors there has been an increase in collective power (from .139 at Time 1, to .293 at Time 2, for 030T triads). For these groups, both the relational changes and the im-provement in survival overtime, are consistent with our theory: that reducing energy and increasing collective control will enhance stability. On the other hand, a slight reduction in collective power (of 9%, to .452 by Time Two) seems to have accompanied the rechanneling of love from the collective to the interpersonal level in the young charismatic survivors: less energy generated by communion means less control to maintain stability.

For the noncharismatic survivors, we can see that with the exception of a relatively small (.027) actual increase of *loving* 300 triads in the young cohort, there is a decline in the collective structuring of affect and power and an increase in interpersonal bonding. These changes may signal a deterioration in collective organization overtime, that, should it continue, could result in a breakdown in group cohesion culminating, eventually, with dissolution. However, it appears from the triadic structure of the old cohort (see Figure 7:8) that the level of collective organization required for the survival of these noncharismatic systems is relatively small.

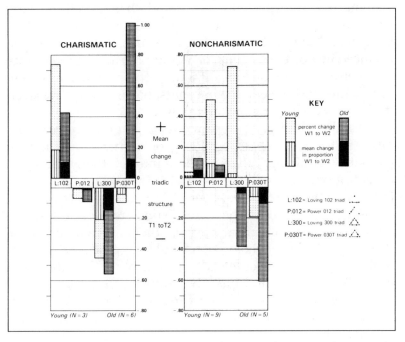

7:9 *Change in Triadic Structure (T1 to T2) of Love and Power for Charismatic and Noncharismatic Communes by Age*

Summary

Throughout this book, we have argued that, structurally, charisma is a social form that mobilizes and aligns huge quantities of social energy. This energy is highly volatile and, unless contained by power, will jeopardize group stability. In the earlier chapters, we found that charismatic structures are comprised of highly interlocking bonds of positive affect (communion) and a strong hierarchy of power relations (control). Now, in this chapter, we have seen that the structuring and interrelation of these two relational systems has implications for the stability of charismatic groups; that how these relations are patterned has direct consequences for survival.

Somewhat unexpectedly, we found that something very similar may be at work in noncharismatic systems; here, too, the data indicate that bonds of positive affect must be counterbalanced by power relations for a group to have a good chance of survival. In these groups, though, the evidence also suggests a linkage between the interpersonal and collective levels in the structuring of affect and power.

But rather than being separate relational dimensions with different functions (Parsons, 1951), or having a basic incompatibility requiring differentiation into mutually exclusive organizational domains (Heider, 1958), our findings show that love/affect and power/control are fundamentally interrelated. So that while they are distinct relational systems, with different functions and forms, they are cojoined at the deeper level of the whole. This would suggest that not only is the order of each enfolded into the other, but the order of their interrelation must be enfolded in all relations throughout the whole. Such an interrelation would provide the mechanism that regulates movement back and forth between the two domains — the oscillation between energy generation and energy control that drives the process of social transformation.

But to understand the nature of this order we must adopt a very different way of looking at social organization than that provided by the present perspectives of social science. As we will see in Part Four, the critical clue to this order already lies before us as a question about the power hierarchies we have discovered: namely, why do we find coherent images of global structure when data measuring only dyadic relations are aggregated?

NOTES

1. There is a subtle but important difference between Turner and myself on the relationship between communitas/communion and stability. He sees communitas as an enlivening, regenerating force in an existing, ongoing community. It is one pole of a dialectical process in which "men are released from structure into communitas only to return to structure revitalized by their experience of communitas. What is certain is that no society can function adequately without this dialectic." For Turner, communitas suspends structure only in order to rejuvenate it, to reaffirm it: "maximization of communitas provokes maximization of structure" (1969:129). There is no fundamental undermining of structure or risk of instability here.

   On the other hand, my interest is in *transformation* — the role communion plays in breaking the mold that holds individuals to an existing social order thereby releasing energy in the form of a raw, free-flowing potential that is now available for use in almost any kind of social activity. Since this energy can be reinvested in an established structure, or be used to build a new order, or even be used for further *de*-structuring, it is "unstable" — that is, available, *potentially,* for any social activity.

2. Two factors complicate verification of these expectations. First, because the propositions are interdependent, verification cannot be made on an individual basis; validity must be assessed for the set as a whole, and then only after all the relevant evidence has been examined. For example, Propositions 7:1, 7:2, and 7:3 can hold only if the conditions postulated in Propositions 7:4 and 7:5 do not obtain. Second, the small number of resident charismatic ($N=6$) and high charismatic potential ($N=6$) communes places severe constraints on verification for these categories. Consequently, systematic statistical analysis has only been possible for the more general charismatic-non-charismatic classification.

3. A further indication of this can be seen in the data on mean commune age for each category also given in Figure 7:1.

4. With only one exception, all of the resident charismatic groups were less than two years old.

5. Zablocki's analysis (1980:146-186), is aimed at identifying factors that account for the stability of communes as social entities themselves. Our concern is different (the stability of charismatic groups), and requires that we undertake a systematic analysis of the determinants of the survival of charismatic and noncharismatic communes.

6. As will become clear in Part Four, since I have a very different use in mind for membership turnover, I have not employed it here as a measure of group stability.

7. While Zablocki and I agree about the destabilizing consequences of communion, we seem to disagree on its structural basis. He argues that the "cathexis effect" is an outcome of dyadic relationships, rather than the result of the collective patterning of communion, as I am suggesting. Furthermore, he contends that the dyadic measure is the appropriate "unit of analysis", citing my doctoral research (Bradley, 1980) to support his claim that "there is no evidence of an association between triad patterns ... and either of our measures of stability" (this was not a question I examined in my dissertation). Therefore, since "triadic measures do not help to predict stability, ... measures defined on higher-level subgraphs will do no better" (Zablocki, 1980:167). As we will see in a moment, however, not only is there solid evidence of a relationship between the triadic structure of *loving* relations and the survival of charismatic groups overtime, but this relationship is also apparent when the communes are simply divided into survivors and nonsurvivors.

8. While the numbers of cases are small, the higher stability of the charismatic communes in the 41-60% *loving* dyads category (the only region where there is reasonable overlap between the two types of groups), suggests that these findings are not just the result of relational biases in the charismatic and noncharismatic subsamples.

9. The reader will recall that this "relaxed" operational measure of power includes: acknowledged dominance relations, where i claims *power* and j defers; uncontested dominance, where i claims *power* but j says "don't know" or "no answer"; and uncontested deferences, where i says "don't know" or "no answer" and j defers *power* to i.

10. The "unrestricted" measure of *power* adds to what is already included in the "relaxed" definition (see Note 9 above) those dyads in which only one individual provides information about the hierarchical order of the relation and the other sees the relation is "equal" or "neutral". See Chapter Eight, pages 199 to 205, for a discussion of the "strict", "relaxed", and "unrestricted" operational definitions of *power*.

11. The 102 and 012 triad types, which each involve only one relation among the three members of a triad, are being used as structural indicators of dyadically-specific, *interpersonal*

patterns of *loving* and *power* relations, respectively. The 300 and 030T triad types, involving a connection among all three members of a triad, suggest relational patterns more consistent with *collective* forms of social organization.

12. With only 2 charismatic nonsurvivors in the second test year for which we have relational data, we can conclude little from a comparison with the 14 charismatic survivors. On the other hand, the triadic data suggest that the change in the relational structure of the surviving charismatic communes may well have contributed to an enhanced likelihood of stability in the second test year. Both the 38% reduction in the mean proportion of *loving* 300 triads, and the corresponding 53% increase for *power* 030T triads in these groups between Time One and Time Two, are changes we would expect from our theory that should improve stability. We will examine further evidence on the relationship between changes in relational structure and stability in a moment.

13. There are not enough cases in the subcategories to divide the communes in this way for the second test period.

14. Although there had been a move from collective to interpersonal bonding, these resident charismatic survivors were still averaging relatively high levels of collective love (.322 for the 300 triad) and collective power (.380) by the second wave of data collection.

15. This analysis has been restricted to surviving communes as we have too few charismatic and noncharismatic nonsurvivors to be able to group them by commune age. This means that we cannot say whether or not any observed differences in triadic structure improved or reduced the likelihood of commune survival; at best, we can only say that the data are either consistent or not consistent with the theoretically expected pattern for stable (surviving) groups.

PART FOUR

TRANSCENDENCE

The collective consciousness is the highest form of the psychic life, since it is consciousness of the consciousnesses. Being placed outside of and above individual and local contingencies, it sees things only in their permanent and essential aspects, which it crystallizes into communicable ideas. At the same moment of time that it sees from above, it sees farther; at every moment of time it embraces all known reality; that is why it alone can furnish the mind with the moulds which are applicable to the totality of things and which make it possible to think of them.

Emile Durkheim, *The Elementary Forms of Religious Life*
(1915: 492).

Chapter Eight

BEYOND KNOWN ORDER*

Introduction

In the early part of the summer of 1974, we were busy on the Communes Project designing and pretesting the measurement instruments that would be administered later that summer for the first wave of data collection. Of the numerous instruments we constructed, one was especially important to me. This was the Relationship Questionnaire. I remember hurrying back with Benjamin Zablocki after pretesting it in a commune on the Lower West Side of New York, and how, with excited anticipation, we went straight to the power question to convert the respondents and their answers into the circles and arrows of a sociogram. But, we asked each other, is there any evidence of a power hierarchy?

---

*With his healthy scepticism of my hypothesis of holonomic social order, and his advocacy for the efficacy of existing sociological theory, Joel Nelson made a significant contribution to this chapter. Of course, he bears no responsibility for what I have done here.

197

A feeling of awe and amazement came over me as a single, transitively-ordered structure gradually appeared as we carefully drew the sociogram. It seemed as if something almost magical had happened; from our mapping of each member's specific relationship with every other individual we had constructed a view of power for the group as a whole. A feeling deep inside told me that there was something very important here; but nearly ten years would pass before I would see the paradox in the relation of what we had measured to what we had found, and its importance.

There were two problems: one was technical and the second a matter of perspective. The first involved developing the necessary operational technology that would reveal the underlying hierarchical order that Zablocki and I had caught a glimpse of in that New York commune. In many communes, however, such order remained elusive, masked by ideological contamination and other sources of measurement error. As we have seen, finding the operational key to this problem resulted in one of the major findings of this research: the discovery of strong, clearly articulated power hierarchies in the charismatic communes (see Figure 6:4(a), page 150, above).

However, given the measurement procedures employed, this finding is paradoxical: the data from which these images of power are constructed were not measured at the group level; they were generated by mapping the social relation between each pair of members. This should mean more disjointed subsets and cliques, more intransitivity — patterns that reflect idiosynchratic individual or interpersonal realities, rather than the forms we have found which are more consistent with a collective order. How is it, then, that by measuring dyads and aggregating them together we obtain a view of the organization of power in the group as a whole? Why do such coherent images of global structure emerge from mappings of dyadic relations?

In this chapter we will find that by further relaxing the operational definition of power, even more dramatic images are revealed, and that the high degree of global order and coherence, that is so striking about the charismatic groups, is also present in many of the noncharismatic communes. Although the generality of such order was unanticipated, it suggests that we are not just dealing with an order that is distinctive to charismatic systems but potentially something of a more fundamental nature. There is also much more than the methodological issue of multi-level measurement involved here since the central question it raises concerns the relation of parts to a whole: what does it mean that an image of the social whole can be constructed from information contained in its parts? And what, potentially, might this reveal about the fundamental nature of social organization?

In this chapter we classify the images of power into communes with little global order and coherence and those with globally coherent patterns. Then we attempt to explain the differences using four existing sociological theories; historicist, interactionist, normative, and stratificational. Because we find little empirical support for the accounts of global coherence offered by these explanations, we move beyond conventional sociological wisdom in Chapter Nine to pursue a novel, more fruitful idea: that social organization is holonomic — that each part contains information from which an image of the whole can be constructed.

While I have attempted to keep the analysis rigorous, the largely subjective classification of global coherence, the small numbers of cases in some tables, and the more basic issue of the implications of using a very relaxed operational definition of power, mean that the findings and inferences made in this and the following chapter should be treated with caution. Thus the ideas and material presented in what follows are presented in a speculative vein.

Operational Considerations

Relaxing the Measurement of "Power"

So far, in our analysis of power relations, we have considered two ways of operationalizing our sociometric measure of power; a "strict" operational construction in which both individuals in each dyad agree about the hierarchical order of their particular relation, and a "relaxed" construction in which relations where only one individual answered in terms of the hierarchical order (the other responding with "don't know" or "no answer") also are included. For a number of reasons[1] we found the relaxed definition to be a more valid measure and, consequently, have employed it in our analysis to this point. It is possible, however, to relax the operational criterion even further to include an additional set of dyads; those in which only one individual provides information about the hierarchical order of the relation and the other sees the relation as "equal" or "neutral".[2] Despite the disagreement implied in these dyads,[3] this third "unrestricted"[4] criterion results in images of power that possess even more global organization and seems reflective of a collective or holistic order.

Figures 8:1 and 8:2 compare the three different images[5] of power that result from using the strict, relaxed, and unrestricted operational definitions for a noncharismatic and charismatic commune, respectively.[6] Not only can large increases in the incidence of dyads for both communes be seen as the operational definition is increasingly relaxed, but greater coherence in the global organization of power is revealed. A reduction in isolates and disjointedness, and an increase in the number of levels of hierarchy (measured by the longest transitive path), occurs in both communes.[7] For example, the image for commune C, with 24 members, changes from one of 4 isolates and 8 distinct levels of hierarchy with a strict definition, to no isolates and 15 levels using an unrestricted definition; the corresponding images for commune K (29 members) changes from 2 isolates and 12 levels, to no isolates and 21 levels.[8] What is especially intriguing about these examples is that they show how more global hierarchical coherence and order is uncovered as nonmutual perceptions of power are included in the definition.

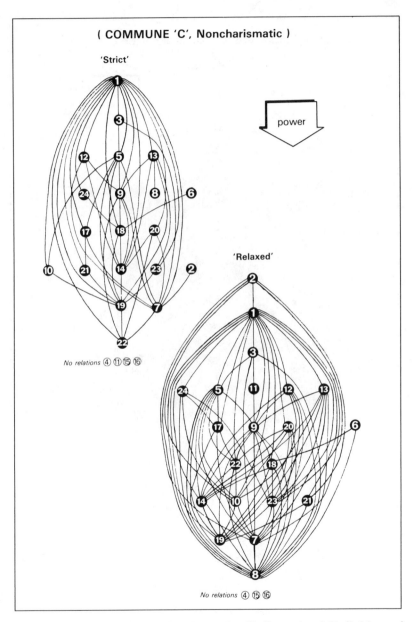

8:1 *"Strict", "Relaxed", and "Unrestricted" Operational Definitions of Power for a Noncharismatic Commune* (continued p. 202)

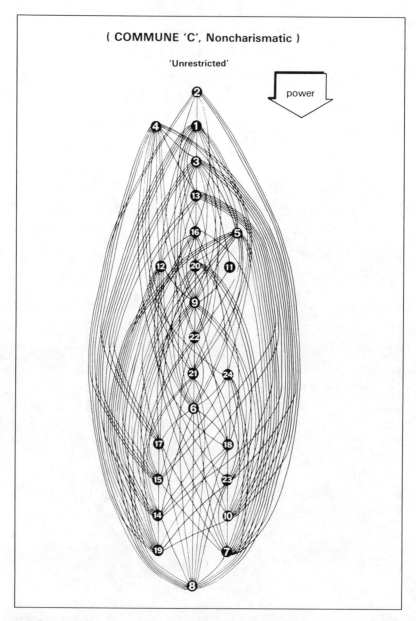

(COMMUNE 'C', Noncharismatic)

'Unrestricted'

power

8:1 *Continued*

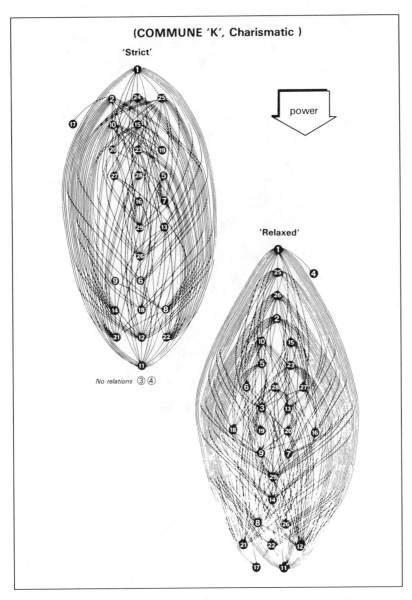

(COMMUNE 'K', Charismatic)

'Strict'

power

'Relaxed'

No relations ③ ④

8:2 *"Strict", "Relaxed", and "Unrestricted" Operational Definitions of Power for a Charismatic Commune*   *(Continued p. 204)*

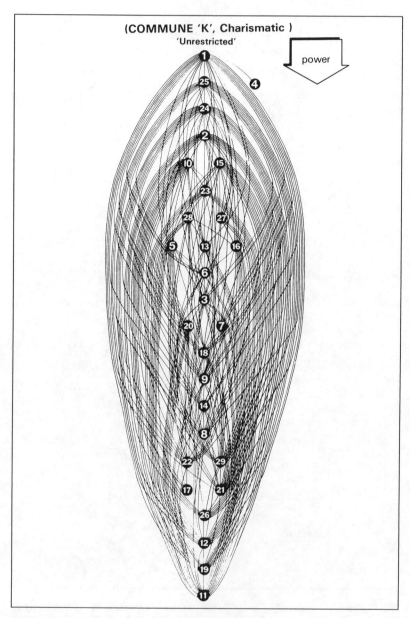

8:2 *Continued*

Measuring Global Coherence

Applying the unrestricted definition to the rest of the communes reveals, in general, more relations and more structure. There is an increase in mean dyadic connectedness of *power* relations for all 46 communes from .361 to .604 when moving from the relaxed to the unrestricted definition. The overall increase in structure can be seen by comparing the images in Figure 8:3 with those in Figures 6:4(a) and 6:4(b) (see pages 150 and 151, above), and by considering the results of the triadic analysis presented in Table 8:1. Thus while an average 68% of all relations for the relaxed definition are either null triads (the 003) or triads involving isolated pairs (the 012), only 36% of the relations enumerated by the unrestricted definition are distributed in these triad types — types that reflect minimal global organization. The most interesting difference is that on average just under a quarter (24%) of all relations for the unrestricted definition are patterned as 030T triads — indicative of a high degree of collective integration. Only 8% of the relations for the relaxed definition have this form.

Before continuing, it is important to note that it is unlikely that the patterns are an artifact either of the data gathering procedures or of aggregating the dyads together for each commune. In regard to the former, *i* and *j*'s responses to our sociometric instrument were gathered in a way to ensure that their answers are independent; strict supervision of the data gathering by field workers made collusion between *i* and *j* impossible. And for latter to be plausible, that each dyad is a discrete reality, one would expect much less global coherence; more cliques and disjointed sets, more intransitivity — patterns that reflect idiosynchratic individual or interpersonal realities, rather than forms more consistent with a collective order. If anything, the data gathering procedures have worked against the discovery of such globally coherent patterns; the commune members were asked only about their particular relation with each adult member, considered one by one. *They were not asked at all about the global pattern of relations for the group as a whole* (see the "Relationship Questionnaire," Appendix B).

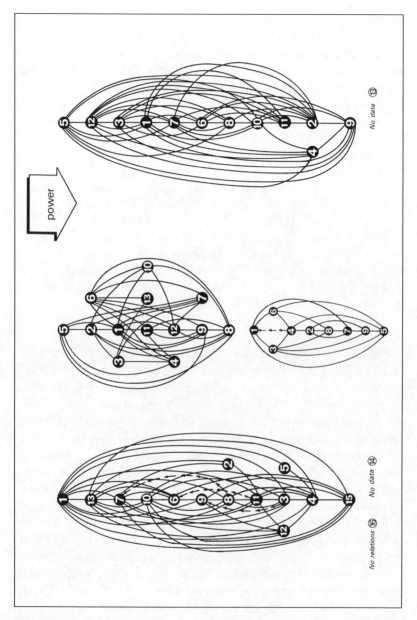

8:3(a) *Selected Examples of Coherent ("Unrestricted") Power Structure, Wave One*

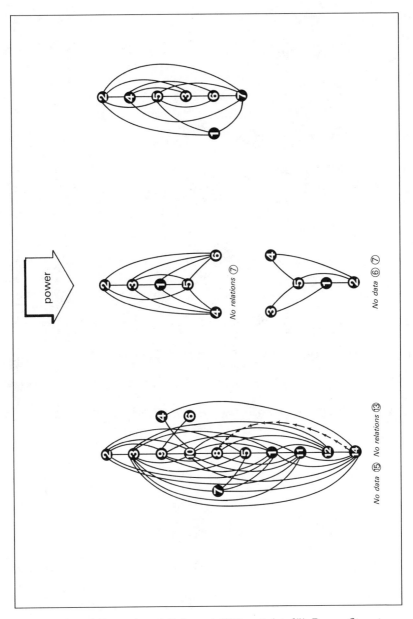

8:3(b) *Selected Examples of Coherent ("Unrestricted") Power Structure, Wave Two*

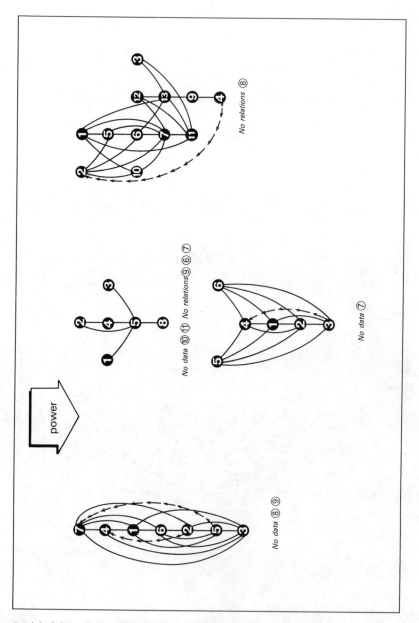

8:3(c) *Selected Examples of Incoherent ("Unrestricted") Power Structure, Wave One*

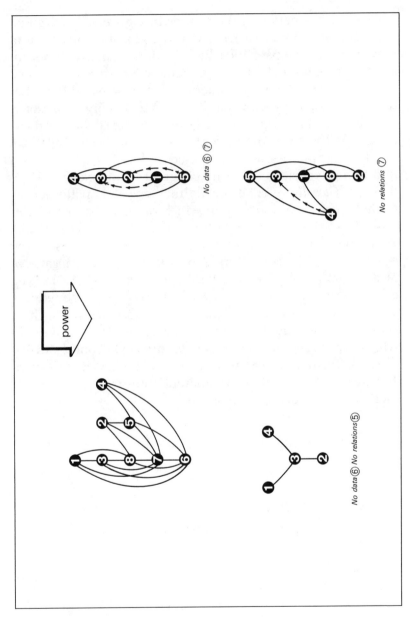

8:3(d) *Selected Examples of Incoherent ("Unrestricted") Power Structure, Wave Two*

Closer examination of the images in Figure 8:3 shows that there is quite a lot of variability in the global organization of power; some groups exhibit highly connected structures coalescing around a single, long, transitive path; some groups have multiple sociometric leaders and more lateral differentiation; and some groups manifest more disjointed patterns with isolates and intransitivity. Using the variability in these images as the base, the sociograms of unrestricted relations for all 46 communes were examined and tentatively classified into two categories:[9] "globally coherent" and "globally incoherent." *Globally coherent* means that power is patterned as a single, cohesive structure in which order flows unambiguously from the top to the bottom. This means a lack of disjointedness, cliques, isolates, and intransitivity (see the examples in Figures 8:3(a) and 8:3(b)). *Globally incoherent* means that power does not have collective integrity, lacking cohesion and possessing, instead, structural disjointedness and structural ambiguity. This means substructures such as cliques or disjointed subsets, isolates, and intransivity in which order flows in a cycle (see Figures 8:3(c) and 8:3(d)).

Three further criteria were used to finalize classification. To be classified as "globally coherent" the structure of power must meet the following conditions:

a) Be free of cliques, fractures, and disjointed subsets

b) Have no more than 10% of the group's members as isolates

c) Have no more than 5% of all possible triads patterned as intransitive triads (030C triad) in a triadic analysis.

This resulted in classifying 25 communes as globally coherent and 21 as globally incoherent.

To substantiate this classification we can use triadic analysis (Table 8:1). Clear differences in triadic structure are apparent, especially for the 012 triad and for the 030T triad.

TÁBLE 8:1 TRIADIC STRUCTURE OF "UNRESTRICTED" POWER CLASSIFIED BY GLOBAL COHERENCE, AND TRIADIC STRUCTURE OF "RELAXED" POWER (WAVE ONE)

GLOBAL COHERENCE	"UNRESTRICTED" DEFINITION				"RELAXED" DEFINITION	
	Coherent (25)*	Incoherent (21)	Total (46)		All Groups (46)	
Asymmetrical Triad Type	Mean Triad Incidence (proportions)[1]			Mean τ	Mean Triad Incidence	Mean τ
003	.068	.131	.097	.669	.317	1.122
012	.209	.322	.261	−.161	.362	−.740
021D	$.160^{2.083'}$	.111	.137	1.154	.116	1.725'
021U	.117	.108	.113	.398	.071	.266
021C	.122	.138	.129	−1.311	.051	−1.360
030T	$.317^{2.807''}$	.155	.243	1.803'	.075	1.206
030C	$.006^{-2.134'}$	.036	.020	−1.334	.008	−.415
Total	.999	1.001	1.000		1.000	

*N = ( ).
1. Mean τ for these subcategories listed only when statistically significant. Symbols denote the following $pr.$ values:
' .05
'' .01

211

The groups in the globally coherent category average nearly a third (32%) of all triads in the latter form, while those the communes with incoherent structures have the same proportion for the former. These structural differences suggest different processes of social interaction might be present in these groups — collective and interpersonal, respectively. We will see further evidence for this interpretation in Chapter Nine.

Our objective in what follows is to explain this structural variability — viz, the presence of a coherent global order of power in some communes and not in others. This goal means that two things must be considered at every step in the analysis. One concerns the issue of the *association* between the global coherence of power and the explanatory variables we consider. To keep things simple and direct, contingency table analysis comparing percentage distributions of the coherent and incoherent communes will be used. The second consideration, however, is more complicated and concerns the further question of actual structural differences: that in addition to the distribution of coherent and incoherent groups in relation to the explanatory variables, there also is systematic evidence of *structural differences* between these groups in the global organization of power relations. This requirement, and the need for a safeguard against the subjective nature of the measurement of global coherence, means that triadic analysis will be conducted as well. This will enable us, as the analysis proceeds, to see the extent to which subsets of groups within our two categories of global coherence continue to exhibit their expected structural differences.

Explaining Global Order

Structural Bias

Before we consider four existing sociological explanations, there are two factors, group size and dyadic connectedness, that as potential sources of structural bias, could account for the differences. As mentioned above (see Chapter Six, pp. 153–157), larger groups have more members which may mean more relations which in turn may mean greater structural cohesion and complexity. Similarly, groups with higher densities of relations may exhibit greater structural order simply because there are more relations available for bonding.

Taking size first, Table 8:2 shows that while the communes in the coherent category are equally likely to be found in all three size ranges, the incoherent groups are heavily concentrated in the smaller size ranges. And although differences in triadic structure exist, there is a decrease in collective organization (030T triad) and a corresponding move toward pair bonding (012 triad) for both types of groups as size increases. Despite this, however, residual structural differences still remain between the coherent and incoherent groups that are independent of size. Finally in Table 8:2, a comparison of all groups in the coherent and incoherent categories with their corresponding subsamples matched on dyad connectedness, shows an independent residual difference in triadic structure between the coherent and incoherent communes as well.

Existing Theories

But even if we can discount such methodological effects, there are four existing sociological theories that should be examined before we consider a holonomic alternative: historicist, interactionist, normative, and stratificational. Let us examine the evidence for each of these in turn.

Historicist Hypothesis

The historicist theory of social organization postulates that all patterns of social interaction, whether social relationships, institutions, or collectivities, require time to be learned and constructed as a stable, self-perpetuating order. The more complex the social order the greater is the time and

TABLE 8:2 COHERENCE OF POWER BY SIZE, DYADIC CONNECTEDNESS, AND AGE (WAVE ONE) — TABULAR ANALYSIS AND TRIADIC STRUCTURE

	TABULAR ANALYSIS				TRIADIC STRUCTURE[1]						
GLOBAL COHERENCE	Coherent (25)*		Incoherent (21)		Coherent (25)			Incoherent (21)			Total (46)
					Triad Type			*Triad Type*			
					012	021D	030T	012	021D	030T	
COMMUNE SIZE	mean	%	mean	%							
≤6 members	5.5	32.0	5.3	61.9	.088	.181	.406	.365	.127	.127	(21)
7-10	8.9	36.0	7.6	33.3	.239	.150	$.344^{2.828''}$	.224	.091	.225	(16)
≥11	13.1	32.0	13.0	4.8	.297	$.149^{4.067''''}$	$.196^{4.624'''''}$	.444	.038	.042	(9)
Total	9.2	100.0%	6.4	100.0%							(46)
DYADIC CONNECTEDNESS	mean		mean								
sub-sample:[2]											
≥.250 but ≤.375	.314		.297		.234	$.191^{2.573''}$	$.237^{2.134'}$	.312	.152	.140	(26)
	(16)		(10)								
full sample	.335		.261		.209	$.160^{2.083'}$	$.317^{2.807''}$	.322	.111	.155	(46)

214

COMMUNE AGE (years)	mean	%	mean	%							N
founded 1972 or earlier	4.1	60.0	4.3	33.3	.261	$.171^{2.858''}$	$.212^{2.910''}$	.322	.169	.159	(22)
founded 1973 or 1974	1.6	40.0	1.5	66.7	.131	.143	$.474^{2.653''}$	.322	.082	.154	(24)
Total	3.1	100.0%	2.4	100.0%							(46)

*N = ( ).

1. Mean triad incidence (proportions); mean τ scores (small figures) given only when statistically significant. Symbols denote the following p.r. values:
    ′   .05
    ″   .01
    ‴‴‴   .00005

2. This is a sub-sample and includes groups only if dyadic connectedness for power ("unrestricted") fits the range specified.

215

resources that must be invested by a group. Furthermore, time will also screen out problematic and less viable social forms (Stinchcombe, 1968:101-129). Since the coherent power hierarchies, are complex transitive orderings which require that every individual knows their own and everyone elses' relative position, this theory would lead us to expect a positive association between the global coherence of power and the longevity of a commune. The data in Table 8:2, however, show that this is only partly the case.

As expected, the coherent groups are nearly twice as likely as the incoherent groups to be found in the older category (60% compared to 33%). However, when examining the triadic structure we find, contrary to the historicist hypothesis, that it is the younger coherent communes that exhibit more collective forms of power (030T triad type). Thus, the young coherent groups average 47% of their relations in the 030T form, which is more than double the 21% for the coherent groups founded in 1972 or earlier. The fact that the young groups exhibit more of this pattern than the older communes, suggests that quite complex hierarchical patterns can be established relatively quickly.

Some indication of just how rapidly such order can emerge in small groups, at least, can be seen in some preliminary results from another study of 41 task groups I am at present undertaking with Nancy Roberts. In Figure 8:4, images of power relations are presented for two groups of undergraduate students that met for an hour once a week to work on a class-related group project. Using the same measurement procedure as was employed in the Communes Project, relations among the students in each group were mapped across nine consecutive weeks at the end of the weekly meeting.[10] You can see that hierarchical order emerges very rapidly, and, in the case of Group X, the pattern that is established in the very first week (i.e., after just one hour of interaction) more-or-less persists right to the end.[11]

What is interesting is that coherent collective order can emerge quite quickly; that it does not require time to be

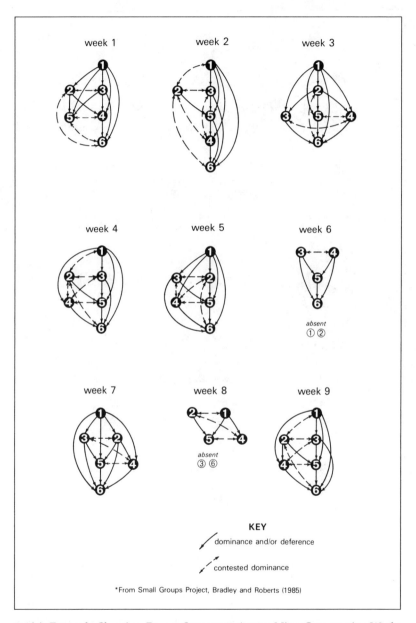

8:4(a) *Example Showing Power Structure Across Nine Consecutive Weeks in Group "X"**

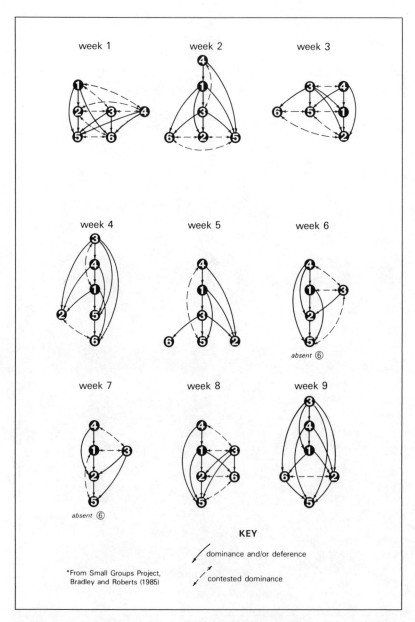

8:4(b) *Example Showing Power Structure Across Nine Consecutive Weeks in Group "Y"**

socially constructed by group members. This raises the possibility that certain basic relational orders are carried in the minds of individuals as relational gestalts. When socially activated under certain conditions, these fundamental structures provide an immediate initial order to an otherwise complex and confusing social world. They may then be modified through other secondary processes of interaction.

Interactionist Hypothesis

A second explanation is the interaction hypothesis: that by a process of pairwise interaction, individuals arrive at an agreement about the nature and ordering of each specific relation in which they are involved. It is through a series of particularized pairwise negotiations or contests that the order among group members is established; global organization is simply a reflection of the dominance ordering established in dyadic interaction. This hypothesis would lead us to expect a hierarchical order built up from dyads of consensus — in our terms, strict relations in which both individuals agree about the specific relation between them. But, because this process of pairwise interaction takes time, we would not expect this form in newly created groups. And insofar as individuals are pursuing primarily self-oriented rather than collective-oriented relations, we should find fragmented, disjointed patterns reflecting the diverse needs and interests of individuals.

The data provide little support for these expectations. First, as we discovered much earlier in this book (see pp. 90–93), the strict operational definition reveals very little coherent global order in the communes. Indeed, only 6 (13%) of the 46 groups have coherent structures of power built from dyads of mutual agreement, and four of these are charismatic with a collective rather than an interpersonal orientation. Second, as we have just seen for both the communes and some small task groups, globally coherent hierarchy can emerge very rapidly; time for a process of pairwise social construction does not seem necessary.

The fact that the unrestricted image yields globally coherent order is at odds with the third expectation. Because the unrestricted image includes nonmutual perceptions of power, which are presumed to reflect the idiosynchratic interests of the individual, fragmented, disjointed patterns should be evident. However, the globally coherent order we see in many of the unrestricted images, suggests that a different ordering process is at work. It suggests a reality beyond a shared interpersonal construction of order. It points to a process by which information about the relational order of the collective is enfolded into the minds of group members as a global *whole*.

Normative Hypothesis

The third explanation is the normative hypothesis: that hierarchical order is established by the culture of a group. It is a relational pattern that has been collectively prescribed and institutionalized, inculcated and maintained by socialization, ritual, and collective sanction. From this perspective we can expect a relationship between the content and orientation of group culture, and global organization.

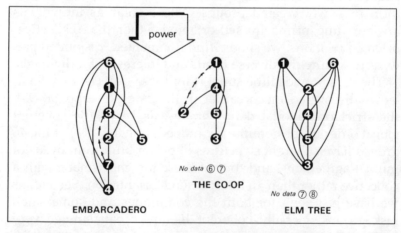

8:5 *Power Hierarchy (Wave One) in Three Communes With "Egalitarian" Ideologies*

Taking the content first, we can see from the examples in Figure 8:5 of three political, counter-cultural communes with strong Marxist ideologies of equality, that the relational reality of power in these groups is at odds with their ideology. For Elm Tree and Embarcadero especially, a clearly articulated power hierarchy is apparent despite ideological prescriptions to the contrary. Patterns such as these not only raise questions about the often assumed deterministic relationship between culture and social structure, but more importantly, suggest that some other force is at work.

As far as cultural focus is concerned, the normative hypothesis would lead us to expect that groups with collectively oriented cultures, in terms of ideology and formal organization, will exhibit greater global coherence. Table 8:3, however, shows that this does not hold for three of the four variables presented (viz, ideological orientation, degree of ideological consensus, and new member admission requirements).

For the two measures of ideology in Table 8:3, it is apparent that neither a "collective" ideological orientation nor a "high" degree of ideological consensus is related to global coherence. On the first measure, both types of groups were most likely to have a "collective" ideology (76% and 67%, respectively), and on the second measure the coherent groups were just as likely to have a "high" as a "low" level of ideological consensus. Although there is evidence that collective forms of hierarchy (030T triad type) are more likely when the ideology is focussed on group interests, the triadic analysis indicates that structural differences still remain for the coherent groups.

A similar result is found for the relation between the presence of formal rules and a coherent structure of power, with the coherent communes being equally likely to have "some" or "few" rules. And again, while the coherent groups with a more formalized culture exhibit greater hierarchical interconnection (030T triad) than the coherent groups with a more informal culture, they are still structurally distinct from the incoherent groups.

TABLE 8:3 COHERENCE OF POWER BY IDEOLOGICAL FOCUS, IDEOLOGICAL CONSENSUS, PRESENCE OF RULES, AND MEMBERSHIP REQUIREMENTS (WAVE ONE) — TABULAR ANALYSIS AND TRIADIC STRUCTURE

GLOBAL COHERENCE	TABULAR ANALYSIS Coherent (25)*	TABULAR ANALYSIS Incoherent (21)	TRIADIC STRUCTURE[1] Coherent (25) Triad Type 012	Coherent 021D	Coherent 030T	Incoherent (21) Triad Type 012	Incoherent 021D	Incoherent 030T	Total (46)
IDEOLOGICAL FOCUS									
Collective	76.0%	66.7%	.196	$.172^{2.312''}$	$.351^{3.272''}$	.332	.110	.158	(33)
Individual	24.0	33.3	.249	.121	.209	.302	.112	.150	(13)
Total	$\overline{100.0\%}$	$\overline{100.0\%}$							$\overline{(46)}$
IDEOLOGICAL CONSENSUS									
High	44.0	28.6	.195	$.187^{3.268'''}$	$.312^{4.015''''}$	.325	.130	.145	(17)
Low	56.0	71.4	.220	.138	$.321^{1.858'}$	.321	.103	.159	(29)
Total	$\overline{100.0\%}$	$\overline{100.0\%}$							$\overline{(46)}$

FORMAL RULES

								N
≥some	52.0	.211	.141[2.563]''	.389[4.213]''''	.335	.084	.113	(19)
≤few	48.0	.207	.180	.238	.317	.121	.172	(27)
Total	100.0%							(46)

NEW MEMBER REQUIREMENTS

								N
Strict[2]	72.0	.227	.136[1.955]'	.333[3.138]''	.338	.125	.157	(24)
Relaxed[3]	28.0	.162	.220[2.413]''	.275[1.956]'	.316	.105	.155	(22)
Total	100.0%							(46)

*$N = (\ )$.

1. Mean triad incidence (proportions); mean $\mathcal{T}$ scores (small figures) given only when statistically significant. Symbols denote the following p. values:

  ' .05
  '' .01
  ''' .001
  '''' .00005

2. "Strict" means closed to new members: noviliateship, trial membership, or certain trait/s required.
3. "Relaxed" means exposure to group, group readiness, or, if space is available.

223

Turning to the fourth variable, the strong association shown in Table 8:3 between global coherence and admission requirements for new members does not hold when longitudinal data are examined. Taking the 16 communes coherent at wave one for which data were available one year later at wave two,[12] while 12 (75%) were still judged to be coherent at wave two, they were just as likely to have "strict" requirements for new members as the 4 that had become incoherent by that time (9 out of 12, and 3 out of 4, respectively). Overall, apart from evidence of more collective structural forms for the coherent groups that possess more elements of a collective culture, little understanding of global coherence is offered by the normative hypothesis.

Stratification Hypothesis

A fourth explanation, a hybrid of the interactional and cultural theories, is the stratification hypothesis: that hierarchical order merely reflects the ubiquitous process of social stratification. Thus, the specific position an individual occupies is either the result of a stratifying mechanism within the group, or alternatively, the result of one penetrating the group from society. The length of time an individual has belonged to commune,[13] and whether the individual holds a college degree are indexes of these mechanisms. To measure the degree of hierarchy, we can divide the number of links in the longest transitive path for *power* by the number of members in a group.

Table 8:4 confirms what we already know from the images in Figure 8:3 above: that both the coherent and incoherent communes are quite stratified. And although the coherent groups have an average of 22% more hierarchy, there is still about one level for every two individuals in the incoherent communes. However, neither measures of stratifying mechanisms are strongly associated with the degree of hierarchy or the triad counts of the structural analysis. For example, taking the internal stratifying criterion first, and excluding the outlying cases so that the remaining groups have similar and approximately-even proportions of older and newer members, a slight increase in hierarchy (about 10%) occurs for both kinds of communes. But while the coherent groups average almost a 30% decline in the proportion of 030T triads, they still remain structurally distinct from the incoherent groups. And when subsamples are matched for an approximately-even distribution of members with and without college degrees, the increased difference in hierarchy is mainly due to a decline of hierarchy in the incoherent groups. Overall, there is little evidence of a clear, independent association between these indicators of stratifying forces and the global coherence of power.

Conclusion

It is now clear that the four sociological theories we have examined are unable to explain the presence of coherent global order in the communes; none of them are supported by the results of our analysis. And while it might be argued that our measures are too crude to be a "reasonable" test of these theories, there is evidence, nonetheless, that points toward a very different perspective. It is appropriate, therefore, to consider this alternative.

The evidence is our paradoxical finding that images of global order can be constructed from mappings of dyads. This suggests that social organization *may* be like a hologram: it is possible to derive a view of the group from dyads because the parts (dyads) contain all information about the organization of the whole (the group). Thus, the relation between part and whole is *holonomic* (one-to-one correspondence) — that at one level (that of information) the dyad is the same as, or equivalent, to the group. This means that not only does each dyad reflect the order of the specific relation between the particular individuals involved, but it also reflects the interrelation

TABLE 8:4   COHERENCE OF POWER CONTROLLED BY LENGTH OF MEMBERSHIP AND EDUCATION, AND BY DEGREE OF HIERARCHY (WAVE ONE) — TABULAR ANALYSIS AND TRIADIC STRUCTURE

GLOBAL COHERENCE	TABULAR ANALYSIS				TRIADIC STRUCTURE[1]						
	Coherent (25)*		Incoherent (21)		Coherent (25)			Incoherent (21)			Total (46)
					Triad Type			*Triad Type*			
	mean	degree of hierarchy	mean	degree of hierarchy	012	021D	030T	012	021D	030T	
PROPORTION JOINED 1973 OR EARLIER											
Sub-sample:[2] ≥.200 but ≤.600	.455 (13)	.687	.410 (11)	.576	.268	$.149^{1.914'}$	$.255^{2.924''}$	.293	.082	.178	
Full sample	.532	.633	.373	.518	.209	$.160^{2.083'}$	$.317^{2.807''}$	.322	.111	.155	(24)

PROPORTION WITH COLLEGE DEGREE

	mean	degree of hierarchy	mean	degree of hierarchy						
Sub-sample:[3] ≥ .300 but ≤ .700	.500	.654 (11)	.439	.484 (7)	.174	.144	$.358^{2;.334''}$	.319	.075	.170 (18)
Full sample	.505	.633	.536	.518	as above			as above		

*N = ( ).
1. Mean triad incidence (proportions); mean T scores (small figures) listed only when statistically significant. Symbols denote the following $pr.$ values:
    ' .05
    '' .01
2. The proportion of members that joined in 1973 or earlier had to be in the range specified for a commune to be included in this sub-sample.
3. This is the proportion of members in a group with a college degree. This sub-sample does not include the Boston groups (N = 11). Problems were encountered with some data files when transferring tapes between computer systems. A replacement data tape arrived too late to correct this deficiency.

227

among *all* dyads as they are enfolded into the global order of the group. In effect, it would seem that what we have uncovered is a relational order that both enfolds and is enfolded by the individual; a level of order that transcends individual interests and interpersonal construction; a level of order more immediate than time and more fundamental than culture; a level of order in which parts and whole are one — a collective consciousness, a "social hologram".

NOTES

1. The reasons are discussed above on pages 90 to 93.
2. This third set are refered to as "unacknowledged" dyads in Figure A:8(b) on page 317 of Appendix A. The strict and relaxed definitions are represented in this model (Model IV) as "acknowledged" dyads and "incomplete" dyads, respectively.
3. It is only recently (in the last three years or so) that I have undertaken an extensive analysis of the implications of including this set of dyads in the operational definition. In my earlier efforts I had little success in finding how to use the hierarchical information contained in these dyads. Consequently, my initial analysis pursued a more consensually based operational criterion.
4. The label "unrestricted" is relative to the strict and relaxed categories. It does not mean that this operational criterion had no conditions; for example, it does not include the three types of mutual dyads ("acknowledged dominance," "acknowledged null," "mutual missing") shown in Figure A:8(b) page 317, below.
5. The rules that I used to draw the hierarchical sociograms, in trying to reduce the arbitrariness and subjectivism that inevitably accompanies such graphic representations of structure, are given in Appendix C.
6. I have selected these groups as examples because they are the largest communes in the study for which relational data are available. Finding such a degree of global order from mappings of dyads in smaller groups would be less surprising, since with fewer people there is more opportunity and time for social interaction. In larger groups, this is less likely so that the degree of global order that emerges from mappings of dyads is more remarkable, and shows that the upper bound for such order is above the largest commune ($N = 29$) considered here.

7. While there is some increase in intransitivity in both communes (from 2/2024 to 21/2024 triads in commune C, and 2/3654 to 43/3654 in commune K — not shown in Figures 8:1 and 8:2), the results of a triadic analysis indicate that this is well below that expected by chance (*pr.* <.00005).

8. It is interesting to note the greater proportion of consensual bonds in the charismatic commune. Commune K had almost twice the percentage of strict dyads in its unrestricted image than commune C (61% and 31%, respectively).

9. Although the visual inspection and classification of sociograms suffers from subjective bias and arbitrariness, the hierarchical sociogram provides the only means of viewing the patterning of *actual* relations (i.e., uncontaminated by more formal network analysis techniques of data aggregation, such as block modelling or smallest space analysis) in the group as a whole. To reduce to impact of such spuriousness and provide a more rigorous and systematic basis to this classification, triadic analysis was performed on all groups.

10. I should point out, that the groups were stratified by gender, age, and seniority (freshman, sophomore etc.) and students were assigned using random number tables. Also, that no one reported knowing anyone else in the large class (N = 273) prior to enrollment, and that, at least for the groups shown here, no student reported that their group met outside the weekly, class-assigned hour.

11. Compare these patterns for Group X and Group Y (Figure 8:4(a) and 8:4(b) to those for domestic fowl in Figure 10:N1, page 297, below.

12. Of the 25 communes that were coherent at wave one, 6 had dissolved by wave two and a further 3 provided no relational data for the second study year.

13. Given the wide cultural and ideological diversity among the communes in this research, finding a single, common stratifying mechanism is difficult. In communes, however, as in many collectivities, length of membership is generally seen as one of the bases for seniority and prestige (see, Zablocki, 1980; Goode, 1978).

Chapter Nine

WHOLE IN PART*

... so long as some part of the surface of the striate cortex (the projection field of the ... retina ...) remained intact, there was no loss of habit. Any small part of the region was capable of maintaining the habits. ...

In later experiments ... discrimination of visual figures could be learned when only one-sixteenth of the visual cortex remained.

K. S. Lashley, "In Search of the Engram," in *The Neuropsychology of Lashley*, F. A. Beach, D. O. Hebb, E. T. Morgan, H. W. Nissen (Eds.), 1960:491.

Introduction

Two things are clear from the last chapter. First, the commune data do not support any of the explanations for coherent global order offered by four major sociological theories. And second, that the essential property of this order bears a close resemblance to that of a hologram, in that information about the organization of the group seems somehow enfolded into all dyads.

* I would like to express my gratitude to Karl H. Pribram, who both made helpful comments on earlier drafts of this chapter and also kindly provided copies of his articles and recent manuscripts. Lois Erickson and Nancy Roberts deserve special mention for their contributions to this chapter as well.

But, rejecting a theory from one scientific area, and identifying an "apparent" similarity between observations and a concept from another domain, means only that the latter *may* be useful as a metaphorical analogy. To go beyond this, we must demonstrate that the principle of holonomic order has empirical utility as sociological explanatory tool; we must find some way of subjecting it to an objective empirical test; we must give it, too, the opportunity to be falsified.

One way of doing this is to create a test condition, analogous to the procedure of removing cortical tissue, that neuropsychologists employ in experiments to determine brain structure and function. It was the paradoxical results that his mentor, Karl Lashley, obtained with this technique (see the epigram above), that convinced Karl Pribram (1966; 1969) that memory is processed by the brain like information is encoded and stored in a hologram. Thus, if we can demonstrate that the order of the group is contained in each and every relation, by showing that this information is not lost when the individuals are removed, then we will have compelling evidence for the hypothesis of holonomic social order.

For the neuropsychologist, evidence of holonomic order is established when, for example, an animal shows it can still perform a variety of visual discriminations despite having most of the cortex removed — in Lashley's experiment, retaining the memory of how to get through the maze. Because it is broadly equivalent, we will use maintenance of global order as the test condition for the communes in this research — that a coherent structure of power endures, over time, despite losing relations through high membership turnover.

In what follows, we will see that the results of our analysis are broadly consistent with this crude test of the hypothesis of holonomic social order. We will find, also, that not only is there an independent positive effect of coherent power on commune survival over time, but that high levels of communion must be accompanied by coherent power to reduce the likelihood of dissolution. But first, let us introduce the concept of the hologram and briefly describe how Pribram employed it to revolutionize our understanding of perception and memory.

Hologram: Metaphor For Wholeness[1]

As an optional device that can create a highly realistic, three-dimensional representation of an object from information encoded on a glass (holographic) plate (Figure 9:1), most of us are familiar with the hologram.[2] Most recently we have encountered it as a vivid, life-like image of an object that seems mysteriously projected away from the two dimensional surface of a bank/credit card, or from that of the so-called "stickers" that are presently popular with children. Such "optical holograms" are only one among a number of different examples of a more general kind of organization described in physics as *holonomic* (Gabor, 1948).

At first glance, holonomic organization seems perplexingly paradoxical: all parts are distributed over the whole, and the whole is enfolded in all parts. It also seems counterintuitive, for if each contains the other, then part and whole must be equivalent. But how can a piece be the same as the whole of which it is only a part? It cannot be geometrically isomorphic, for we can "see" the difference — the lack of correspondence in size, shape, volume etc.. But there is a second kind of isomorphism, which is algebraic and transformational, involving linear and reversible correspondence in information: that *information about the order of the whole is "stored", in a coded (i.e. transformed) form, in the part.* It is this property that makes it possible not only to encode a transform of the whole in all parts, but also to reverse the process — to back-transform from the encoded information — and recreate the whole.

In an optical hologram, the three-dimensional image of the object is encoded on the holographic plate as overlapping concentric rings representing interference patterns of light waves (see Figure 9:1). The interference patterns are created by light

A: ENCODING THE OBJECT

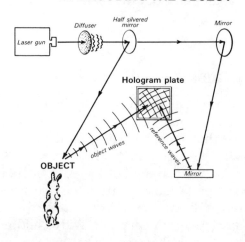

B: DECODING TO CONSTRUCT IMAGE*

The holographic plate records, coded in its interference patterns of concentric rings, a three-dimensional image of the rabbit. The interference patterns have been produced by light bouncing off different features of the object. The patterns encode those features. By shining a laser beam through the plate, the encoding can be retrieved so that the rabbit seems to appear in space. This can also be done by shining a beam through only a piece of the plate.
(*Figure 9:1(B) and text is from Briggs and Peat (1984:110), reproduced here with permission of the publisher, Simon and Schuster, Inc.)

9:1 *Example of an Optical Hologram*

waves from a laser gun bouncing off the object *en*-coding the object's features on the plate. When a laser beam is shone through the plate the encoded information is then *de*-coded into a three-dimensional image of the object. Because the encoded information about the entire object has been recorded everywhere, an image of the whole object can be obtained even when a laser is shone through only a piece of the plate: "The plate can be broken down into small fragments, and each piece will reconstruct the entire object" (Leith and Upatnieks, 1964:1297). However, because smaller fragments carry only a narrow beam of light, a weaker signal, there is some loss of resolution. But "even the blurred image, reconstructed from the tiny chip, is still an image of the whole scene" (Pietsch, 1981:63).

Waveforms are the mechanism by which information about the whole is distributed to all parts (Figure 9:2). Each wave carries information that, upon interaction with other waves, is exchanged creating additional waves of interference. Each point on every wave thus interacts with every point on all other waves, so that all information about everything is distributed everywhere throughout the whole. It is like throwing two pebbles into a small pond. The waves, created by the pebbles' impact, radiate outwards as two sets of concentric rings. As the wave rings from each set intersect with those of the other set, they interfere with or reinforce each other, creating a complex interference pattern. The interference pattern contains, in a coded form, information about the whole process. Decoding this information, by reversing the process, means that an image can be created of the original objects. "If one took a movie of the whole process, from pebble to interference pattern, one could show the film in reverse so that the pebbles would seem to be produced from the ripples" (Pribram, 1983:35).

Mathematically, the holographic process can be described by a Fourier transform function (Gabor, 1948; 1972). This function decomposes the interference pattern into a set of component waveforms, the elements of which are completely regular sine waves. These component waveforms are thus a code for the interference pattern and it is these that are stored on the holographic record. By representing a particular waveform component of the entire interference pattern, each point on the record contains information about the complete image. In this way, the whole image is enfolded and distributed to every point.

To make a hologram, two or more (Fourier transformed) records must be linearly superposed (e.g., Figure 9:2(a)). Mathematically, this means convolving (i.e., adding) the records together so that each point encoded on the resultant product contains information (relative phase, angle, degree) from both waveforms (moirés c and d, Figure 9:2(a)). Decoding the holographic record, to retrieve the image, simply requires applying the Fourier transform function a second time (Figure 9:2(b)). This is because the function is invertible: it not only converts images into waveforms, but can convert the waveforms back into images (Pietsch, 1981:153-161).

Holonomy and the Brain[3]

In his ground-breaking book, *Languages of the Brain*, Karl Pribram (1971) used the hologram as the basis for a revolutionary model of brain function.[4] In a brilliant insight, he saw a number of basic properties that the brain shared in common with the hologram that would explain the paradoxes that had perplexed Lashley right to the end of his life: viz, distributed information store; gigantic storage capacity; image constancy and highly textured, three-dimensional, parallax reconstruction; associative image retrieval; image projection away from the record's surface; independent of "physical waves".[5] Accordingly, Pribram boldly predicted that rather than storing memory in a particular location, the brain transforms information into a code — "the neural network performs holographic transformations on sensory input" — and stores the encoded image everywhere, throughout the cortex (Pribram, 1982:281).

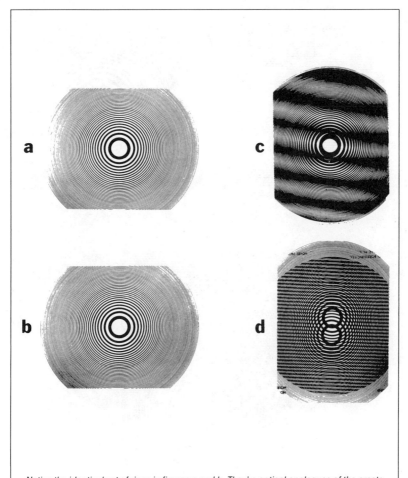

Notice the identical set of rings in figures a and b. They're optical analogues of the crests of ripples on a pond. I superimposed these two sets of rings out of phase to produce the moiré patterns in figures c and d. The moirés are interference patterns, and the phase difference is how off-center the two sets are relative to each other. If we compare figures c and d, it is apparent that the frequency of beats, as well as their widths and spacings, vary with the phase shift. When the two centers lie closer together, as in figure c, the stripes are coarse, widely spaced and of low frequency. Where the phase difference is great, as in figure d, frequency is high, spacings are narrow, and the stripes are thin. The stripes are precisely determined by the phase shift. And these stripes represent the phase code in transform space (page 155).
(From: Pietsch (1981: 154–155), figures and text reprinted by permission of the publisher, Houghton Mifflin Company.)

9:2(a) *Hypothetical Example of Holographic Record: Encoding Information*

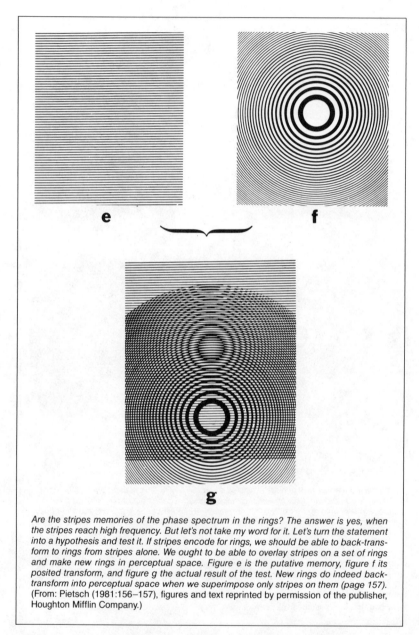

Are the stripes memories of the phase spectrum in the rings? The answer is yes, when the stripes reach high frequency. But let's not take my word for it. Let's turn the statement into a hypothesis and test it. If stripes encode for rings, we should be able to back-transform to rings from stripes alone. We ought to be able to overlay stripes on a set of rings and make new rings in perceptual space. Figure e is the putative memory, figure f its posited transform, and figure g the actual result of the test. New rings do indeed back-transform into perceptual space when we superimpose only stripes on them (page 157). (From: Pietsch (1981:156–157), figures and text reprinted by permission of the publisher, Houghton Mifflin Company.)

9:2(b) *Hypothetical Example of Holographic Record: Decoding Information*

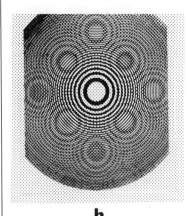

h

What do we mean by stripes? They are beats, yes. But stripes are periodic patterns of light and dark, a harmonic array of alternating densities. Given this, the memory of rings shouldn't literally be confined to stripes. The memory is a periodicity, a wavy logic. We should be able to back-transform rings from, say, dots. Figure h shows that dots on rings will indeed create new rings (page 157; emphasis in original).

I am presenting this dot experiment for another reason as well. Perhaps the rings are just a matter of luck. Maybe the various dots are spaced fortuitously to interact with the correct arcs. If we look at figure h carefully, we see that not all rings are the same. In fact, those on opposite ends of the vertical and horizontal axes, thus lying on perspective arcs of the same circles, are mirror images of each other: where one ring has a dark center, the corresponding ring is light. If the "maybe" speculations above were right, these rings would be identical. But they are not (page 158).

Let's shift our focus back to the nature of the phase code, which in our ring system is the preservation of ring information by periodic patterns. The ring memory is not limited to dots and stripes. When we react rings with too great a distance between their centers, we do not produce stripes. Instead, something interesting happens. Inspect figure i, and notice that rings are forming in the regions of overlap. Built into the higher-frequency rings is a memory of rings closer to the center. ...The phase code is not literally stripes or dots, but rather a certain periodicity, a logic. Our rings are much like ripples on a pond; they expand from the center just as any wave front advances from the origin. ...Each point in a wave contributes to the advancing wave front. The waves at the periphery contain a memory of their entire ancestry. When we superimpose sets of rings in the manner shown in figure i, we back-transform those hidden, unsuspected "ancestral" memories into perceptual space. Figure i shows that no necessary relationship exists between the nature of a phase code and how the code came into being (pages 158–159).

(From: Pietsch (1981:157–160), figures and text reprinted by permission of the publisher, Houghton Mifflin Company.)

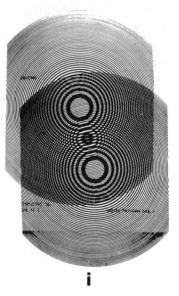

i

9:2(b) *(Continued)*

It was the mathematical properties of this process that were important. For Pribram realized that to show the holographic approach was more than a novel metaphor, *that it actually had explanatory power*, meant comparing the mathematics of holography with the mathematics of brain function. Empirically, this would require demonstrating that a set of neural signals is transformed and enfolded into every part of the cortex by a transform function that can be described by the linear wave equations of Fourier mathematics.

Since he first made this prediction, some twenty years ago (Pribram, 1966), a consistent body of strong, confirmatory, experimental evidence has accumulated (e.gs., Campbell and Robson, 1968; Blakemore and Campbell, 1969; Pribram, Newer, and Barron, 1975; Movshon, Thompson, and Tolhurst, 1978; De Valois, De Valois, and Yund, 1979; Marcelja, 1980; Pietsch, 1981; Daugman, 1985), indeed, to such an extent that it is often taken for granted in recent work (e.g., Eich, 1985; Murdock, 1985).

Very briefly, this evidence shows that the functioning of the neural microstructure (i.e., the interaction between vertical, axonal transmission pathways and the horizontal dentritic networks), for several sensory systems (viz; visual, auditory, somatosensory, and olfactory), can be described by linear wave equations — a result consistent with the holographic model. Also, that while the other major theories of the neurophysiology of perception are either directly contradicted (field theory), or are unable to fully explain the evidence (feature correspondence theory), the holographic theory is strongly consistent with the data: viz, the actual transfer functions by which auditory, visual, olfactory, and tactile input is enfolded into the neurophysiological structures of memory, have been shown to conform to the Fourier mathematics of a holographic process (Shapley and Lennie, 1985).[6] In other words, there is no isomorphism between phenomenal experience and brain structure; instead, sensory and bodily inputs are processed into neural patterns by a holonomic transformation. We can best sum it all up in Pribram's own words:

In the fifteen or more years since this striking resemblance between holography and certain brain/behavioral processes was noted, much evidence has accumulated to show that what began as a metaphorical simile has been developed into a precise neurological model. ...

Such a theory is thoroughly grounded in the structures and functions of the microanatomical connectivity of the nervous system and provides a mathematically sophisticated formulation of the relationship between anatomy and the images of perception, and also between anatomy and memory structure.

... There is little remaining doubt that some brain processes are characterized by holonomic transformations that result in algebraic isomorphisms between image/object on the one hand and the holographic transform domain on the other. (Pribram, 1983:36; 1982:274.)

While Pribram's remarkable achievement can serve as an inspiration, we must establish the explanatory potential and appropriateness of the holonomic metaphor for social phenomena on sociological grounds. This will mean a journey into new territory, for, apart from some interest in the hologram's metaphorical utility among a few pioneers in management and organization,[7] the concept's potential does not seem to have sparked the imagination of other social scientists.

Holonomic Social Order: An Hypothesis

Just how closely the hologram fits as a model for social order can be seen when its six essential properties are compared with some basic characteristics of social organization. Let us consider the match between each of these in turn.

The first property is the independence of a holographic process from the actual presence of "real" waves — that while holonomic order can be described mathematically by the equations of wave mechanics, there is no necessity that waves be physically present. There are no "waves" in computer simulations of optical information processes (see Figure 8-9 in Pribram, 1971:151), for example, and there are "not necessarily" discernible wavefronts in the response of dendritic networks to neuron excitation in the brain (Pribram, 1982:275). What does hold though, is that when compared with alternative mathematical descriptions, a waveform model is the best fit to the data.

There is already strong evidence that many social processes behave in a wave-like manner — viz, business cycles in the stock market; political swings of leader/party popularity; the sways of public opinion; periodic outbursts of collective violence and war etc., etc.. What is required in future research, is to show that a holonomic transform of information from parts of a system will yield a view of the whole system.

This brings us to the second property, a distributed information store — that information about the whole is distributed everywhere, in all parts. As already mentioned, this means that an image of the whole can be reconstructed from any part, and it is this back-transforming capability that seems to have been captured in the mappings of dyadic relations from the communes.

Such information redundancy is highly functional for a system because a holographic store is extremely resistant to damage. The code for the whole, being present in every part, can survive all-but-total destruction. This would explain a paradox, documented by studies from diverse contexts, that has frustrated conventional sociological wisdom: namely, the resilience and durability of social organization in the face of "contrary" conditions. Some examples: the persistence of operational effectiveness in isolated military units that have suffered very heavy casualties (including leadership); an unyielding fabric of community despite massive devastation to populations and living environments wrought by natural or human causes; the germination of social cohesion among highly transient slum populations, or among the waves of urban squatters who arrive in Third World cities with only poverty and hope in common; the resistence of social structure to interventions aimed at securing so-called "planned social change"; and more benignly, the flourishing of community in the middle class neighborhoods of suburbia in the face of high rates of social/geographic mobility. The paradox that these situations share is the persistence of social order under highly disruptive conditions — either conditions where an established order endures despite the destruction of much of its parts, or conditions where a new order is established among disparate and previously "unrelated" elements. This is the property that we will test for, in a moment, by examining the impact of membership turnover on the persistence of coherent global structure in the communes.

A third property of holograms is that huge quantities of information can be encoded and concentrated into a small holographic space,[8] while object identity and integrity is preserved. This is accomplished by successively superimposing the unique codes for each object in the holographic store. Sociologically, there are some interesting parallels.

For even the most simple of social situations, as the interactionists have shown, a vast amount of very specific, "taken-for-granted" information concerning the particulars of positions, roles, interaction sequences etc. is required by social actors to construct the appropriate relations that make it a "reality" (e.g., Goffman, 1971). And when one considers the back-to-back sequences of often discontinuous, complex, and sometimes diametrically opposed frames of interaction through which social actors move, we are talking in terms of mountains of highly detailed information.[9]

This unimaginably enormous body of relational material must not only be stored with the identity and integrity of each interaction sequence intact, but it also must be instantly retrievable as a whole. Think about our subjective experience of social reality for a moment. Each social situation — irrespective of size, complexity, degree of conflict, and rapidity of succession from one frame to the next — is usually experienced as a "complete" reality in itself. Moreover, our experience of the transition from one situation to the next, even those patterned antithetically, is usually immediate without adjustment or disorientation over the disjunction actually involved.

A fourth property is that image reconstruction is three-dimensional and is highly textured in terms of detail. The image itself displays constancies, remaining invariant no matter from what part/s it is reconstituted. It also displays parallax, in that "hidden" parts of the object are revealed as the angle of view is changed. Again, there are some interesting sociological analogues.

While, as an object, social reality cannot be reduced to the spatial dimensions of the physical world, it nonetheless has a dimensionality that enables it to be constructed and perceived as "real". It is projected and experienced as if it has, in a sense, a "solid" existence — an existence that, while it involves and includes us, it is also separate and apart: it is "out there". Moreover, despite our unique involvement as individual actors, and the change in our awareness as "new" features are revealed as we move among positions and roles, certain aspects and patterns remain mysteriously familiar and constant — a kind of intangible invariance. Yet, no matter how close or apart our place in the structure, this invariance is experienced as something constant, something fundamental that binds us all together.

This brings us to a fifth property of holograms: namely, that the object image is not coextensive with the holographic record, but is projected away from its surface. In other words, when we see the image (say, that on the two dimensional surface of a credit card) we perceive it as if it actually has a third dimension of depth, projected up or down from the record surface. A similar phenomenon occurs with the perception of stereophonic sound; the auditory system of the brain takes the sound signals from two separate sources (speakers), and combines them into a single auditory image projected into the space between the speakers.[10] Yet the projected image, of course, is an illusion of perception.

As alluded to above, this is analogous to the construction of social reality by social actors. While, on the one hand, it is stored, perceived, and experientially interpreted "inside" — in the mind of the individual, social structure also has an external, independent existence "outside". It is not coextensive with the individuals or the relations from which it is constructed. Rather, it is projected away from these elements as a separate, domain. It has a depth and dimensionality that seems all-encompassing. And yet there is a sense of something synthetic, of something partial and incomplete. Subjectively, it seems paradoxically both "real" and "solid", and yet also "unreal" and "ethereal". It is unreal because it is a construction; only the projection of an image of what "should be". It is real by virtue of our beliefs; we treat the image as real. In doing so, we make illusion reality.

The sixth and final property is that a holographic store is associative. Once objects are encoded in the store, it is possible to retrieve an image of a missing object from the information on another object. For example, from a hologram made of two objects, "subsequent illumination of the stored hologram by light reflected from only one object will reconstruct a ghost image of the missing object" (Pribram, 1982:276). Thus, not only is there an enfolding whole-in-part order for every object encoded, but there is also an enfoldment of the order of each object throughout all of the others (Bohm, 1980: Chapter 6). Again, there is an interesting sociological parallel.

When social systems are damaged by the loss of relational patterns, positions, roles, or social actors, there is very often a capacity to rebuild the missing entities from elements in other social systems. For example, an imperiled corporation, that has lost its economic viability (e.g., Chrysler), may regenerate by decoding the order for profitability from an implant (Iococca) from another corporate system. In this way the implant enables the system to retrieve and actualize an encoded order that it appears to have "lost". Another example is when a social system continues to perpetuate the order for a position or pattern even though the latter has been vacated or disrupted. It preserves the order for the missing element by projecting the element as a potential until it can be restored and actualized. A good example of this phenomenon is membership turnover. Although relational patterns may be suspended because no replacements are currently available when social actors vacate positions, the patterns are usually reactivated when the positions are reoccupied.

By now it should be apparent that there is good reason to take the holographic metaphor seriously and explore its explanatory potential as a model of social organization. It should be clear, in particular, why a holonomic theory is needed to explain the images of global order constructed from mappings of dyadic relations in the communes.

I. Holonomy and Dyadic Relations

In essence, the fundamental postulate of the holonomic hypothesis is that of whole-in-part correspondence in information — that all parts (social actors and relations) contain the encoded order of the whole (the group).[11] Viewing dyads as the parts and the power structure of a group as a whole, a holonomic order means, therefore, that any subset of dyads (even a single dyad) carries the code for the complete order of power enfolded into the specific ties between each pair of individuals. With the information about its global organization distributed this way, the group can thus regenerate or recreate its structure just from a few parts. In other words, the ability of the group to perpetuate its form is *not* compromised by the loss of individuals and their relationships.

The most direct way to test this hypothesis is to see whether a group can maintain a coherent order of power as an increasing proportion of members are removed. Removal of members means the group loses the particular dyads in which these individuals are involved. If social organization is holonomic, this should not mean loss of information about the global order of power, since the information is encoded into and retained by the remaining elements. On the other hand, removing an increasing proportion of members from a nonholonomic system should result in a loss of information about global order. This loss should impair the group's capacity for self-regeneration.

While circumstances in which a collectivity loses members, such as war, accidents, and natural disasters, may provide natural research sites, experiments employing this procedure in real groups are morally and ethically unacceptable. Even without these limits, though, the post hoc nature of this part of the commune study makes it impossible.

An alternative procedure, which is still broadly consistent with this idea, is to use the turnover of members as analogous, in a very approximate sense, to the removal of individuals. Member turnover still involves the destruction of the specific dyadic bonds that exist prior to a change of individuals. In contrast to conventional sociological thinking, from a holonomic perspective we would expect membership turnover to have little impact on a group's ability to maintain a coherent global order over time.[12] This hypothesis can be tested by measuring the effect of membership turnover,[13] between Waves One and Two, on the global coherence of power at Wave Two.[14] The results of two analyses presented in Table 9:1 are consistent with this hypothesis.

The first analysis (Table 9:1(a)) shows that the amount of membership turnover has little association with the coherence of power at Wave Two. For example, while a majority of the communes, coherent at the second wave, had "low" turnover (mean = 52% turnover), as many as 42% had greater than 100% turnover and averaged 137% change to their first wave population. And, although triadic analysis reveals some association between turnover and relational structure for the coherent groups (012 and 030T triads), strong structural differences are still evident when they are compared with the incoherent communes.

TABLE 9:1(a) COHERENCE OF POWER (WAVE TWO) BY MEMBER TURNOVER AND MEMBER GROWTH (W1 TO W2) — TABULAR ANALYSIS AND TRIADIC STRUCTURE

GLOBAL COHERENCE	TABULAR ANALYSIS: Coherent (19)*	TABULAR ANALYSIS: Incoherent (12)	TRIADIC Coherent (19) 012	Coherent 021D	Coherent 030T	TRIADIC Incoherent (12) 012	Incoherent 021D	Incoherent 030T	Total (31)²
MEMBER TURNOVER³ *(mean turnover)*									
Low (≤.99)	.515 (57.9%)	.464 (50.0%)	.125	.210	$.349^{1.868\,\prime}$	.398	.120	.064	(17)
High (≥1.00)	1.367 (42.1)	1.325 (50.0)	.255	.120	$.311^{6.403\,\prime\prime\prime\prime\prime}$	.362	.050	.155	(14)
Total	.846 (100.0%)	.895 (100.0%)							(31)
MEMBER GROWTH BY WAVE TWO⁴ *(mean change)*									
Decrease⁵	-.269 (42.1)	-.271 (58.3)	.179	.206	$.275^{2.636\,\prime\prime}$	.410	.114	.033	(15)
Increase⁶	+.181 (57.9)	+.159 (41.7)	.180	.148	$.374^{4.608\,\prime\prime\prime\prime\prime}$	.337	.044	.217	(16)
Total	-.009 (100.0%)	-.092 (100.0%)							(31)

*N = ( ).

1. Mean triad incidence (proportions); mean T scores (small figures) given only when statistically significant. Symbols denote the following pr. values:
   ' .05
   '' .01
   ''''' .00005
2. This analysis excludes 15 communes; 9 had dissolved and 6 provided no relational data for wave two.
3. Member turnover = ((leavers + joiners) ÷ (population at wave 1)).
4. Member growth is computed as the proportion of population change in a commune using the wave one population as the base.
5. "Decrease" means less than the population at wave one.
6. "Increase" means greater than or equal to the population at wave one.

In the second analysis, presented in Table 9:1(b), we can see that membership turnover has no impact on the maintenance or achievement of coherent global order over time. Of the 16 groups coherent at Wave One, 78% and 71% of those in the "low" and "high" turnover categories, respectively, had maintained a coherent power structure through the second wave. Furthermore, the 15 incoherent at Wave One were just as likely to maintain or achieve global coherence in Wave Two, no matter how much turnover had occurred. Finally, despite some decline in collective bonding (030T triad) for the high turnover groups that had maintained coherence, structural differences still distinguish those maintaining or achieving coherent order in Wave Two from communes remaining or becoming incoherent during that time.

But, while the aggregate amount of member turnover is unrelated to global coherence, there is still the question of location — that information about the whole is not just stored in particular locations, but distributed everywhere, in all parts. A distributed store, consistent with a holonomic order, would mean that the structural integrity of the group is not affected by the loss of relations in particular locations. Accordingly, we can hypothesize that the hierarchical location of member turnover will be unrelated to the maintenance or achievement of coherent global order. On the other hand, if the information store is localized (nonholonomic), then loss of relations in key locations should jeopardize the group's ability to maintain a coherent form. To test these alternatives, the amount of turnover occurring among individuals in the top half of the first wave power hierarchy was calculated,[16] and then the communes were divided into "low" and "high" turnover categories.

Table 9:2 shows some relationship between the location of turnover and the global order of power over time. This is strongest for low turnover communes coherent in Wave One; all nine of them remained coherent through the second wave. However, 3 of the 7 groups (43%) in the high turnover portion of this category, maintained a coherent order despite averaging

TABLE 9:1(b) WAVE ONE COHERENCE BY WAVE TWO COHERENCE BY MEMBER TURNOVER AND MEMBER GROWTH (W1 TO W2) — TABULAR ANALYSIS AND TRIADIC STRUCTURE

TABULAR ANALYSIS

GLOBAL COHERENCE: wave 1	Coherent (16)*		Incoherent (15)	
GLOBAL COHERENCE: wave 2	Coherent (12)	Incoherent (4)	Coherent (7)	Incoherent (8)
MEMBER TURNOVER				
Low (≤.999)				
mean turnover	.557	.709	.441	.341
% row subtotal	77.7%	22.2%	50.0%	50.0%
subtotal	(9)		(8)	
High (≥1.000)				
mean turnover	1.223	1.272	1.432	1.352
% row subtotal	71.4%	28.6%	42.9%	57.1%
subtotal	(7)		(7)	

TRIADIC STRUCTURE[1] (wave two)

Triad Types	Coherent (16)		Incoherent (15)		Total (31)[2]
	Coherent (12)	Incoherent (4)	Coherent (7)	Incoherent (8)	
012	.124	.375	.127	.409	
021D	.147	.250	.320	.055	
030T	$.365^{2.248,,}$	0	.320	.097	(17)
012	.274	.350	.224	.368	
021D	.122	.050	.117	.050	
030T	$.271^{8.711,,,,,}$	.050	$.376^{2.557,,}$	.207	$\frac{(14)}{(31)}$

MEMBER GROWTH (W1-W2)

Decrease[3]

mean change	−.265	−.401		−.276	−.173
% row subtotal	62.5%	37.5%		42.9%	57.1%
subtotal		(8)			(7)

Increase[4]

mean change	+.208	+.200		+.134	+.149
% row subtotal	85.5%	12.5%		50.0%	50.0%
subtotal		(8)			(8)

Triad Types

Decrease[3]

	012		021D		030T	
	.173	.383	.139	.200	$.275^{2.851}$''	.033
	.190	.430	.317	.050	$.276^{2.278}$''	.032
subtotal						(15)

Increase[4]

	012		021D		030T	
	.196	.300	.135	0	$.363^{6.433}$'''''	0
	.152	.347	.170	.055	.395	.272
subtotal						$\frac{(16)}{(31)}$

*N = ( ).

1. Mean triad incidence (proportions); mean T scores (small figures) given only when statistically significant. Symbols denote the following pr. values:
   '' .01
   ''''' .00005
2. This analysis excludes 15 communes; 9 had dissolved and 6 provided no relational data for wave two.
3. "Decrease" means less than the population at wave one.
4. "Increase" means greater than or equal to the population at wave one.

251

more than two thirds change in personnel at the top. Among the incoherent groups, achieving coherence by the second wave is more likely when turnover here is low. It would appear, then, that coherent global order is not completely independent of the location of turnover; there is some vulnerability to a change of individuals in the upper regions of the group. Since this is a change to each of the specific dyads in which these members are involved as well, let us see, therefore, to what extent this vulnerability is specific to the most important position in a group, that of leadership.

It is clear from bottom row of Table 9:2, that losing the sociometric leader/s jeopardizes neither the maintenance nor the achievement of coherent order over time. Nearly half (5) of the 12 communes, coherent at both waves, had lost their leader/s, and of the 7 achieving coherence in Wave Two, more than half (4) had had this happen. So overall, these results suggest that while coherent order is not influenced by either the aggregate amount of turnover or the leaving of leaders, there is some adverse impact by upper level mobility. This suggests that the persistence of coherent global order is related to the stability of a critical infrastructure in the higher echelons of a group. In other words, that information about the whole may not be distributed everywhere, but appears to be specific to a particular region of the group. Clearly, this would be contrary to a holonomic order.

But there is another interpretation of these results that is still consistent with the holonomic hypothesis. This is that it is *not* the template for coherent order that has been "lost" with the turnover in this particular location, but rather the capacity to actualize the order. From this viewpoint, our crude turnover test for holonomy unfortunately confounds together two quite distinct domains of social reality: a domain of potential, the full array of movements of energy encoded into the group as possibilities; and a domain of action, the actualized patterns of social activity. As we will see below (Chapter Ten, pages 286 to 290), these domains are structured quite differently: the former is a nonlocalized order of potential

TABLE 9:2 WAVE ONE COHERENCE BY WAVE TWO COHERENCE BY UPPER HIERARCHY TURNOVER, AND LOSS OF WAVE ONE SOCIOMETRIC LEADER — TABULAR ANALYSIS AND TRIADIC STRUCTURE

TABULAR ANALYSIS

GLOBAL COHERENCE: wave 1	Coherent (16)*		Incoherent (15)	
GLOBAL COHERENCE: wave 2	Coherent (12)	Incoherent (4)	Coherent (7)	Incoherent (8)
TOP ½ MEMBER TURNOVER[3]				
Low (≤.499)				
mean turnover	.215	0	.146	.067
% row subtotal	100.0%	0%	57.1%	42.9%
subtotal		(9)		(7)
High (≥.500)				
mean turnover	.683	.709	.675	.783
% row subtotal	42.9%	57.1%	37.5%	62.5%
subtotal		(7)		(8)
LEADER/S LEFT COMMUNE[4]				
percentage of groups affected	41.7%	75.0%	57.1%	37.5%

TRIADIC STRUCTURE[1] (wave two)

	Coherent (16)		Incoherent (15)		Total (31)[2]
Triad Types	Coherent (12)	Incoherent (4)	Coherent (7)	Incoherent (8)	
012	.175	0	.127	.545	
021D	.133	0	.320	.073	
030T	.315[4.970'''']	0	.320	.129	(16)
012	.221	.363	.224	.294	
021D	.149	.150	.166	.040	
030T	.358[4.852''''']	.025	.376[2.557'']	.166	(15)

*N = ( ).
'' .01
''''' .00005

1. Mean triad incidence (proportions); mean τ scores (small figures) given only when statistically significant. Symbols denote the following *pr.* values:
2. This analysis excludes 15 communes; 9 had dissolved and 6 provided no relational data for wave two.
3. This is member turnover in the top half of wave one power hierarchy.
4. This is whether the sociometric leader/s (wave one) had left the group by wave two.

253

patterns of action enfolded throughout the group; the latter, the action domain, is an order localized in time and context — the specific movements into which the energy of the group has been structured. From this perspective, the adverse impact of upper-level turnover on coherent order reflects a reduction in actualization capacity rather than loss of the encoded template. Stability, here, is more than likely a prerequisite for the actualization of order, while it is probably less important for encoding group structure.

Coherent Power and Stability

As a structure for extraordinarily efficient collective action, coherent order requires complete alignment with the group. It involves the interrelation of all parts in an harmonious alignment that synchronizes everything to the movement of the whole. It is a fusion of relations that both energizes and aligns the collective and empowers the individual as well. Accordingly, we should expect evidence of greater functional effectiveness when coherent order is present, not only for the group but also for the individual.

For a collectivity, the first imperative is survival; before anything it must attempt to secure the future. Without this everything else, both collective objectives and individual aspirations, is in question. To ensure the future a group must establish relational forms that enhance its chances of survival. We have argued that functional effectiveness is greatest when coherent order is present. Consequently, we expect a relationship between the global organization of power and durability: that coherent power results in a higher likelihood of commune survival.

Starting, briefly, with the persistence of global structure, Figure 9:3 shows that, once a pattern for power is established, it tends to persist over time. While this holds for both categories of communes surviving through Wave Two, it is more likely for groups with coherent power (75% versus 62%).[17]

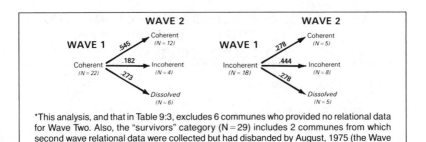

*This analysis, and that in Table 9:3, excludes 6 communes who provided no relational data for Wave Two. Also, the "survivors" category (N = 29) includes 2 communes from which second wave relational data were collected but had disbanded by August, 1975 (the Wave Two "test" point).

9:3 *Probability of Maintaining Global Coherence, First Test Year*[*]

Turning to survival, Table 9:3(a) shows, with the exception of the first test year, that a coherent order of power gives quite a boost to a commune's chances of survival. Not only do the groups coherent in Wave One enjoy a higher overall survival rate by the third wave (64% compared to 50%), but there is evidence of a strong advantage when the accumulated effects of this disposition are examined (Table 9:3(b)). So that while 92% of the twelve groups maintaining coherent power across waves one and two are still in extistence one year later, this is true for only 63% of the eight communes remaining incoherent for both waves.

Finally, there is some evidence that the global organization of power also may have consequences for the behavior of individuals. In the pilot study to the Small Groups Project (Bradley and Owens, 1980), a student's performance on the final exam was found to be related to the global pattern of power in the class work group to which the student belonged (see Figure 9:4). The sociograms of power in Figure 9:4(a) are of groups in which 50% or more of the members achieved a grade of "A" or "B" on their final exam. Compared with the sociograms in Figure 9:4(b), these groups exhibit a more coherent order with fewer conflict bonds ("mutual claims" in which *i* and *j* both claim the greater power), less intransivity, and an absence of multiple sociometric leaders. The groups shown in Figure 9:4(b) are those in which 50% or more of the group received a final exam grade of "C", "D", or "F".[18]

TABLE 9:3 TIME-SPECIFIC AND ACCUMULATED
EFFECTS OF COHERENCE OF POWER ON
COMMUNE SURVIVAL

a) TIME-SPECIFIC EFFECTS

COHERENCE STATUS	number of communes	SURVIVAL RATE (percentage)
Wave One		*Wave Two*
Coherent	22	72.7%
Incoherent	18	72.2%
Wave Two		*Wave Three*
Coherent	17	88.2%
Incoherent	12	66.7%

b) ACCUMULATED EFFECTS

COHERENCE STATUS		number of communes	SURVIVAL RATE (percentage)
Wave One	*Wave Two*		*Wave Three*
Coherent +	Coherent	12	91.7%
Incoherent +	Coherent	5	80.0%
Coherent +	Incoherent	4	75.0%
Incoherent +	Incoherent	8	62.5%

While these results are tentative, the relationship between the global order of power and individual behavior is quite strong. It is by empowering individuals through alignment with the collective, or by rendering them ineffective by channeling individual energies into contraposing patterns and conflict, that group structure can facilitate or inhibit individual achievement.

II. Holonomy and Multiplex Relations

So far, we have considered only one of the ways by which the order of the social whole is encoded into its parts — namely, enfoldment in dyads. But dyads are only one of the elements that constitute a group. A second is multiplexity, the order of interrelation among the different content dimensions of social structure. Insofar as social organization is holonomic, the order of each content system will be encoded into that for every other. Therefore, we should expect the relational order for love to be enfolded into the order for power, and vice versa.

We have already uncovered two pieces of evidence that are consistent with this idea. First, in Chapter Five, we found that love and power are coexistent contents in charismatic communes: convolved together — cojoined by an *AND* function — rather than differentiated or conditionally related. The second appeared in Chapter Seven where we found a balance between the structures of love and power in the stable groups. Both pieces of evidence suggest the possibility that these content systems are related by a more fundamental unity, related by some kind of holonomic process.

Evidence of a holonomic linkage is a reciprocal interrelation between the two content systems — that the order of each is directly tied to the order of the other. In other words, there should be one-to-one correspondence between love and power. As argued above, functional effectiveness will be higher in groups where such multiplex holonomy exists. Consequently, we should see the effect of this interrelation between love and power on group stability.

Communion, Coherent Power, and Stability

Starting with the relationship between communion and the global organization of power, Table 9:4 shows that the coherent communes have, on average, a greater proportion of their *loving* bonds structured collectively (300 triad), and that they are distributed evenly across the three categories of communion. The incoherent groups, however, are concentrated primarily in the lower categories. A difference is also apparent in the triadic structure of *power*, and, as expected, is related to the presence of communion; the coherent groups tend to manifest more collective control (030T triad) as the degree of communion (300 triad) increases.

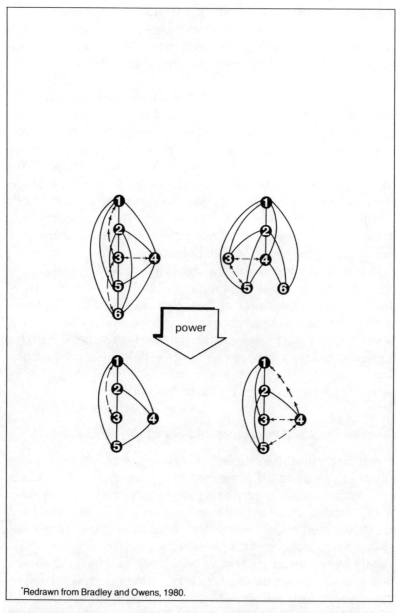

9:4(a) *Power Structures of Groups With ≥ 50% of Members Whose Final Exam Grade was "A" or "B"**

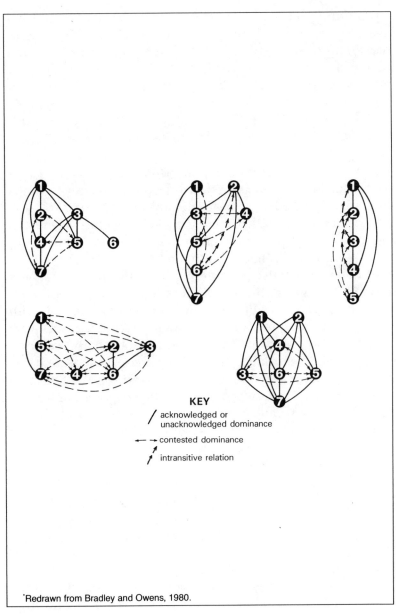

KEY

/ acknowledged or
unacknowledged dominance

←- -→ contested dominance

↗ intransitive relation

*Redrawn from Bradley and Owens, 1980.

9:4(b) *Power Structures of Groups With ≥ 50% of Members Whose Final Exam Grade Was "C", "D", or "F"**

Examining the joint effect of communion and the global organization of power on group stability (Table 9:5), we find that, overall, the results confirm our expectations. Viewing the survival rates first, we find that both the coherent and incoherent groups with "low" communion enjoy relatively high survival rates of 75% or more across the two test years. For the groups with "high" communion, however, it is a different story. As expected, here those with coherent power have a considerable advantage that actually improves over the two test years. These groups jump from a 71% to a 89% survival rate during this period, while the incoherent groups drop slightly to 50% from an already low rate of 56%. It is clear from these data that there is a strong interactive effect of communion and power on group stability that persists over time — a finding in line with the holonomic hypothesis.

Although we must be cautious with the triadic analysis in Table 9:5, given the small numbers in the "dissolved" categories, these results, too, are broadly consistent with a holonomic interpretation of the data. Taking the survivors first, with the exception of the incoherent, "high" communion subset, the triadic structure of these groups remains quite stable over the two test years. And, as we found in Chapter Seven, there is also evidence of a reciprocal interrelation between love and power in both the form and relative proportion of these relational systems. This multiplex holonomy is most apparent in the first test year for the ten coherent groups with "high" communion. These communes have on average about the same proportion of *loving* 300 triads (.311) as they do for *power* 030T triads (.281), and a similar match for the *loving* 102 and *power* 012 triads (.271 and .228, respectively). For the other survivors (except those with "high" communion), there seems to be some counterbalancing of dyads of love with both interpersonal and collective forms of power. This, too, suggests a holonomic process is operating.

Interestingly enough, it also is evident even in the incoherent survivors (Table 9:5) at the interpersonal level, in the close ratio of power to love across both test years. For the *power* 012

TABLE 9:4   COHERENCE OF POWER BY COMMUNION (WAVE ONE) — TABULAR ANALYSIS AND TRIADIC STRUCTURE

GLOBAL COHERENCE (wave one)	TABULAR ANALYSIS				TRIADIC STRUCTURE[1] OF POWER						Total (46)
	Coherent (25)*		Incoherent (21)		Coherent (25) Triad Types			Incoherent (21) Triad Types			
COMMUNION (wave one) Mean Proportion	mean propn.	percentage	mean propn.	percentage	012	021D	030T	012	021D	030T	
	.022	36.0%	.013	47.6%							
Loving 300 Triad	mean propn.	percentage	mean propn.	percentage	012	021D	030T	012	021D	030T	
Low (≤.099)	.121	28.0	.157	33.3	.191	.131	$.307^{2.830''}$	.294	.011	.168	(19)
Medium (≥.100 – ≤.249)	.529	36.0	.447	19.0	.285	$.171^{1.722'}$	$.250^{2.356''}$	.321	.102	.168	(14)
High (≥.250)	.232	100.0%	.144	99.9%	.167	$.180^{3.100'''}$	$.370^{3.135'''}$	.393	.123	.104	(13)
Total	.232	100.0%	.144	99.9%							

*N = ( ).

1. Mean triad incidence (proportions); mean τ score (small figures) given only if statistically significant. Symbols denote the following pr. values:

' .05
'' .01
''' .001

261

TABLE 9:5 COMMUNE SURVIVAL BY COHERENCE OF POWER BY COMMUNION FOR FIRST AND SECOND TEST YEARS—TABULAR ANALYSIS AND TRIADIC STRUCTURE[1]

A) FIRST TEST YEAR SURVIVAL STATUS (wave two)

COMMUNION (wave one)[2]	Survived (35)*				Dissolved (11)				Total (46)
	Loving Triads		Power Triads		Loving Triads		Power Triads		
	102	300	012	030T	102	300	012	030T	
Low Communion (≤.100)									
POWER (wave one)									
Coherent									
mean proportion	.462	.044	.197	$.324^{2.875''}$	.300	0	.075	.425	
percentage of row total	81.8%				18.2%				100.0% (11)
Incoherent									
mean proportion	.391	.021	.323	.161	$.700^{2.71''}$	.100	.250	.250	
percentage of row total	91.7%				8.3%				100.0% (12)
High Communion (>.100)									
POWER (wave one)									
Coherent									
mean proportion	.271	$.311^{3.662'''}$	.228	$.281^{2.565''}$	.157	$.575^{1.636'}$	.256	$.338^{2.725''}$	
percentage of row total	71.4%				28.6%				100.0% (14)
Incoherent									
mean proportion	.353	$.204^{1.750'}$	.366	.074	.203	$.417^{2.023'}$	.285	.218	
percentage of row total	55.6%				44.4%				100.0% (9)

262

B) SECOND TEST YEAR SURVIVAL STATUS (wave three)

COMMUNION (wave two)[3] Low Communion (≤.075) POWER (wave two)	Survived (23)				Dissolved (6)				Total (29)[4]
	Loving Triads 102	Loving Triads 300	Power Triads 012	Power Triads 030T	Loving Triads 102	Loving Triads 300	Power Triads 012	Power Triads 030T	
Coherent									
mean proportion	.423	.021	.197	.286[5.425†]	.400	0	.100	.300	
percentage of row total		87.5%				12.5%			100.0% (8)
Incoherent									
mean proportion	.444	.006	.364	.148	.750	0	.200	.050	
percentage of row total		75.0%				25.0%			100.0% (8)
High Communion (>.075) POWER (wave two)									
Coherent									
mean proportion	.354	.212[2.121']	.168	.357[3.165'']	.345	.176[2.939'']	.248	.248[2.793'']	
percentage of row total		88.9%				11.1%			100.0% (9)
Incoherent									
mean proportion	.575	.175	.500	.100	.350	.150	.486	.065[2.017']	
percentage of row total		50.0%				50.0%			100.0% (4)

*N = ( ).

1. Mean triad incidence (proportions); mean T score (small figures) given only if statistically significant. Symbols denote the following pr. values: ', .05; '', .01; ''', .001. The reader is reminded that the T scores for loving triads may not be valid (see Chapter Six, pp. 142–143, above).
2. Measured by the proportion of loving 300 triads.
3. The cut-off criterion of >.100 for the "high communion" category in Wave One, has been relaxed to >.075 to boost the number of groups in this category. The mean proportion of loving 300 triads for all communes dropped from .232 in Wave One to .093 by Wave Two.
4. Excludes six communes which provided no second wave relational data.
† This value is inflated due to the particularly high T for one group; the median T is 2.690, with pr. at the .01 level.

triad and the *loving* 102 triad, the ratios are virtually identical (all in the .830 to 1.00 range) for all categories of communion. This pattern of almost a one-to-one correspondence between these two relational systems, is a pattern we saw earlier in Chapter Seven. Again, it points to a category of groups that seem primarily based on dyadically-specific, interpersonal interaction rather than on more collectively-oriented processes.

For nonsurvivors, there is little indication of a holonomic linkage between love and power. This is clearest in the first test year for which there are more cases. Both the coherent and incoherent groups with "high" communion appear to have insufficient control to contain the energy; they average only a little more than one *power* 030T triad for every two *loving* 300 triads. This contrasts strongly with the almost one-to-one ratio (.904 to 1.00) between these triad types for the ten surviving coherent groups in this category.

These results, like those in Chapter Seven, are strongly suggestive of a holonomic mechanism that interrelates the two orders of love and power. For some groups, there seems to be processes operating separately at the interpersonal and at the collective levels. In others, a process that interlinks the two levels. Irrespective of which of these processes is evident, it seems clear that they function to maintain a balance between the orders love and power, an equilibrium that is associated with greater functional effectiveness — at the very least, with improved chances of survival.

Charisma, Multiplex Holonomy, and Stability

It would seem then, love/affect and power/control are the elements of a more fundamental order, one that transforms and aligns energy into patterns of social activity, and vice versa, by a holonomic process. Since transformation is the essence of a charismatic system, we should find evidence consistent with a holonomic linkage between communion and coherent power in charismatic groups.

Table 9:6 presents the survival rate of charismatic and non-charismatic communes broken down by the global organization of power. In line with the findings of Chapter Seven, we can see that power is usually coherent in charismatic systems. This reflects the strong, collective foundation of charismatic systems; transformation to a new level of organization means aligning all elements to work in unison. On the other hand, with a much greater likelihood of an interpersonal and/or individual orientation, power in the noncharismatic groups may often-as-not be incoherent.

For stability, Table 9:6 shows that coherent power is associated with a high likelihood of survival across both test years for charismatic groups (86% and 88%, versus 57% and 67% for the incoherent). But, the pattern is not consistent for non-charismatic communes. It reverses from a 22% survival advantage for the incoherent in the first year to the same advantage one year later for the coherent communes. As we will see from triadic analysis, this is explained by structural differences which suggest a holonomic linkage between love and power in the survivors.

For the charismatic groups, as expected, there is good evidence that multiplex holonomy is associated with survival. The twelve coherent survivors (first test year) have almost a one-to-one correspondence between love and power at the interpersonal level (.275 and .233, respectively) and at the collective level (.254 and .284). However, there appears to be some leeway in this interrelation in a few charismatic groups. So that while the four incoherent survivors (first test year) exhibit holonomy at the interpersonal level (.354 and .395), they also have on average a four-to-one ratio favoring love (.217 and .055) at the collective level.[19] Although such imbalance is not typical of charismatic survivors, it would seem that below a certain threshold some uncontained pressure from communion can be tolerated. It is certainly clear from the five that dissolve, that imbalances at much higher levels of communion (around .500 and above) are likely to be fatal.

TABLE 9:6 SURVIVAL STATUS BY CHARISMATIC GROUPING BY COHERENCE OF POWER FOR FIRST AND SECOND TEST YEARS—TABULAR ANALYSIS AND TRIADIC STRUCTURE[1]

A) FIRST TEST YEAR
SURVIVAL STATUS (wave two)

CHARISMATIC GROUPING

	Survived (35)*				Dissolved (11)				Total (46)
	Loving Triads		Power Triads		Loving Triads		Power Triads		
	102	300	012	030T	102	300	012	030T	
POWER (wave one)									
Charismatic									
Coherent									
mean proportion	.275	$.254^{3.457'''}$	.233	$.284^{3.587'''}$	.110	.587	$.295^{1.927'}$	$.298^{3.205'''}$	
percentage of row total	85.7%				14.3%				100.0% (14)
Incoherent									
mean proportion	.354	$.217^{1.754'}$	.395	$.055^{1.723'}$	.194	$.480^{2.194''}$	.371	.119	
percentage of row total	57.1%				42.9%				100.0% (7)
Noncharismatic									
POWER (wave one)									
Coherent									
mean proportion	.510	.066	.179	.333	.253	.281	.146	$.402^{1.634'}$	
percentage of row total	63.6%				36.4%				100.0% (11)
Incoherent									
mean proportion	.388	.032	.316	.160	.485	$.165^{1.629'}$	.140	.385	
percentage of row total	85.7%				14.3%				100.0% (14)

266

B) SECOND TEST YEAR
SURVIVAL STATUS (wave three)

CHARISMATIC GROUPING

Charismatic POWER (wave two)	Survived (23)				Dissolved (6)				Total (29)[2]
	Loving Triads (102)	Power Triads 300	012	030T	Loving Triads (102)	Power Triads 300	012	030T	
Coherent									
mean proportion	.385	.161[4.804'''']	.214	.373[7.613†]	.345	.176[2.939'']	.248	.248[2.793'']	
percentage of row total	87.5%				12.5%				100.0% (8)
Incoherent									
mean proportion	.525	.125	.250	.250	.200[1.965'] .200		.371	.029[3.416''']	
percentage of row total	66.7%				33.3%				100.0% (3)
Noncharismatic POWER (wave two)									
Coherent									
mean proportion	.387	.090	.153	.280	.400	0	.100	.300	
percentage of row total	88.9%				11.1%				100.0% (9)
Incoherent									
mean proportion	.461	.023	.448	.098	.667	.033	.333	.167	
percentage of row total	66.7%				33.3%				100.0% (9)

*N = ( ).

1. Mean triad incidence (proportions); mean τ score (small figures) given only if statistically significant. Symbols denote the following pr. values: '.05; ''.01; '''.001; ''''.00005. The τ scores for loving triads may not be valid (see pp. 142–143, above).
2. Excludes six communes which provided no second wave relational data.
† This value is inflated due to the particularly high τ for one group; the median τ for one group is 4.867, with pr. at the .00005 level.

A final point in Table 9:6, concerns some indication of a holonomic process interlinking love and power across the interpersonal and collective levels. For instance, the high incidence of dyadic love (102 triad), in the coherent noncharismatic survivors, is counterbalanced across both test years by a collective structuring of power (030T triad). (Compare this to the incoherent nonsurvivors (second test year). These noncharismatic communes seem to lack sufficient power at either level to contain their high level of dyadic love.) To some extent, a similar interlinkage between collective power and interpersonal love is evident in the coherent charismatic survivors of the second test year. But the reverse form, matching interpersonal power with communion, does not seem successful (e.g., the defunct, incoherent charismatic groups (first test year)). This suggests that effective regulation of the energy released by love is primarily a collective process, not an interpersonal one.

It is clear from these results that a coherent structure of power improves the stability of charismatic groups by acting as a counterbalance to communion. This one-to-one correspondence between love and power is consistent with the earlier findings of Chapter Seven, and also with our expectation of a holonomic linkage between the two relational systems. Since there is evidence of this interrelation in the noncharismatic survivors as well, it is likely that such multiplex holonomy is a more general phenomenon. However, here it operates between the interpersonal and collective levels, while in the charismatic groups it is fundamentally a collective order.

Summary

In these last two chapters we have attempted to understand a basic paradox raised in the earlier chapters by our findings about power: that from information about dyadic relations a view of the structure of the group can be constructed.

In Chapter Eight we sought to resolve this paradox with four major sociological theories. But they offered little explanation for what we found: a coherent order of power can be created almost immediately, without the time necessary for socialization and institutionalization; it occurs in groups with widely different cultures, ideological orientation, and formal organization; it is an omnipresent order encoded into the particularized relations of the individual's interpersonal reality; it is not just the intrusion into a group of a ranking of individuals by society, nor is it solely the reflection of the value placed on each member by the group itself. In short, it is an order that does not seem to be explicable in the terms of existing sociological theory.

Taking, as our point of departure, the principle of organization implied in the paradox itself — that the parts (individuals and relations) contain information about the order of the whole (the group), we had more success in this chapter approaching the problem from a holonomic perspective. Using membership turnover as analogous to the removal of cortical tissue in experiments on brain function, we found that a commune's ability to maintain a coherent order of power over time is not affected by the aggregate level of turnover or a change of (sociometric) leader/s. And while turnover in the upper strata has some negative impact, this more likely reflects an impairment to the group's ability to actualize structure than loss of the relational code for coherent power.

Corroborating the results of Chapter Seven, coherent power functions to counterbalance the destabilizing pressures from energy released by love; communes with high communion but incoherent power do not survive. This is true for the charismatic groups as well. But the evidence also suggests that the mechanism that regulates the balance between love and power operates at different structural levels. So that while this is primarily an interpersonal phenomenon in non-charismatic communes, it is basically a collective process in charismatic groups.

This discovery of a one-to-one correspondence between the orders of love and power suggests that, while different in function and form, these two relational systems are actually complementary — that they are *cojoined* at the deeper level of the whole. The love/affect system is a heterarchic order, and when patterned as communion, is the means by which structure is converted into energy — energy, that is, as potential for social activity. On the other hand, the power/control system is a hierarchic order. It is the system by which energy is aligned and keyed to a particular function, the means for converting energy into structured activity.

The two systems are interlinked by an underlying holonomic process in which the order of each is enfolded into the other. Thus, social organization is the conjunction of both systems in an invertible process of transformation back and forth from one state to the other: structure into energy, energy into structure, and so on. As the mechanism for mobilizing and aligning energy for social activity, this interrelation between both systems — this *wholeness* in order — is fundamental. Without it social organization cannot be; any other order of connection is insufficient.

It is an understanding of the dynamics of this process, the movement of social order, that we seek in the next and final chapter.

NOTES

1. This section owes much to Leith and Upatnieks (1964; 1965), Pietsch (1981, Chapter Three), and Pribram (1971, Chapter Eight; 1982).
2. For a very readable introduction to the hologram, see Chapter 3, "Holograms", of Paul Pietsch's intriguing book *Shufflebrain: The Quest for the Hologramic Mind* (Pietsch, 1981). See *The Holographic Paradigm and Other Paradoxes: Exploring the Leading Edge of Science* (Ed., Wilber, 1982), for a discussion of the holographic perspective in science.

3. While we only have space to examine the use of the holographic metaphor in neuropsychology, it has also been employed fruitfully in physics. David Bohm (1980) has constructed a model of the physical universe as an "implicate" (implicit) order in which an enfolded, fundamental nonspace/nontime interrelatedness of everything to everything else is contained in a perpetual "holo-movement". At the micro level, for example, Bohm's holonomic model offers new understanding of the paradoxical wave/particle duality of subatomic phenomena: the behavior of light in the "double-slit" experiment in which photons seem to act as if they "know" what is happening to one another.

4. See Pribram (1971: "Part One" and pages 140-166; 1982). For a very readable, nontechnical account of Pribram's work and its profound implications, see Chapter Five, "Karl Pribram and the Looking-Glass Mind", of Briggs and Peats' (1984) book, *The Looking Glass Universe: The Emerging Science of Wholeness*. See Edelman and Mountcastle (1978) for an alternative nonholographic, stochastic model of brain function.

5. These properties are discussed in more detail on pages 241 to 246.

6. For example, in a key experiment, testing feature correspondence theory against holographic theory (DeValois, DeValois, and Yund, 1979), it was found that the neurons in the visual cortex (of cats and monkeys) responded to the Fourier transforms of plaid and checkerboard patterns, predicted *exactly* by holographic theory, and not to the patterns' structural features (edges).

   Pietsch (1981) offers a nontechnical account of a set of experiments he conducted to show Pribram's theory to be false. Instead, the results convinced him of the veracity of the holographic theory.

7. See: Loye (1983); Mitroff and Kilman (1983); Morgan and Ramirez (1984); Bradley (1985a); El Sawy (1985); Lincoln (ed., 1985); Mitroff (1985); Ravn, (1985; 1986); Roberts (1985); Glazer (1986); Morgan (1986); and Winograd (1986).

8. Pribram (1971:150) reports that some ten billion *bits* of retrievable information have been stored holographically in a single cubic centimeter.

9. Some idea of the brain's capacity to store this and other information is given by Pieter van Heerden. To store as little as one *bit* of information every second during a human lifetime, the brain must perform 3×10^{10} elementary binary (nerve impulse) operations a second (in Pribram, 1971:150).

10. Bekesy (1959) has shown the same sort of thing for the perception of tactile stimulation. Activating the two sets of vibrators he placed on a subject's forearms, Bekesy found that the subject does not perceive the source point of stimulation as being coextensive with the place of skin contact. Instead, after initially perceived as bouncing back and forth, the source point would "jump" into the space a little ahead and between the forearms where it would stabilize.

11. Although the commune data do not provide a reasonable test for the five other similarities we have just described, evidence of a holonomic correspondence between the group and its parts will increase the plausibility of the untested parallels.

12. The reasoning underlying most of the existing sociological work on member turnover would result in postulating the opposite effect to the one I derive here from the holonomic perspective (see Bluedorn, 1982).

13. Membership turnover was measured by taking the leavers and joiners during the twelve months between the first and second waves as a proportion of group population at Wave One.

14. Of the 46 communes at Wave One, 31 were still in the study by Wave Two; 9 had dissolved and 6 provided no second wave relational data. Using the same procedure as used for the first wave (in an independent application), 19 communes were classified as having globally coherent power images and 12 incoherent at Wave Two. Of the former, 63% (12) had maintained coherence across both waves, while 33% (4) of the latter had been coherent in Wave One.

    The triadic analysis in Table 9:N1 (see page 274) shows little change in triadic structure for the total sample and for the coherent communes when compared to the first wave (see Table 8:1, page 211). The changes for the incoherent groups (decreases in 030T, 021C, and 021D, and increases in 012, and 021U triad types) suggest a reduction in collective organization.

15. The results of an analysis not reported here, indicate that there is also little relationship between membership growth or decline and global coherence.

16. The power hierarchies were split into "top" and "bottom" halves by dividing the number of levels in the longest transitive path by two.

17. While Aidala (1980) has gathered a third wave of relational data from a selected subsample from the full sample of surviving communes, I have not had access to these data. Consequently, it has not been possible to extend this analysis to a third point in time.

18. The final exam and participation in the work groups were set up as independent activities in the class. The exam covered material other than that the groups had worked on, and it was administered in a class rather than a group context.
19. Of these, one had dissolved and one was still in existence one year later; no information was available about the disposition of the other two.

TABLE 9:N1 TRIADIC ANALYSIS OF POWER CLASSIFIED BY GLOBAL COHERENCE

MEAN PROPORTIONS OF TRIAD INCIDENCE[1]

	003	012	012D	021U	021C	030T	030C	Total
GLOBAL COHERENCE OF POWER (wave two)					Triad Types			
Coherent	.049	.180	.172	.123	$.140^{-2.753''}$	$.333^{3.778''''}$	$.003^{-2.703''}$	(19)
Incoherent	.090	.380	.085	.194	.092	.110	.050	(12)
Total all communes	.065	.257	.138	.150	$.122^{-2.013'}$	$.246^{2.502''}$	$.021^{-1.714'}$	(31)*

1. Mean τ scores (small figures) given only when statistically significant. Symbols denote the following pr. values:

' .05
'' .01
'''' .0001

*N = ( ). This total excludes 15 communes of which nine had dissolved and six provided no relational data for the second wave.

PART FIVE

NEXUS

A human being is a part of the whole, called by us the "Universe", a part limited in time and space. He experiences himself, his thoughts and feelings as something separated from the rest — a kind of optical delusion of his consciousness. This delusion is a kind of prison for us, restricting us to our personal desires and to affection for a few persons nearest to us. Our task must be to free ourselves from this prison by widening our circle of compassion to embrace all living creatures and the whole of nature in its beauty. Nobody is able to achieve this completely, but the striving for such achievement is in itself a part of the liberation and a foundation for inner security.

Albert Einstein.*

*Quoted in: *The Medium, the Mystic, and the Physicist,* by Lawrence LeShan (1972: 143).

Chapter Ten

WHOLENESS AND TRANSFORMATION

... things have a twofold nature: the one invisible, unique, simple, and unworldy, and the other visible, multiple, varied, and distributed throughout the world. There are two kinds of energy: the one primordial, immovable, and intellectual, the other secondary, kinetic, and revolving in relation with the intellect. The one is free from cause and effect; the other contains them.

Proclus, in his fifth-century (A.D.) analysis of Plato's *Timaeus*; from *Commentaire sur le Timée*, translated by A. J. Festugière, 1968 (4:73), Paris: Vrin.

Introduction

We began this journey seeking the demystification of charisma. Using the perspective and methods of sociology, we sought an understanding that has theoretical utility and empirical validity. But, like most voyages of discovery, we have been propelled by deeper currents through uncharted waters, confronting the unanticipated and unknown. As we near our journey's end, it is time to review where we have been, what we have found, and to reflect upon its significance. In this final chapter, therefore, I want to assess what we have learned about charisma and social organization, and also to speculate about the broader implications of this research.

I. Recapitulation

Charisma

Chapter One opened with sketches of three communes. The communes, portrayed in terms of size, membership, organization, ideology, and purpose, are quite different from one

277

another. They do, however, have something in common: a collective belief that their leaders possess exceptional powers or abilities of a supernatural origin.

In this study, we found evidence that this belief existed in 28 of the 57 communes. According to Max Weber, it is this belief about the basis of a leader's rule that establishes charisma. Our efforts, however, have been geared to move beyond such a normative approach and to seek an understanding of charisma's structural foundation. Consequently, we have probed beneath the surface of charismatic beliefs to study the nature and patterning of social relations within the group.

Our objective has been to identify the structural properties that set charisma apart from other varieties of social organization. Thus, we have tried to isolate those aspects of charismatic social organization that not only capture what is essential and distinctive, but also those that are independent of the characteristics of individuals. Our first step was an assessment of current sociological orthodoxy. It is only by showing that an existing theory lacks empirical validity that the door is open for an alternative.

The Limits of Weber's Understanding

In Chapter Two the study began with an empirical evaluation of the *veracity* of Max Weber's model of 'pure' (personalized) charisma. This view sees charisma as antagonistic to formal and routine organization — a communal form with a limited division of labor, little hierarchy, minimal delegation of authority, and a subsistence economy. It is also highly unstable because legitimacy of leadership rests upon the leader's ability to repeatedly prove continued possession of the 'gift of grace'.

But the commune data reveal many contradictions to Weber's description: a social structure composed of many elements of formal and routine organization, an elaborate division of labor, a stable economic base for self-sufficiency, and much delegation of authority. Weber's model is also questionable on theoretical grounds. For if composed solely of the elements in his model, charisma would be little more than a momentary expression of collective desire.

There is a second limit to the Weberian theory. Weber, Shils, and Wilson (among others) have each argued that 'pure' charisma will not be found in modern, rational-technological contexts. However, the existence of nonroutinized charismatic communes in a highly technological society like the United States, is a direct violation of the thesis.[1] Moreover, the data show that charismatic affiliation is only weakly related to an individual's socio-technological context: commune members with high socio-economic/urban backgrounds or current status, may still surrender control of their lives to a charismatic leader.

These findings suggest that charisma is not restricted to the so-called "lower" stages of socio-technological development. Because it is a potential for change enfolded into the order of all social systems, virtually everyone is vulnerable to its magnetic hold.

A Relational Approach

With the ground cleared for an alternative approach, our strategy was to start by identifying charisma's normative elements — the unique attributes of charismatic beliefs. By correlating these elements with properties of the charismatic group's relational patterns, it would be possible to locate charisma's structural base.

i) Normative Elements   In Chapter Three, two normative elements were identified, which together, are empirically distinctive to charisma. The first is a collective belief that a particular individual possesses talents, powers, or abilities that are regarded as truly outstanding or extraordinary. Judged by the wide diversity of "special" qualities mentioned by charismatic members, attribution of charisma can be based on almost any human capability; talent in leadership does not seem to be a necessary condition. What is important, though, is that the followers regard the ability as "exceptional".

A second criterion is required to separate a charismatic individual from one who is seen as a "virtuoso." This criterion is the belief that the extraordinary qualities are derived from a supernatural source. The charismatic's special powers are not understood in everyday terms; they are not based in the reality of the existing moral order. Rather, these powers are derived from a different reality — that of the supernatural. By contrast, the exceptional talents of the virtuoso are seen as natural abilities, rendered exceptional through much learning and practice. Strong evidence of this normative element also was found in the charismatic communes.

ii) Structural Elements   The question of charisma's inherent instability is the key to developing an understanding of charisma. Weber accounted for this in normative terms. He saw instability as the result of the leader's failure to maintain legitimate authority — the need to constantly prove continued possession of 'the gift of grace'. In our model, though, instability is explained by the relational dynamics of social transformation — by the structures a charismatic system uses to mobilize and regulate the enormous amounts of social energy required to achieve radical change.

Two relational patterns involved in this process were postulated and broadly validated by the commune data. First, a system of communion fuses the group together to break down social distinctions and release energy from the existing structure. Empirically, a densely interlocking pattern of highly charged bonds of positive affect was found in the charismatic communes, varying directly with the intensity of charismatic leadership (i.e., more likely with resident charismatic leaders). This communion is built from fraternal love, optimism, and, for the resident charismatic groups, an element of euphoria.

But communion and the highly volatile energy it liberates, is extremely unstable. Unless it is monitored and regulated, it will have destabilizing and often fatal consequences for the group. To survive under these conditions, a charismatic group requires a strong collective power structure. This structure acts to harness the energy, aligning and channeling it to collective ends.

Data from the charismatic communes support this expectation. When compared to the noncharismatic communes, the structure of power is stronger and more coherent: a single, nondisjointed, multi-leveled, transitive hierarchy of direct and indirect ties, with virtually everyone connected to the charismatic leader. For the resident charismatic communes, especially, where measurement is less affected by ideological contamination, a high degree of consensus is also present. By contrast, power structures in the noncharismatic groups are more disjointed, with fewer levels, more intransitivity, and a greater likelihood of multiple leaders. These structural differences were broadly confirmed by Holland and Leinhardts' (1976) triadic analysis.

Finally, our results suggest that the patterns of communion and collective power are not only distinctive to the charismatic communes, but also they appear to be structurally emergent when compared to relations in the noncharismatic groups. Thus, communion and collective power are most closely linked to charismatic beliefs; they are not explained by other collective or individual factors. Furthermore, the results from a multi-level analysis reveal structural residuals associated with charisma that cannot be explained by the properties of lower structural units.[2]

iii) Stability   Verification of our theory, however, requires more than empirical demonstration of an association between charismatic beliefs and the relational patterns of communion and collective power. Evidence of a *causal* connection must be shown between these structures and the stability of charismatic systems. Accordingly, evidence of a direct connection between both the form and changes in these bonds and the commune survival over time, was sought from the analysis of longitudinal data in Chapter Seven.

Two important discoveries emerged from this analysis. The first is that there is reasonable evidence for the veracity of the relational theory. The results show that survival over time is highest for those in which there is a balance in the structuring of love and power among the charismatic groups. This is primarily a process involving a one-to-one correspondence in the order of these relations at the global level — that communion is counterbalanced by collective power. This is something we had a glimpse of in Chapter Five at the dyadic level with the coexistence of love and power.

The second finding was unexpected: a very similar process also seems to be at work in noncharismatic systems. The data show that a counterbalancing in the structures of love and power results in a higher likelihood of survival. While this is largely a collective process in the charismatic groups, there is evidence that this process involves interpersonal and collective elements in the noncharismatic communes.

A common linkage between the structuring of affect and power and group stability, in both charismatic and noncharismatic systems, suggests something fundamental about the nature of social organization. Instead of just being separate relational systems, differentiated as mutually exclusive bonds, love/affect and power/control are actually complementary. At one level, they appear as distinct relational forms with different functions and processes. In fact, they are cojoined in a deeper order at the level of the whole.

Holonomic Social Order

The critical clue providing insight about the nature of this order of interrelation, was already before us as a methodological paradox: *how to explain the construction of global images of communal power structure from the mappings of discrete dyads.* That is, how could a view of the order of the whole (the group) be obtained from information about the parts (dyads)? Implied in this paradox is an ordering principle that led us to consider a radically different way of thinking about social organization in Chapters Eight and Nine.

The principle is that of holonomic order: the whole contains all parts and each part contains the whole. It involves a one-to-one correspondence in information between a part and the whole. Thus, since information about the order of the whole is enfolded into each part, the whole can be reconstituted from a part. In this way, social order is like a hologram: *an image of communal power structure can be obtained from dyads because information for the order of the group is contained in all relations.* At a theoretical level, we found a remarkable correspondence between the properties of holonomic order and some basic characteristics of social organization (see above pages 241 to 246).

Two kinds of evidence from the commune data are consistent with this hypothesis. The first, presented in Chapter Eight, is the inability of four major sociological theories — historicist, interactional, normative, and stratificational — to explain the presence of a coherent global order of power in the communes. The data show that coherent global order can emerge rapidly, without the time necessary for institutionalization; that it is unlikely to be the result of pair-wise constructions, negotiations, or contests between individuals; that it is not just a manifestation of more formalized cultural patterns; and that it is not a ranking of individuals according to a group or a societal value.

The second kind of evidence comes from the results of a crude test of the hypothesis conducted in Chapter Nine. Here, membership turnover was regarded, in broad terms, as analogous to the removal of cortical tissue from the brain in neuropsychology. In the same way that rats can still find their way through a maze after most of the cortex has been removed, the communes should be able to maintain a coherent global order of power over time, even though many relations have been destroyed by high membership turnover. It is the property of the distribution of memory of the maze throughout the brain that is tested in the former; it is the distribution of the order of the group throughout all relations that is at issue in the latter.

Despite the limitations to this test, the data are generally consistent with the hypothesis. The level of membership turnover does *not* reduce a commune's ability to maintain a coherent global order of power over time, and neither does a change of (sociometric) leader(s). And while turnover in the upper strata has some negative impact on the perpetuation of this order, this more likely reflects a reduced organizational capacity than the loss of relational information for coherent power.

In addition to these results, there is other evidence consistent with the holonomic hypothesis. Corroborating the findings for the charismatic communes, a coherent order of power offsets the destabilizing effects of love. While the earlier evidence in Chapter Seven for a one-to-one correspondence in these relations is from the triadic level, here, it is at the global level (the organization of relations for the commune as a whole).

This complementarity in the structuring of these two relational systems, is not just a property that is present solely at one level or another in the group. Rather, it is an order that we have found evident at all levels — dyadic, triadic, and global. It is an order of interrelation for the group as a totality that is enfolded throughout all parts.

A Caution

Before we consider broader implications and speculate about the meaning of what *may* have been discovered in this study, a note of caution is in order regarding the interpretation of the findings of this research.

The results reported in this book, and their implications for the sociology of charisma, must be interpreted within the context of an important limitation. While it is the uniqueness of our research site, the urban commune, that has enabled most of what has been accomplished here, it also constitutes the study's most serious limitation. Certainly, given the sampling methods employed, there is little doubt that the results probably extend to urban communes in general (see Zablocki, 1980: 358-389). However, there is still the question of how typical the relational patterns and processes identified here are of charismatic systems in general.

The urban commune is a social entity that is quite rare and unusual when compared to the forms of collective organization that are predominant in society today (viz; government and corporate bureaucracies, political parties, social movements, voluntary associations, communities, etc.) Although occasional glimpses of similar relational patterns are silhouetted in accounts of revolutionary change (Skocpol, 1979), charismatic leadership (Schweitzer, 1984; Willner, 1984), and charismatic cults (Lofland, 1966: Bugliosi, 1974), it is only future empirical research that can assess the validity and the generality of the model of charisma we have developed in this book. Future work will require a focus on charismatic social organization instead of the traditional concern with charismatic leaders.

A second limitation of this research, relevant to charisma, concerns transformation. With our relational theory, we have sought to understand charisma by viewing it as a structure by which a collectivity may achieve a quantum change in social organization. However, due to the short time frame of this research, this is something that we have not been able to assess empirically. Consequently, it remains for future research to seek evidence of a direct relationship between the relational systems of communion and collective power and the actual transformation of the charismatic group.

There is a different question to consider for the holonomic results: namely, the meaning of the data and how to interpret the relational patterns. There are two issues here. One concerns the behavioral reality of the power structures we constructed from dyad mappings. That is, are the hierarchical orderings "real" in terms of the social distribution of rights, status, influence, etc., or are these patterns an ordering of individual perceptions — an alignment of minds?[3]

Although the observational evidence on the communes suggests there is some behavioral reality to these hierarchies, it lacks sufficient detail to be conclusive. But this is not the point, because either way — whether it is a reflection of behavioral reality or a psychic one — the data clearly show that such hierarchical orderings have objective consequences for group stability. The basic question, therefore, is how and why do these orderings have such a fundamental impact on the group?

This question raises the second issue. We have treated communal power structures as if they are "real" in some basic sense; that they are not an artifact of measurement error, and therefore, have validity as a "fact". Taking into account some errors and shortcomings that may remain, despite efforts to be operationally and procedurally rigorous, the overwhelming order and consistency in the data lead us to regard the communal power structures as valid. As a consequence, the issue for us has been *how to explain* these relational patterns.

After consideration of alternative theories, our answer is to propose a "new" holonomic explanation — new, that is, in its application to sociological phenomena. Although there may be questions and reservations about the adequacy of our operational indicators of these theories, and our interpretation of the results, the patterns that we have found still remain. If the holonomic hypothesis is *found wanting,* an alternative should be proposed; the data still require explanation.

II. Interface

If we put the study's limitations to one side momentarily, and adopt a more speculative viewpoint, there are some potentially important implications of our findings with a significance beyond sociology. Not only do the results point to a very different understanding of social organization than current perspectives,[4] but they also suggest some striking parallels with forms and processes at other levels of reality. Accordingly, I want to take the last few pages of this book to step back and view the findings from a much broader perspective. We will begin with the remarkable similarity between the organization of different kinds of brain function and that of the two patterns of social organization this research has uncovered.

Localized and Distributed Organization

Two very different patterns of neurological organization have consistently emerged from research on brain functions. One of these, a *distributed* order, has already been encountered in the review of Pribram's holonomic model of perception and memory (see Chapter Nine, pages 236 to 241). This order involves a linear and reversible process by which information from perception is transformed and encoded everywhere throughout the cortex as a distributed memory store. The second is a *localized*, nonlinear order, in which neurological activity is confined to particular systems of the brain that are specialized by function. The problem is how to resolve the paradox that emerges from these contradictory views: brain functions appear to be both distributed *and* localized.

Pribram's (1982) ingenious solution is to regard these seemingly opposing orders as complementary, linking them together into a single, integrated model of brain activity. Each order is a separate domain that handles a fundamental neurological function. Based on very different processing logic, each has a distinct form. The perception/memory domain operates to receive and store information in a manner that both preserves object identity, and yet, is easily retrievable for immediate use. Accordingly, it is a linear order in which information is converted into a reversible code and stored as a nonlocalized memory available to all brain systems. On the other hand, the decision/action domain discriminates particular pieces of information required by the specialized systems that regulate and direct bodily decision and action. It is a localized, nonreversible order — a one-way process for retrieving specific material from the distributed memory store. Although the order of each appears antithetical to the other, they are complementary; together, they comprise a whole:

> The persistant puzzle that brain functions appear to be both localized and distributed is thus resolved. Memory storage is shown to be distributed (while the) decisional operators involved in coding and retrieval are localized. These (decisional) operators can be conceived as separate brain systems, genetically inherent in their function but dependent on sensory input from the environment to trigger and shape their development (see, e.g., Chomsky, 1980; Pribram 1971b). In short, there are "boxes in the brain," each "box" corresponding to a "faculty of mind." But these "boxes" operate on a distributed matrix that is nonlocal and therefore available to all. (Pribram, 1982: 291; quotes and citations in the original; my additions.)

These two neurological orders closely parallel the two patterns of social organization that we have found: love/affect and power/control. Each is a separate system handling different aspects of group function, structured in relation to one another as contraposing forms. Generally referred to as the lateral (or horizontal) and hierarchical (or vertical) dimensions of social organization, they are usually thought of as mutually exclusive (Weber, 1978, Vol. 1; Parsons, 1951; Heider, 1958). However, we have found these seemingly incompatible forms to be fundamentally interrelated as a complementary order at the level of the whole.

The relational systems are the channels that link two fundamental domains of social reality: (1) a domain of energy and information, of raw unused potential; and (2) a domain of structure and action, where social behavior is actualized (see Figure 10:1). The domains are quite different.

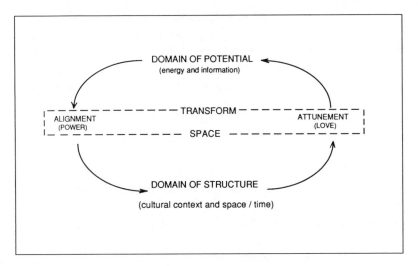

10:1 *Love and Power as Transformers of Energy and Structure*

The energy/information domain is the domain of potential and possibility. It is the full array of movement that energy, when manifested as action, can assume. It is bound by neither cultural context nor time, but exists as a nonlocalized order of potential, enfolded throughout the group. It is the domain from which particular patterns of social action are selected and keyed by the socio-cultural order — patterns programmed for activation when certain conditions prevail.

The structure/action domain is the domain of manifest social reality. It is the specific movement of activity into which the energy of the group has been structured. Triggered and shaped by worldly circumstance, it is localized in terms of time and context. It is a differentiated order, an order in which energy is enacted as structure by functionally specialized elements in the group.

Love/affect and power/control are separate but complementary systems that link the two domains. The love/affect system unlocks the energy that is used up in existing patterns of social activity. It *de-*structures the energy by breaking down prescribed patterns and institutional forms, converting them back into unused potential. Through this process, everything is enfolded everywhere throughout the group, so that there is complete freedom in the movement of energy and information among all elements. Thus, it is the means by which structure is converted into energy — a bridge from the domain of structured activity to the domain of energy and potential. Its form is *heterarchical*, a bonding of all elements in equality. It is a holonomic order of one-to-one correspondence between all parts and the whole.

On the other hand, the power/control system operates as a movement in the other direction. It converts energy into manifest patterns of action. Out of all that is potential and possibility, it actualizes a particular pattern of social activity. It is the process by which energy is localized in time and context as action. Therefore, it is a selective, directed process which keys energy for actualization into structure by functionally specialized systems of the group. It is *hierarchical* in form — a differentiated order of interdependence in which the whole is emergent and different from the parts. While it too is a conversion process, the movement is from the nonmanifest domain of potential to the worldly domain of action. Energy is transformed into structure.

Together, the two systems comprise a transform space, a space in which movement between the domains of energy/potential and structure/action occur. This space is the conjunction of everything; the union of love and power, the oneness of energy and structure — a "perfect synthesis":

> ... we meet with the notion of a perfect synthesis of communitas and hierarchical structure. It was not only Dante and Thomas Aquinas who pictured heaven as a hierarchical structure with many levels of sanctity and, at the same time, as a luminous unity or communitas in which no lesser saint felt envy of a greater nor greater saint any pride of position. *Equality and hierarchy were there mysteriously one.* (Turner, 1969: 182; emphasis mine.)

The Movement of Social Order

Social organization is therefore an ongoing process of movement back and forth through this transform space, from the
domain of potential to the domain of action. It involves a
reversible process of transformation and back-transformation
— energy into structure, structure into energy, and so on — a
recurring cycle of oscillation between potential and actuality:
"Society... seems to be a process rather than a thing — a
dialectical process with successive phases of structure and
communitas" (Turner, 1969: 203). Although they are separate
conduits, each processing a different direction of the movement, love and power are related holonomically as an order of
invertible transforms.

This movement of social order is a fundamental process
in which social systems are aligning to the totality of
forces that move the natural world — to the whole movement of the universe itself. The natural order is something that is constantly evolving and changing. No form
is fixed or static; everything is in transition and flux — from
sub-atomic particles dancing momentarily between creation and annihilation, to the cosmological tug-of-war
between energy and gravity — all is process, all eternally
becoming (Whitehead, 1969). This matrix of movement
reaches everywhere and touches everything; nothing in
the universe is unaffected for there are no boundaries, just
relations and interrelations — the connection of everything
with everything.

Nested in this larger movement, the social order mediates
collective and individual actions with the ever-changing reality of the natural order itself. It is a never-ending process
of interaction between a social system and the natural order,
alignment and realignment, adjustment and readjustment.
It involves the corresponding structuring and restructuring
of the system's elements, of the interrelation among the
elements themselves, and of their interrelation with the
natural order. It is a holistic mode that lies outside time and

cultural context, a movement in which social organization is indivisibly co-evolving with nature:

> In the immediacy of existence, linear and irreversible time become suspended. The experienced processes of the past and the visions of an anticipated open evolution are directly grasped in a four-dimensional present. Poetic reality breaks into the profane reality of everyday life.
> ... the sequential order of information, corresponding to a specific sequence of events, is suspended, too. A state is generated which resembles the cyclical time concept of archaic cultures. Events are no longer connected in a sequential mode, but in an associative mode. (Jantsch, 1980: 302.)

This is the movement of wholeness.

This wholeness of social order is ever present as the totality of relations between a social system and the natural world. It exists as a collective consciousness that envelops all social elements, and it is enfolded into all relations and the minds of all individuals. Thus, it is an order of truth and genuine potency in action that is always accessible. While it is generally circumscribed by cultural prescription, there are occasions when the movement of wholeness is transcendent. Then, as a free-flowing *unfoldment* of form in harmony with the natural order, it maximizes human potential yielding true knowledge, extraordinary collective achievement, and personal fulfillment:

> In the field of group endeavor, you will see incredible events in which the group performs far beyond the sum of its individual talents. It happens in the symphony, in the ballet, in the theater, in sports and equally in business. It is easy to recognize and impossible to define. It is a mystique. It cannot be achieved without immense effort, training, and cooperation, but effort, training, and cooperation alone rarely create it. Some groups reach it consistently. Few can sustain it. None can define it. We should be content to eternally strive for it and enjoy it when it occurs. (Dee Hock, Chief Executive Officer, Visa International; quoted in Schlesinger, Eccles, and Gabarro, 1983: 486.)

Although the movement of wholeness is fundamental and omnipresent, it is often eclipsed by the cultural order — the arbitrary, incomplete social constructions of reality. These are worlds of social illusions: images based on culturally selected, fragmentary sensory perceptions, holographically projected[5] images of reality that are socially defined as "real". These are artificial social worlds of internal contradiction and inconsistency, synthetic constructions yielding conflict and stress, never in complete congruence with the natural order. They waste much natural and human potential by locking social energy into ossified structures of domination and repression.

When artificially bound by the illusions of culture, this wholeness, the full potential of movement, is held in check — eclipsed by a fragmented, conflicted social construction fraught with stress from internal disorder and from *disunion* with nature. This fragmented movement is based on culturally prescribed positions and roles which are elaborated as systems of social differentiation. Here, love and power are segmented. The former is particularized to certain "special" bonds in which affect is used as a reward-control mechanism; the latter as authority in which the illusions of the past are given collective reign through coercion and constraint. Thus, the fragmented order limits the movement of social energy, restricting it by locking it up in institutionalized patterns; it excludes much social potential.[6] In David Bohm's words:

> I ... call attention to the general problem of fragmentation of human consciousness. ... the widespread ... distinctions between people (race, family, profession, etc., etc.,) ... now preventing mankind from working together for the common good ... have ... their origin in a kind of thought that treats *things* as inherently divided, disconnected, and 'broken up' into yet smaller constituent parts. Each part is considered to be essentially independent and self-existent.
>
> When man thinks of himself in this way. ... he cannot seriously think of mankind as the basic reality, whose claims come first. Even if he does try... he tends to regard humanity as separate from nature, and so on. ... but if he can include

(think of) everything coherently and harmoniously in an overall whole that is undivided, unbroken, and without a bor-
der... from this will flow an orderly action within the whole.
(Bohm, 1980: xi (italics in original.)

As a means for radical change and realignment with the
movement of the natural order itself, charisma is potentially a
bridge to wholeness. Seen as the fusion of love and power,
charisma embodies the transform space in which a radical
change of social systems — a quantum realignment[7] — *can* take
place. But realization of this awesome potential requires alignment with the universal forces that move the natural world.

However, linkage with the abstract order of the universal
demands transcendence of worldly perception and interest
and the complete surrendering of ego and the self:

> ... the self (is) seen from the distance of the cosmic or
> infinite. ... we identify ourselves with the cosmic or infinite
> perspective itself; we value life from its standpoint. ... what is
> ordinarily background becomes foreground and the self is no
> longer figure to the ground. We sense the unity of the whole
> and ourselves part of that unity. (Kohlberg and Power, 1981:
> 234; my addition.)

Without this order of truth, charisma becomes but a collective
fantasy, a delusion spawning despotism and malevolence.
While there are less risky noncharismatic bridges to wholeness,[8] these transformations also require transcendence of
the illusionary constructions of culture and self for nexus
with the universal.

Synthesis

Two central themes have run throughout this book: *transformation* and *wholeness*. Each has been used in two distinct ways
in different sections of the book; the one serving as perspective, the other as an explanatory principle. It is their fundamental connection that is the basis of the new understanding
we have sought to develop here.

Our initial concern was to build an empirically-valid account of charisma with transformation as the perspective and wholeness as the explanatory principle. It is the connection between charisma as a means for radical change, and the global interrelation of love and power, that is critical to an understanding. Thus, as a system for transformation, charisma uses communion to liberate energy from existing structure, and power to channel and mold the energy into a new social form. Stability, as we found during this delicate process, requires that these two relational patterns be complementary.

In seeking an explanation for the global images of communal power structure obtained from mappings of discrete dyads, the roles are reversed. Wholeness, in the form of holonomy, becomes the perspective, while transformation, as an informational encoding-decoding process, becomes the explanatory mechanism. Again, it is the connection between the two that is key to an understanding. Thus, by transforming information about the global organization of relations into an encoded form, the group is able to enfold its order as a whole in all parts.

In this final chapter, we have brought the connection between the two themes into central focus. We have done this by attempting a general synthesis of our findings with the goal of understanding the basic movement of social order: to explain why social organization is an ongoing process of alternation between energy/potential and structure/activity, and to understand what role charisma plays in this process. We also have noted some striking parallels in the organization of social order and structure at other levels of reality. For both, a holonomic perspective has been the key.

From a broader perspective, this should not be surprising since the hologram is the metaphor that has yielded new, basic understanding of the two realities adjacent to the social realm: that of mind-brain and that of the physical universe. Not only is Pribram's (1971) holonomic theory of the brain the foundation for the present understanding of perception and memory, but his most recent work postulates a basic (holo-nomic) uniformity between certain transform functions in the brain and certain quantum processes at the subatomic level (Pribram and Carlton, 1985(a); 1985(b)).[9] And not only does Bohm's (1980) theory of the "implicate order" (a model in which cosmic and subatomic realities are indivisibly inter-twined in a single all-encompassing "holomovement") explain phenomena that elude the current theories of physics, but his holonomic model also connects human consciousness with the order of physical reality itself (see Bohm, 1980, Chapter 7). Consequently, as a bridge, the social realm must possess some fundamental unity between physical and mind-brain reality. It is reasonable, therefore, to expect a basic congruence between the order of these realities and that of social reality. At present, this underlying congruence seems best captured by the metaphor of the hologram.

NOTES

1. See, also, Schweitzer, 1984: Table 1.1, pp. 14-15.
2. There also is good evidence throughout the analysis of finer structural differences (broadly consistent with our relational model of charisma) among the four-way charismatic break-down of the communes. However, space does not permit us to go into these details here. The interested reader should consult the appropriate sections in Chapters 4-6.
3. These power structures have the same underlying geometry as what is found in the dominance orders of domestic fowl. For example, compare the hierarchical orderings in Figure 10:N1 (particularly the 32nd week and that for weeks 36-51) with those in Figures (8:1 through 8:3). However, based on the data presented in Chapter 8, one difference is that such hierarchical forms appear to be generated much more quickly in human groups.
4. See, for example, the recent discussion of the current "crisis" of sociological theory by Coleman (1986), Collins (1986), and Wallerstein (1986).

5. This is a process of holographic image projection. In Chapter 9 we reviewed the neurophysiological mechanisms by which sensory perceptions (viz; auditory, vision, tactile, taste) are holonomically transformed and stored in the brain as memory codes, and then decoded by the same (Fourier) transform process to be holographically projected as images. In the same way that the hologram projected from the surface of a bank/credit card is an optical illusion — it is an *image* of reality, *not* reality itself — the images "seen" by the brain are illusions; they are convincing reproductions of pieces of reality. This same process is at work when the brain is processing socio-cultural information. At the neuropsychological level, socialization involves the holonomic transformation of socio-cultural material into the brain, and the corresponding holographic projection of this information as an image to be "seen". Thus, social reality is an illusion created out of culturally-keyed (selective) perceptions that the brain constructs into reality-like images.
6. Ravn (1986) has an interesting discussion of the moral implications of these two constructions of social reality. He argues that wholeness (harmony with a larger existential or social whole) is "good", while fragmented social constructions (conflicts between parts of the human mind or parts of society) are "bad".

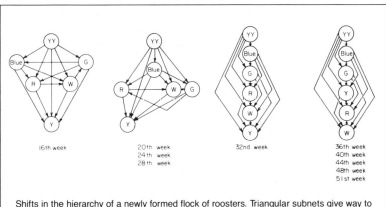

Shifts in the hierarchy of a newly formed flock of roosters. Triangular subnets give way to a more stable, linear order. The letters and the name "Blue" designate the individual roosters. (From: Wilson (1980, Figure 13-2:138), reprinted by permission of the publisher, Harvard University Press.)

10:N1 *Evolution of Dominance Hierarchy Among Domestic Fowl*

7. Our theory, of charisma as a system that generates and aligns social energy in a process of collective transformation, has some interesting parallels with Ilya Prigogine's theory of "dissipative structures". Prigogine and his collaborators (Nicolis and Prigogine, 1977; Prigogine and Stengers, 1984) have found that open (far-from-equilibrium) systems are able to defy the second law of thermodynamics. This is achieved by a process of energy generation and fluctuation that dissipates entropy enabling a quantum leap to stable, more complex forms of order.

The basic idea is that by moving to a very high state of energy, a system self-generates a new and totally discontinuous form of organization. The system achieves this complete transformation by synchronizing the energy fluctuations to a point where a sudden jump occurs from a simple to a more complex order. To keep a new form, these structures must constantly disperse the entropy that would otherwise build up and dissolve them with equilibrium. Extending this principle to a charismatic system, communion would be the mechanism that dissipates entropy. It does this by liberating the energy from existing structure, thereby recharging the system with energy to keep entropy at bay.

During the process of energy fluctuation, the system creates a new catalytic element which enables both further fluctuation and, eventually, structural transformation to occur. This self-generation of a catalyst Prigogine labels "autocatalysis." In broad terms, it seems analogous to the spawning of a charismatic leader by a social system when it undergoes radical change.

According to Prigogine, the energy fluctuations reach a point at which they no longer average out, but instead are "amplified" to a new and critical level — the "bifurcation" point. At the bifurcation point, the system may move in any one of a number of directions, and Prigogine contends that chance determines the order attained. Beyond the bifurcation point, is a new level of order, stable and resistant to further energy fluctuation. Additional structural change only can occur if another round of intense energy fluctuation is triggered.

While every caution must be excised when making an analogy between two totally different levels of reality, the parallels are quite remarkable (see Loye and Eisler, in press). In his book, *The Self-Organizing Universe*, Erich Jantsch (1980) employs Prigogine's model to build a theory of the co-evolution of life and human social organization. To take a specific example, he uses it to explain how certain socio-ecological processes generate discrete and discontinuous levels of growth as a hierarchy of urban centers in a large metropolitan system (e.g., the Paris metropolitan region).

There are, however, some interesting points of difference. One concerns the mechanisms that regulate and stabilize a system as it moves towards the high energy state required for transformation. Based on the data presented in this book, it appears that this mechanism is internally generated in charismatic systems, in the form of a strong, coherent power structure. But for bio-chemical systems, Prigogine and his associates find that the regulator is external — the growing interdependence the structure has with its environment through its need for new supplies of energy. This raises an important question concerning the degree of interdependence or autonomy dissipative structures at different levels of reality may possess in relation to their environment.

Higher-order dissipative structures, like a charismatic system, appear to have an internal mechanism that both triggers and regulates fluctuation. In this sense, they can be seen as having a relatively high degree of autonomy. On the other hand, the bio-chemical systems that Prigogine describes, such as the Belousov-Zhabotinsky reaction, appear to have little autonomy: the regulator is external in the form of the availability of energy from the environment. Does this mean that relatively autonomous dissipative structures, such as charismatic systems, emerge only at higher levels of organization? If this is true, to what extent is the presence of an internal regulator related to the development of social organization in a system?

8. See, for an example, the study of "community healing" among the Kalahari Kung of Africa by Richard Katz (Katz, 1982). A hunter-gather society in the Kalahari Desert, the Kung use "healing" as a way of realigning everyone and everything in their community to the order of their whole environment:

> ... Healing pervades Kung culture, as a fundamental integrating force. The culture's emphasis on sharing and egalitarianism, its vital life of the spirit and strong community, are expressed in and supported by the healing tradition. The central event in this tradition is the all-night healing dance (page 34).
>
> The dance is a community event in which the entire camp participates. ... All who come are given healing (page 34).

The Kung do not look upon their healing dances as separate from the other activities of daily life. Like hunting, gathering, and socializing, dancing is another thing they do (page 34).

For the Kung, healing is more than curing, more than the application of medicine. Healing seeks to establish health and growth on physical, psychological, social, and spiritual levels; it involves work on the individual, the group, and the surrounding environment and cosmos (page 34).

... healing deals with the whole person, in all aspects and situations. Healing is thus directed as much toward alleviating physical illness in an individual as toward enhancing the healer's understanding; as much toward resolving conflict in the village as towards establishing a proper relationship with the gods and the cosmos. A healing may be specifically directed toward one of these focuses (sic), but the healing in fact affects them all (page 53).

... Participating in the dance, the camp can experience a communal transformation. Individuals are healed, and the camp, as a unity greater than the sum of its members, is also healed and set right in its environment (pages 205-206).

9. "It may yet turn out that this mathematical similarity between the quantum mechanics and neural mechanics has a basis in neurophysiological reality. ... the mathematics used to describe quantum events is also useful in describing receptive field properties that are produced by the junctional interactions occurring in dendtritic networks. ... What has occurred between retina and primary visual cortex is a transformation into Hilbert space ... . The transformation is akin to that which characterizes the quantum domain in physics ... ." (Pribram and Carlton, 1985(a): 21, 22.)

APPENDICES

APPENDICES

Appendix A

DYADIC MAPPINGS OF NETWORK STRUCTURE: OPERATIONAL MODELS

Introduction

At present, empirical images of network structure must be constructed by aggregating mappings of dyadic relations. These relations can be *undirected*, as a nominal link between a pair of social actors, or they can be *directed* in terms of an asymmetric ordering in the flow of relational content. Not only does each type of relation have a distinct sociological meaning, but each requires different operational logic.

Images of networks of directed or undirected ties are accurate insofar as measurement captures the actual organization of these relations. In small, bounded groups, this involves complete enumeration of all possible dyadic relations for each content of theoretical interest. Complete enumeration entails mapping each dyad independently, from both sides of the relation. In doing so it is essential that clear, unambiguous measurement of the actual presence or absence of a bond is achieved. This requires explicit identification of all dyads involving incomplete or missing data.

303

Different patterns of dyadic bonding may denote structures of deeper sociological significance. Thus, while dyadic agreement (normative consensus; see pages 83 through 88, above) may indicate network norms proscribing or prohibiting certain ties, or point to institutionalized relations, dyadic disagreement can mean ambiguity or conflict for a given content, or even be one element of a higher order (substantively different) multiplex form. Valid inference of these structures requires that relational data contaminated by measurement error be separated and interpreted with caution.

Since the three existing operational models used by networks researchers do not, in various ways, achieve these imperatives, a fourth approach has been developed for the relational analysis undertaken in this book. These imperatives will be used to assess each of the models in turn.

Operational Models of Dyadic Relations

The four models are compared in Table A:1. The first three are procedures that have been used routinely by network researchers. The fourth is the one developed for this study. All models involve just a single a content (i.e., are uniplex) and distinguish only between two states of relational strength or intensity: a relation either exists or it does not.

The primary difference among the models is in the degree to which each achieves logically exhaustive and mutually exclusive classification of the kinds of uniplex dyads possible. Operationally, this difference is the degree to which the presence or absence of a tie between two actors, i and j, is explicitly measured and independently verified by both actors. This produces quite different images of network structure, which appear to be the result of differences in measurement error among the four models. This can be demonstrated illustratively by applying the operational logic of each model to one of the communes (Loch Lomond) in this study.[1]

TABLE A:1 COMPARISON OF FOUR MODELS OF UNIPLEX DYADS ON SELECTED RELATIONAL PROPERTIES

MODEL	Complete Network Enumeration?	Determination of State of Relations?	Types of Relations?	Mutuality (consensus between i and j)?	Utility for Multiplex Models?
I: *Nonrelational/ Nonconsensual*	No: ego-anchored relations only; (N-1)	Existence measured only; nonexistence confounded with "missing" data	Cognitive map only	Not determined	None
II: *Quasi-relational/ Nonconsensual*	Sometimes <(N(N-¹))	Same as Model I	Undirected relations only	Not necessarily ascertained	Very little
III: *Relational/ Quasi-consensual*	Yes: N(N-1)	Same as Model I	Confounds undirected and directed relations together	Determined partially for undirected relations	Limited; only with difficulty
IV: *Relational/ Consensual*	Yes: N(N-1)	Existence and nonexistence measured and separated from "missing" data	Separate procedures for undirected and directed relations	Determined for undirected and directed relations	Some; for duplex content interrelation especially

MODEL I: Nonrelational and Nonconsensual

Operational Logic

The first model (Figure A:1) is the simplest mapping that can be made of a uniplex dyad. It has been used primarily in social surveys to gather systematic data about the network of relations in which the respondent is enmeshed. It presents an ego-centered view and is usually restricted to the direct ties that respondents hold with other members of their network. This means that only N-1 of the possible N(N-1) dyadic relations (where N = the number of actors) in each respondent's network are measured. Because each dyad is considered just from one actor's perspective, the model is a social-psychological view — at best, a cognitive map.

Without measuring the relation from both sides of the dyad, the extent of agreement among the two actors, the degree of normative consensus, cannot be established. This means that the presence of norms about relations in a network may be overlooked.

While it can be used to obtain individual perceptions of undirected and directed ego-anchored networks, without a mapping of these relations from the other members, little can be ascertained sociologically about the structure of the network as a whole. This also holds for mappings of individual perceptions across different contents: little can be inferred about multiplex structure when this model is employed.

A further problem is that only one state of relational intensity is explicitly measured: a tie between two actors, i and j, is "present" if i indicates a tie with j — otherwise the tie is presumed "absent". This means that, while the conditions for a tie's existence are specified, those for its nonexistence are not. An "absent'" bond is really a residual category, inferred rather than directly measured. It is also ambiguous since it is not clear what is meant when a tie is "not present". Does it mean that actor i said, explicitly, that the tie does not exist

MODEL I
NONRELATIONAL AND NONCONSENSUAL

	Actor i:	Actor j:

KEY

I = Relation is present

O = Relation is absent
or information is missing

▨ = Relation : *(i→j=1)*

▢ = No relation : *(i→j=0)*

A:1 *Operational Logic for Model I*

with *j*? Or instead, did *i* respond with "don't know", or "no answer"? The former is a definite statement about the actual nature of the relation. The latter is at best, ambiguous — incomplete information — or at worst, measurement error.

Clear, unambiguous measurement of the nonexistence of a relation is just as essential as good measurement of its existence. This is because valid inferences about the patterning of absent or null bonds cannot be made so long as such measurement error is included. Stronger, more definitive images of the boundaries of social structure can be constructed when both the presence and absence of relations are explicitly measured.

Empirical Application

An assessment of Model I's empirical accuracy for mapping networks can be made quite effectively with a small, bounded network, such as a commune, where the relations for all dyads have been enumerated from every member's viewpoint. This makes it possible to compare a given actor's perception of their involvement with the perceptions of other members. This is done in Figure A:2 for *sexual* ties[2] among the members of Loch Lomond. By comparing perceptions for each pair of members, an index of the congruence in perceptions can be computed.

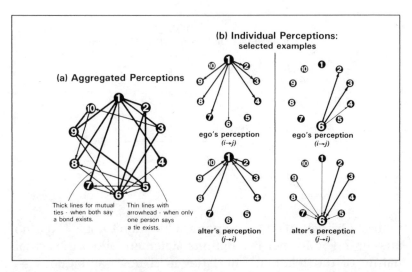

A:2 *Model I: "Sexual" Relations Example*

Of the 21 *sexual* relations mentioned by individuals, only 11 (53%) are corroborated by the other person implicated in each of these claims (Figure A:2(a)). When calculated for individuals and then averaged for the group, the lack of congruence in perceptions, at .466, is quite high. Of the ten members, only one person (#2) has perceptions that are in complete agreement with the others. For half the group, the majority of their perceptions are at odds with those of their fellow members.

The two extremes of the situation are exemplified in Figure A:2(b) by members #1 and #6. The sociograms at the top show how each individual sees their *sexual* ties, and those at the bottom how others see these relations. While the perceptions of member #1 are highly consistent those of the rest of the commune, the perceptions of member #6 are not. The issue here is not that one set of perceptions may be more accurate than the other; the situation between member #6 and the others may actually involve such discordance (there is ethnographic evidence to this effect). The real problem is that this, the discordance, is something that is not evident from any one person's perceptions alone. Consequently, images of network structure based solely on one actor's perceptions run the risk of serious, undetected distortion.

MODEL II: Quasi-relational and Nonconsensual

Operational Logic

The basic difference of Model II from Model I is that the dyad is measured from each actor's perspective. This is important for it means, potentially, that the focus has moved from the social-psychological to a sociological level of analysis. Unfortunately, however, this is only partially achieved.

By defining a relation as "present" if either i or j reports the tie exists (Figure A:3), the measurement criterion is weakened back to the socio-psychological level where only one actor's perception is involved — hence the "quasi-relational" label for this model. This "either/or" criterion may result in less than complete enumeration of a network's dyadic relations. And while complete enumeration may not be possible in difficult research sites, there are some important implications of the either/or criterion that severely limit the model's utility for constructing images of social structure.

The first implication is that because all three cells (Figure A:3) in which a relation is present between i and j are classified as the same, the directionality of a tie cannot be established. This also reduces the model's utility for analyzing multiplex patterns. Because the directionality of contents is not explicated, only a very simple form of multiplexity can be explored: namely, the coexistence of different contents as multiple ties between i and j. Important questions about how contents are interrelated, for instance, as patterns of exchange relations, cannot be addressed.

A second implication is that the weak either/or criterion means that only one of the four cells in Figure A:3 achieves unambiguous measurement of consensus. This is the top left-hand cell where both i and j indicate that a tie exists between

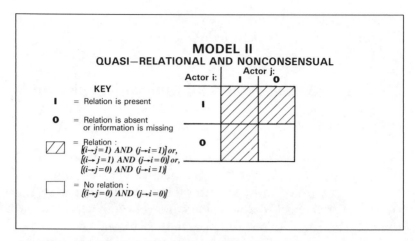

A:3 *Operational Logic for Model II*

them. But this cell is lumped together with the two in which either *i* or *j* indicates a relation, with the result that the consensual property of the former is diluted and lost. Moreover, because only the presence of a tie is explicitly ascertained, little can be said with confidence about the patterning of absent ties in the lower right-hand cell. This cell is a residual category; while it may include bonds that are actually not present between *i* and *j*, it also includes bonds for which information is incomplete or missing. Consequently, this model cannot be used for inferences about network norms proscribing or prohibiting certain relations.

Empirical Application

Figure A:4 presents an empirical application of the model. The two images of *sexual* ties in Loch Lomond depict the two relational states of this model — the sociogram on the left representing ties that are present, and the other residual category of absent bonds. Since the two categories are mutually exclusive, the pattern in each sociogram is the obverse of the other. Because I want to make a comparative assessment of the empirical accuracy of each model, I will keep further comments until after I have presented the other two models.

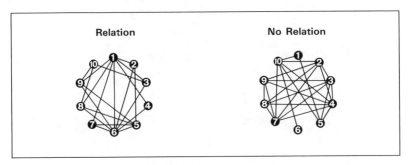

A:4 *Model II: "Sexual" Relations Example*

MODEL III: Relational and Quasi-consensual

Operational Logic

The third model is that employed by Holland and Leinhardt (1970; 1976) in their "triadic analysis". As Figure A:5 shows, it is identical to Model II with one key difference: the three cells showing presence of a tie are divided into two separate categories. The first is a *mutual* tie in which both *i* and *j* indicate that a relation exists. This is the upper left-hand cell in Figure A:5. The second category is an *asymmetric* tie in which either *i* or *j* says that the relation is present. The two cells in the off-diagonal are in this category. The lower right-hand cell of absent bonds is the same as in Model II, except that it is labelled as a *null* relation. In sum, three kinds of relations are distinguished by Holland and Leinhardt: Mutual, Asymmetric, and Null ties, denoted by the acronym *MAN*.

The creation of the asymmetric category is important for it represents an attempt to capture the directionality of relations. And while this is an advance over the second model, it unfortunately contains a flaw in conceptual logic that limits the model's utility.

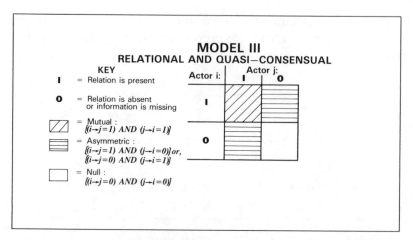

A:5 *Operational Logic for Model III*

The problem is that undirected and directed ties are two distinct kinds of relations each based on a different dimensionalizing logic. For the former, only the presence or absence of a tie is established. Undirected ties, therefore, either exist or do not exist as a connection between i and j. For directed relations, however, an additional operational step is required: not only must the presence/absense of a tie be measured, but also, if present, the tie's *ordinality* with respect to i and j. Directed relations, by definition, involve an explicit dimension of order — e.g., relational inequality, such as greater or lesser power; or relational flow, like more resources going one way than the other, etc. It is not just that a bond is present between i and j, but that, in addition, the bond is so organized that i and j are placed in an ordered relation with respect to each other. As distinct types of relation, these must be kept conceptually and operationally separate.

Unfortunately, this is not done in Model III. Because the additional requirement of specifying ordinality is missing, the underlying dimensional logic is actually that for undirected ties. The directionality attributed to the asymmetric tie is only inferred from the asymmetry in the responses of i and *j;* it is not actually measured. Moreover, this attempt to infer directionality results in another problem: that a more justifiable sociological interpretation of the two "asymmetric" cells, as undirected ties, is overlooked. An interpretation that does not require the presumption of directionality, is that *i* and *j* just disagree; another is that information is incomplete (missing). The problem, then, is that by attempting to measure two distinct kinds of relations in the same dimensional space, the model confounds them together and ends up not accomplishing either. The conceptualization of relations, either as symmetric (undirected) or asymmetric (directed) dyads, thus, is not logically exhaustive.

The second problem with this model is a limitation mentioned above for Models I and II. This is the lack of a distinction between ties that are actually measured as absent, and therefore legitimately belong in the null category, and those ties which are treated as "absent" because information is missing or incomplete. As in Models I and II, this problem of ambiguous absent ties means that normative consensus cannot be inferred. In this model, explicit measurement of a normative property is only achieved for one cell: i.e., the mutual tie. For both the asymmetric tie and the null bond, measurement error in the form of incomplete or missing data cannot be separated out.

A consequence of this is to reduce the model's utility for analysis of multiplex patterns, especially those involving asymmetric and null ties. Unless the relations that actually do not exist are distinguished from those contaminated by measurement error, spurious images of multiplex structure can result.

Empirical Application

Since the model attempts to be applicable to both undirected and directed relations, Figures A:6 and A:7 present an empirical example of each: *sexual* ties and *power* relations, respectively. For both contents, three sociograms are drawn to represent the pattern for each of the mutual, asymmetric, and null ties. As there is no change in concept, the images for absent and null *sexual* ties, produced by Models II and III, respectively, are identical. But the distinction between mutual and asymmetric ties in the latter does make a difference.

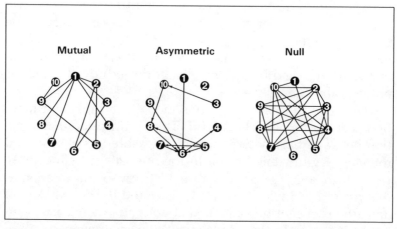

A:6 *Model III: "Sexual" Relations Example*

This can be seen by comparing the images generated by Model III (Figure A:6) with those rendered by Model II (Figure A:4, above). Almost half (48%) of all *sexual* ties shown as "present" in Model II, turn out to be bonds that are not seen as existing by both individuals in each dyad. Furthermore, when the pattern of relations produced by the two models is compared, it can be seen that while members 1, 5, and 6 are shown as dominant in Model II, only #1 remains so in Model III, with twice the number of mutual ties as anyone else. Finally, most (63%) of the eight relations that Model II shows member #6 involved in, are "asymmetric" ties from other individuals.

Overall, it is clear that the two models provide quite different images of network structure. It is clear, too, that Model III provides a more accurate image by clarifying some of the

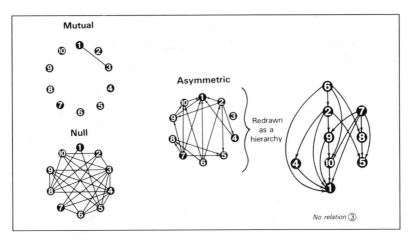

A:7 *Model III: "Power" Relations Example*

ambiguity of the second model. I will hold my comments on *power* until after the fourth model has been presented.

MODEL IV: Relational and Consensual

Operational Logic

In an effort to overcome these problems, I developed the fourth model presented in Figure A:8 that has been employed in the research reported in this book. There are two important differences of Model IV when compared to the others (see Table A:1, above). The first is a distinction between two fundamental kinds of relations: *undirected* ties, in which only the presence or absence of a relation between i and j is established; and *directed* ties, in which both the presence *and* the ordering of the tie between i and j is identified. Independent measurement of the bond between i and j, from both sides, means that complete enumeration of the $N(N-1)$ dyadic relations in a network is accomplished. Because the conceptual and operational logic is different, a separate model for each kind of relation is necessary (see Figures A:8(a) and A:8(b)).

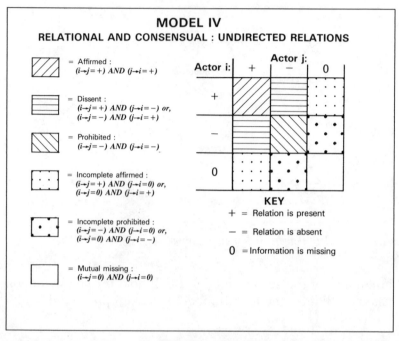

A:8(a) *Operational Logic for Model IV: Undirected Relations*

The second difference is that both the presence and the absence of a relation are measured and kept operationally distinct. For undirected ties, this means that a three-way classification of the relation between i and j is employed: a tie is present; or, it is absent; or, data about the relation is incomplete or missing. For directed ties, there are four categories: a tie is present, and is more for i than for j; or present, but less for i than for j; it is absent; or, information is missing or incomplete.

Three valid categories of undirected dyads are identified (Figure A:8(a)); a tie between i and j can be *affirmed* (both say it exists), or be *dissented* (one says it exists and the other says it does not), or be *prohibited* (both say it does not exist). A fourth category of relations for which only partial measurement has

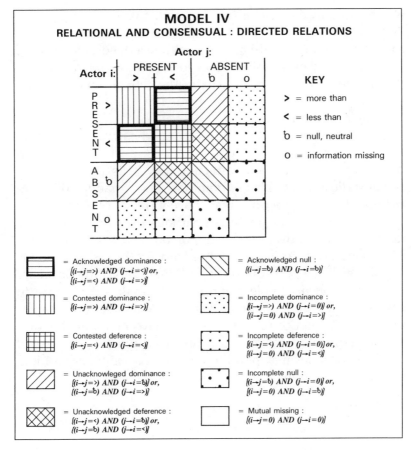

A:8(b) *Operational Logic for Model IV: Directed Relations*

been achieved, due to incomplete or missing observations, is identified in the marginal cells.

The additional requirement of specifying ordinality results in four kinds of directed dyads (Figure A:8(b)): *acknowledged dominance* (where *i* claims dominance and *j* acknowledges *i*'s claim); a *contested tie*, comprised of two subtypes of "contested dominance" (both *i* and *j* claim dominance) and "contested deference" (they both defer dominance to the

other); an *unacknowledged tie*, also with two subcategories —
"unacknowledged dominance" (*i* claims dominance and *j*
says the relation is null) and "unacknowledged deference" (*i*
says the tie is null and *j* defers to *i*); and *acknowledged null*
(both agree the tie is null). Again, the cells around the margins are a residual category of dyads involving incomplete or
missing observations.

These changes result in a number of advantages that Model
IV has over the other models. One is a clear distinction
between undirected and directed ties. This provides relational indicators for Blau's "nominal" and "graduated" parameters of social structure, respectively (Blau, 1977:6-11).

A second advantage is unambiguous measurement of the
degree of normative consensus for both kinds of relations.
The shaded cells in Figures A:8(a) and A:8(b) are all relations
about which the perceptions of both members of the dyad are
measured. Such complete enumeration makes it possible to
establish the extent of agreement that exists about the nature
and organization of relations. As we have mentioned above,
when aggregated for the network as a whole, patterns of
dyadic consensus may point to norms proscribing or prohibiting certain relations.

Multiplexity

A further advantage is for building multiplex images of structure that go beyond the coexistence of multiple contents of
Model II or the partial directionality of Model III. Because the
categories within each type of dyad are mutually exclusive
and logically exhaustive, rigorous, substantively interesting
models of content interrelation and interchange can be constructed. The importance of being able to elaborate uniplex
images into multiplex patterns can be shown with a brief
example. Quite different substantive interpretations can
emerge when uniplex configurations for different contents are
combined and analyzed as multiplex forms.

Considering only "dissent" uniplex dyads, Figure A:9
shows the different multiplex patterns that result when the

separate patterns for two contents, A and B, are combined. (The sixteen logical combinations for two contents, assuming each is either present (+) or absent (−), are given in Figure A:10.) It will be recalled that, although the configurations in the two cells in the off-diagonal of Figure A:8(a) are different, they have the same substantive meaning at a uniplex level and are both classified as a dissent dyad.

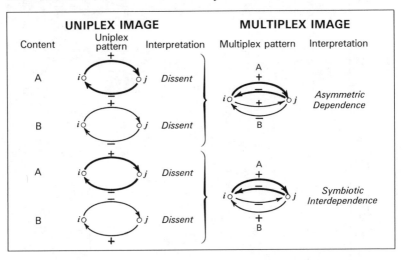

A:9 *Multiple Contents: Uniplex and Multiplex Structures*

From a multiplex view, however, Figure A:9 shows that a different multiplex image emerges depending upon which dissent cell is involved when the two contents are combined. So that if the uniplex pattern is identical for both contents, then only one kind of multiplex structure (that I have labelled "asymmetric dependence") can result. However, this is quite unlike the pattern produced when the configuration for each content is different. In the lower example in Figure A:9 the different dissent configurations for contents A and B form a larger structure, when viewed from a multiplex perspective, in which actor *i* exchanges A for B with actor *j*. I have labelled this pattern "symbiotic interdependence" to emphasize the bond of mutual dependence between the actors.

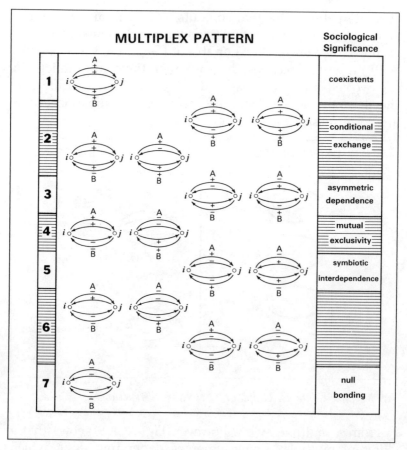

A:10 *Multiplex Dyads Classified by Structural Type*

Multiplex images are important, therefore, not just because they allow the researcher to examine how different contents are interrelated, but also because they offer different substantive interpretations of relational patterns. In studies where networks are mapped across a number of contents, such as this one, it is essential, before accepting a given uniplex image as valid, that multiplex patterns are considered.

Empirical Application

The empirical application of Model IV is presented in Figures A:11 and A:12. For *sexual* ties (Figure A:11(a)), the example of an undirected relation, half the dyads are in the prohibited category (51%). When these are added to the affirmed dyads, we can see that there is consensus about *sexual* ties for three quarters of the dyadic relations possible among members. Although there is dissent over almost as many ties as those that are affirmed (22% compared to 24%), these relations tend to be centered around two distinct cliques that are structured quite differently (Figure A:11(b)).

The clique of affirmed ties is patterned as two tetrads, each with two males and two females involved in multiple heterosexual ties, bridged by the dyad of members 1 and 2. On the other hand, the clique of dissent is comprised of two closed triads joined at the dyad of the two females, #s 5 and 6. The latter are also the bridge to the other clique.

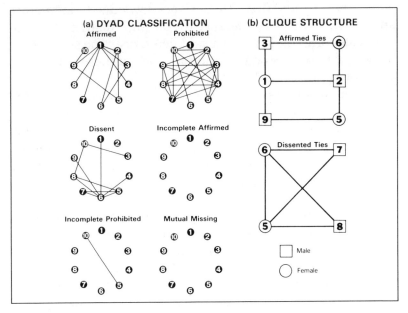

A:11 *Model IV — Undirected Relations: "Sexual" Example*

An advantage of Model IV, when working with problematic data, can be demonstrated with *power* relations in Loch Lomond. We can see in Figure A:12(a), that not only is there little consensus about power, but information is incomplete for as many as 47% of the dyads. With data missing for almost half of the dyadic relations in this group, is it possible to build an accurate image of power structure from the information available? Somewhat surprisingly, this does appear to be the case. (A holonomic explanation for this is presented in Part Four of this book — see Chapters Eight and Nine.)

Starting with the sociomatrix of raw data (see Figure A:N1, page 328 below), this is systematically decomposed into the ten mutually exclusive and logically exhaustive categories of directed dyads identified in Figure A:12(a). The dyads are then recombined, category by category, to form a composite image.[3] This is done by starting with the area of strongest measurement and successively adding weaker and increasingly more problematic data — for example, acknowledged dominance dyads first, then unacknowledged dominance and unacknowledged deference dyads, and finally the incomplete categories of dominance and deference. The sociometric images of *power* in Loch Lomond for each of these three steps are shown in Figure A:12(b).

Although the resulting constructions must be treated with caution, a high degree of structural coherence and order is evident in the two composites; the images are not disjointed and only one intransitive relation is present. Even so, it is essential that such *prima facie* sociological validity be corroborated from other reliable data sources. Thus while, in this example, there is ethnographic evidence in broad terms for the first composite image (upper right of Figure A:12(b)), observations over a four month period by a field worker indicate that members 1, 9, and 10 tend to have less power in the commune than members 4, 6, and 8. Since this is not reflected in the first composite, the second (bottom right) is probably a more accurate image of power in this group.

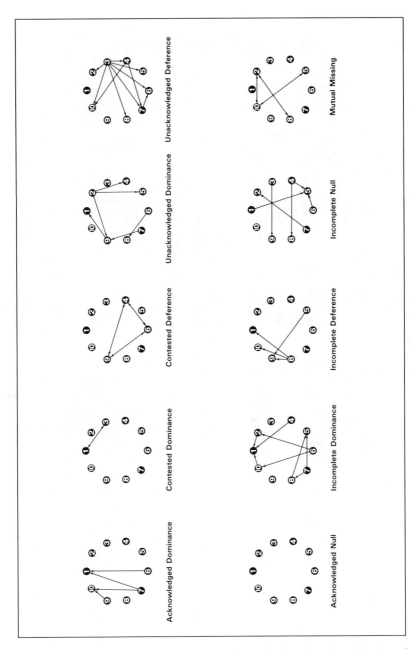

A:12(a) *Model IV — Directed Relations: Example Showing Classification of "Power" Dyads*

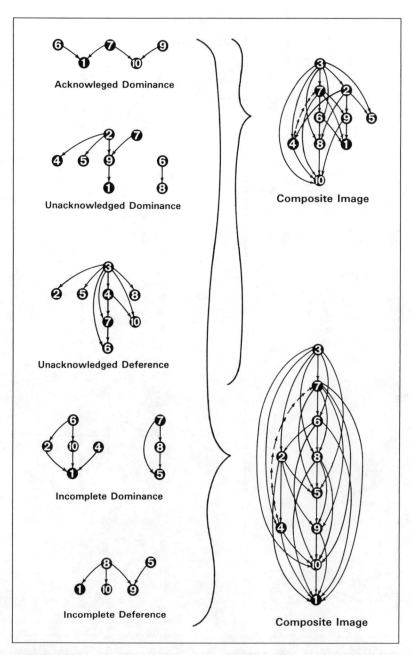

A:12(b) *Model IV — Directed Relations: Example Showing Construction of Composite Images from Dyad Types*

Empirical Accuracy

Finally, I want to make a few comparative comments about the empirical accuracy of the four models. Model I provides an image of an ego-centered network based on one individual's perceptions. As the commune example showed, however, these perceptions may not be in accord with those of the other network members. This means that, while the model may have social-psychological utility by providing cognitive maps of relational patterns, it does not offer a satisfactory means for constructing empirically accurate sociological images.

A more direct comparison can be made among the other three models, since, in varying degrees, they all consider the dyad from the perspective of each actor. With its weak "either i or j" criterion, Model II shows twice as many *sexual* relations as the other two models which use the stricter criterion of mutual choice by i and j. Closer inspection reveals that 48% of the ties Model II classifies as "present" involve error; they are really ties involving disagreement. On the other hand, because a different operational logic is required, the "asymmetric" category of Model III cannot be used to infer directionality for undirected relations. Thus, the flow pattern of asymmetric *sexual* ties shown by Model III is spurious; these relations are really disagreements or part of multiplex exchanges between members. And while it has not occurred for Loch Lomond, there is also the potential for further spurious directionality when such "asymmetry" is inferred from network mappings contaminated with incomplete data.

Although only one dyad is involved in our example, the potential for measurement error is also contained in the absent and null categories of Models II and III. The two categories are based on the same operational logic and classify ties that are actually reported as nonexistent together with ties for which information is missing or incomplete.

For directed ties, only Models III and IV are relevant as directionality is not usually inferred from the other models.

When the former are applied to the kind of relational data gathered in this study, a number of weaknesses are revealed for Model III that seriously detract from its empirical accuracy and create problems with interpretation.

There are two difficulties with the "asymmetric" category. First, because the operational logic does not establish ordinality, directionality cannot be inferred. So that despite the coherent order and transitivity of the 18 asymmetric dyads of power in Figure A:7, valid measurement has not been achieved. A second limitation, directly related to this, is that by classifying the acknowledged, unacknowledged, and incomplete categories of dominance together as asymmetric relations, Model III loses the consensual property of the first, while gaining error from the missing information of the third category.

A problem of interpretation with the "mutual" category emerges when Model III is applied to directed relational data. While, for undirected bonds, this category denotes that i and j agree that a given tie is present, for directed relations a different inference must be drawn. When i and j each claim greater *power* than the other, disagreement exists about the directionality of the relation. Thus, although there is only a single dyad of such "contested dominance" in Loch Lomond, in other cases, where many may be present (e.g., Figure 9:4(b), page 259 above) classification as a mutual tie would result in a spurious interpretation.

Finally, six categories of directed relational information are confounded together in Model III as a "null" tie. Included with those relations that are actually absent are; ties for which information from both i and j is missing, null ties and deference dyads for which information is incomplete, unacknowledged deferences, and contested deferences. An examination of the example in Figure A:12(a) shows how this can distort empirical images of directed networks. Of the 45 *power* dyads possible in Loch Lomond, 26 (58%) are classified by Model III as "null." However, 38% of these are actually unacknowledged deferences, and a further 12% contested deferences.

Although information is missing or incomplete for 29% of the 45 dyads, there are *no* power relations in this group that both *i* and *j* designate as a null tie.

The omission of deference relations by Model III is an unfortunate deficiency. Comparing the images in Figures A:7 and A:12(a), reveals that while Model III's asymmetric category captures some features of Loch Lomond's power hierarchy, it renders a seriously distorted image. In this group, 30% of all dyads are either unacknowledged or incomplete deferences, and it is this information in Model IV that provides the basis for a more accurate image of power. This is best illustrated by the position of member 3 who, although shown as an isolate by Model III, emerges in Model IV as the sociometric leader — a point that is corroborated by the observational evidence on this commune.

Overall, it can be concluded that, for undirected ties, measurement error is present in both categories of dyads in Model II, and that of three kinds of dyads in Model III, only the "mutual" category is able to provide unambiguous measurement of normative consensus. While Model III's "asymmetric" category provides, at a nonconsensual level, a partially accurate image when applied to directed relational data, each of the categories in this model introduces a sizeable amount of measurement error. This is a result of the model's inadequate operational logic for measuring consensual directed relations. For both undirected and directed dyads, therefore, Model IV is superior — not only because of its rigorous measurement of relations of consensus, but also because of its greater empirical accuracy.

NOTES

1. Two relational contents have been selected for this application. The *sexual* content will be used as an example of an undirected (nominal) relation, while *power* as an example of a directed (ordered) relation. (The terms "undirected" and "directed" are discussed and defined on pages 312 and 313, and 315–318.)

The sociomatrices for the "raw" data for both contents are given in Figure A:N1.

				SEXUAL													POWER							
				Actor j													Actor j								
		1	2	3	4	5	6	7	8	9	10			1	2	3	4	5	6	7	8	9	10
	1	-	1	1	1	2	1	1	1	1	2		1	-	0	1	0	3	5	5	5	3	0
Actor i	2	1	-	2	2	1	1	2	2	2	2	Actor i	2	1	-	5	1	1	0	0	0	1	0
	3	1	2	-	2	2	1	2	2	2	1		3	1	3	-	3	3	3	3	3	3	3
	4	1	2	2	-	2	2	2	2	2	2		4	1	3	5	-	3	5	3	3	5	3
	5	2	1	2	2	-	1	1	1	1	0		5	0	3	5	0	-	0	0	0	0	0
	6	2	1	1	1	2	-	2	2	2	2		6	1	1	5	5	3	-	5	1	5	1
	7	1	2	2	2	2	1	-	2	2	2		7	1	3	5	5	1	3	-	1	1	1
	8	1	2	2	2	2	1	2	-	2	2		8	0	0	5	0	1	3	0	-	0	0
	9	1	2	2	2	1	1	2	2	-	1		9	1	3	0	5	5	5	3	5	-	1
	10	2	2	2	2	2	2	2	1	1	-		10	1	0	5	5	0	0	5	5	5	-

KEY

1 = Yes/Sometimes
2 = No
0 = No answer

KEY

1 = Dominance
3 = Neutral/equal
5 = Deference
0 = No answer

A:N1 *Sociomatrices of Raw Data ("Sexual" and "Power" contents) for Loch Lomond Commune, Wave One*

2. For the analysis in this appendix, as elsewhere in this book, the operational criterion for the presence of a *sexual* relation is a response of "yes" or "sometimes" to item *5g* of the Relationship Questionnaire (see Appendix B).

3. While I have shown the relations for each category as a sociogram for visual convenience, the dyad categories (for both undirected and directed relations) were constructed from the raw relational data, as separate sociomatrices, by a computer program, *DAMP* (described in Chapter Five, Note 4, page 126). The relevant subsets were then combined into a single "master" sociomatrix (a separate one for each content) — a composite of the individual dyadic elements. This "master" sociomatrix was then subjected to the various structural analyses reported in this book.

Appendix B

THE RELATIONSHIP QUESTIONNAIRE
(selected items)

Explanatory Note

The following pages in this questionnaire ("page 3") is the source of most of the relationship data used in this book. Each respondent received a questionnaire with multiple copies of "page 3" inserted in it. A respondent in a commune with a population of nine, for example, would receive a questionnaire with eight page 3's, one for each adult person other than himself. Each of these page 3's would have one of the commune member's names typed in at the top. Therefore, in completing this questionnaire each respondent supplied us with a page 3 describing his/her relationship with each other respondent in the same commune.

5. This sheet is about _____

   a. How long have you known the above named person?
      Years _____   Months _____

   b. In you own words briefly characterize the changes which have occurred in your unique relationship with this person as a fellow commune member over the last twelve months or, if less, for the time you have known each other.

   _____

   c. How many hours in a typical week do the two of you spend together just by yourselves? _____

   d. If you happen to know it, state what kind of work (his/her) father did while the person named above was growing up.

   _____

   e. Even the most equal of relationships sometimes has a power element involved. However insignificant it may be in your relationship with this person, which of you do you think holds the greater amount of power in your relationship?

   _____

   f. If this commune did not exist, would you want to have a close relationship with this person? _____

   g. For the list of descriptions below, indicate if the following are involved in your relationship with the person named above by checking the appropriate answer. *Please answer each of the following:*

Description		
Work together	Yes __ No __ Sometimes __	
Spend free time together	Yes __ No __ Sometimes __	
Mind children together	Yes __ No __ Sometimes __	
Sleep together	Yes __ No __ Sometimes __	
Confide in each other	Yes __ No __ Sometimes __	
Loving	Yes __ No __ Sometimes __	
Exciting	Yes __ No __ Sometimes __	
Awkward	Yes __ No __ Sometimes __	
Feel close to each other	Yes __ No __ Sometimes __	
Tense	Yes __ No __ Sometimes __	
Jealous	Yes __ No __ Sometimes __	
Agree on communal policy matters	Yes __ No __ Sometimes __	
Feel estranged from each other	Yes __ No __ Sometimes __	
Exploitive	Yes __ No __ Sometimes __	
Hateful	Yes __ No __ Sometimes __	
Improving	Yes __ No __ Sometimes __	
Sexual	Yes __ No __ Sometimes __	

   h. Do you feel that the overall relationship between the two of you is more important to you, or do you feel it is more important to the above named person?
      ____ More important to you   ____ More important to him/her

   i. In your relationship with this person, does he/she ever act to you as a father or mother, sister or brother, son or daughter, or none of these? _____

j. Although we realize that it may be difficult for you to judge, which of the two of you would you say is held in higher esteem by the communal household as a whole? _____

For the two questions that follow, please indicate your answer by drawing a vertical line through a point on the scaled line below which best represents how close your opinion is to either of the opposing views given.

k. What role do you think the above named person's presence and action play in the commune's survival?

Endanger the |⊢⊢⊢⊢⊢⊢⊢⊢⊢⊢⊢⊢⊢| Is crucial to the
commune's survival   commune's survival

l. Do you feel that this person lives up to the principles of the communal household?

Seldom acts with   Always acts with
any regard for the |⊢⊢⊢⊢⊢⊢⊢⊢⊢⊢⊢⊢⊢| high regard for the
commune's principles   commune's principles

6. Who in your communal household:

_____   a. is energetic

_____   b. is innovative

_____   c. The commune seems to work better when he/she is present

_____   d. knows me in some ways better than I know myself

_____   e. is often aloof

_____   f. has taught me something about how life should be lived

_____   g. is fatherly

_____   h. is motherly

_____   i. The commune seems to feel closer and more together when he/she is present

7. Name the five people who are most significant in your life at the moment, whether or not they are fellow commune members, and describe their relationship to you.

          NAME   RELATIONSHIP

1. _____   _____

2. _____   _____

3. _____   _____

4. _____   _____

5. _____   _____

8. The expression of different views and feelings about things generally occurs when a group of people lives, works, or plays together. Although this may not have arisen so far in your relationship with the commune, would you name *two other commune members* whom you feel you would most turn to for support in the event of a dis-

agreement or problem emerging between you and the rest of the commune.

1. _____

2. _____

9. Do you hold a position in this commune? If so, what are the duties and responsibilities of this position?

_____ Hold no position.

POSITIONS HELD   RESPONSIBILITIES AND DUTIES

_____   _____
_____   _____
_____   _____
_____   _____

10. Who is generally recognized as the leader of this commune?
_____

11. Would you please write the name of one commune member who:

_____ has new ideas for the commune.

_____ is able to help resolve relationship problems which emerge between members from time to time.

_____ something important seems lacking in the commune when he/she is not present.

_____ seems to have an inexhaustible supply of love.

_____ is the person whose advice you generally seek when making an important personal decision.

Appendix C

PROCEDURES FOR DRAWING *POWER* SOCIOGRAMS

Hand-drawn images of group structure from relational data inevitably contain spurious elements introduced during the drafting process. In an effort to reduce such distortion from subjective and arbitrary sources in the graphic representations of power in the communes, the following procedures were used to convert a sociomatrix of dominance and deference relations into the lines and nodes of a hierarchical sociogram. Rather than weighting one more heavily than the other, dominance relations (i.e., where *i* claims *power* over *j*) and deference relations (where *i* defers *power* to *j*) were treated as equivalent when positioning individuals and relations in the sociogram.

Establishing the Longest Transitive Path

As an unambiguous criterion, the longest transitive path was employed to systematically establish a hierarchical order in the *power* relations among commune members. It involved finding the longest unbroken chain of direct relations that connect members in a single order running from the individual at the top of the hierarchy to the person at the bottom. This ordering is "transitive" in that *power* flows only in one direction (i.e., *i* is dominant over *j*, and *j* over *k*, and *k* over *l*, with *i* over *k* and over *l*, and *j* over *l* etc.) and involves no reflextivity; cycles in which *power* flows back up the structure in a closed loop (i.e., *i* over *j*, and *j* over *k*, and *k* over *i*) are excluded at this stage.

To start, the top of the hierarchy was identified by finding the most "dominant" individual. This is the member who is not dominated by anyone else (s/he defers to nobody and no one claims *power* over them) and who holds a dominance relation over at least one other person. As the "sociometric leader", this individual is easily identified in the sociomatrix by no relations (i.e., zeros ("0")) in the column vector and at least one relation (a one ("1")) in the corresponding row vector. In some groups more than one member met this condition. Since these individuals are structurally equivalent, they were placed together at the top of the hierarchy as multiple sociometric leaders.

Next, the second most dominant person — the individual/s at the level immediately below the leader — is signified by two characteristics: first, they are dominated by the sociometric leader, but by no-one else; and second, they are also dominant over at least one other member. Finding the other hierarchical levels below this was accomplished by essentially repeating this process. Thus, the third level is established by someone who is dominated by at least one person from level two, and who had *power* over at least one other member from the rest of the group — and so on, for levels four, five, six etc.

This process is repeated until the bottom of the hierarchy is located: the individual/s who holds power over no-one, but who is dominated by at least one person from the level immediately above. This established the end point of the longest transitive path, and means that the structure's "stem" or "backbone" has been identified.

Positioning Other Individuals and Relations

Individuals left over at the end of the above procedure were then placed one level above the lowest person in the hierarchy over whom they hold *power*. This was done irrespective of whether their dominance is due to their own claim of greater *power* or due to the other member's deference. For those who were dominated but did not hold *power* over anyone else, placement was at the level immediately below the lowest person in the hierarchy who held *power* over them. Relations still remaining at this point, were then filled in by working systematically, level by level, up from the bottom to the relations of the leader, last of all. Finally, isolates (individuals not linked to anyone by *power*), were placed below the bottom of hierarchy under the label "no relations", while those who did not answer the Relationship Questionnaire, were located under the label "no data".

Format: Symmetry

To reduce arbitrary bias in formating the sociograms, a rule of structural symmetry was applied to both the positioning of the nodes representing individuals and the lines representing *power* relations. Equal space was left between each hierarchical level in placing the nodes down the page. Lateral symmetry was employed to position multiple nodes at any one level, with individuals spaced evenly and equally on either side of the stem. Generally, those holding the greatest number of *power* relations over others were placed towards the center of their level; those with fewer, nearer the outer edge. For members holding more than one relation of dominance, the lines were alternated down each side of the stem, distributing the relations equally to both sides of the hierarchy. Thus, the effect of this rule of symmetry in format, its structural bias, is that the pattern of relations and nodes on one side of the stem tends to mirror that on the other.

REFERENCES

Abbott, Edwin A. *Flatland: A Romance of Many Dimensions,* New York: Barnes and Noble Books, 1963.

Abu-Mostafa, Yaser S., and Demetri Psaltis. Optical Neural Computers. *Scientific American,* 1987, 256 (3): 88–95.

Aidala, Angela. Ideological Systems: A Longitudinal Study of Norms, Values, and Ideology in Communal Living Groups. Doctoral dissertation. New York: Columbia University, 1980.

Alba, R. D., and C. Kadushin. The Introduction of Social Circles: A New Measure of Social Proximity in Networks. *Sociological Methods and Research,* 1976, 5: 77-102.

Arabie, P., S. A. Boorman, and P. R. Levitt. Constructing Blockmodels: How and Why. *Journal of Mathematical Psychology,* 1978, 17:21-63.

Axelrod, Robert. *The Evolution of Cooperation.* New York: Basic Books, Inc., 1984.

Bales, Robert F. A Set of Categories for the Analysis of Small Group Interaction. *American Sociological Review,* 1950, 15: 257-263.

Bales, Robert F. The Equilibrium Problem in Small Groups. In: T. Parsons, R. F. Bales, and E. A. Shils, *Working Papers in the Theory of Action,* pp. 111-161. Glencoe, Ill.: Free Press, 1953.

337

Barnes, J. A. Social Networks. Reading, M. A.: Addison-Wesley, 1972.

Barnes, J. A. Network Analysis: Orienting Notion, Rigorous Technique or Substantive Field of Study? In: P. W. Holland and S. Leinhardt (eds.), *Perspectives on Social Network Research*. New York: Academic Press, 1979.

Bekesy, G. von. Synchronism of Neural Discharges and Their Demultiplication in Pitch Perception on the Skin and in Hearing. *Journal of the Acoustical Society of America*, 1959, 31: 338-349.

Bekesy, G. von. *Experiments in Hearing*. New York: McGraw-Hill, 1960.

Bendix, Reinhard. *Max Weber: An Intellectual Portrait*. New York: Anchor Books, 1960.

Bendix, Reinhard. Reflections on Charismatic Leadership. In: *State and Society*, pp. 616-629. Boston: Little, Brown, 1968.

Bensman, Joseph, and Michael Givant. Charisma and Modernity: The Use and Abuse of a Concept. *Social Research*, 1975 (Winter): 570-614.

Berger, Peter L. Charisma and Religious Innovation: the Social Location of Israelite Prophecy. *American Sociological Review*, 1963, 28 (6): 940-950.

Berger, Peter L., and Thomas Luckman. *The Social Construction of Reality*. Harmondsworth, England: Penguin Books, 1966.

Berkowitz, S. D. *An Introduction to Structural Analysis*. Toronto: Butterworths, 1982.

Bernard, H. R., and P. D. Killworth. Informant Accuracy in Social Network Data II. *Human Communications Research*, 1977, 4: 3-18.

Bernard, H. R., and P. D. Killworth. Informant Accuracy in Social Network Data IV: a Comparison of Clique-level Structure in Behavioral and Cognitive Network Data. *Social Networks*, 1980, 2: 191-218.

Bierstedt, Robert. The Problem of Authority. In: M. Berger, T. Abel, and C. Page (eds.), *Freedom and Control in Modern Society*. New York: D. Van Nostrand, Inc., 1954.

Blakemore, C., and F. W. Campbell. On the Existence of Neurones in the Human Visual System Selectively Sensitive to the Orientation and Size of Retinal Images. *Journal of Physiology*, 1969, 203: 237-60.

Blalock, Herbert M. *Social Statistics*. New York: McGraw Hill, 1960.

Blalock, Herbert M. *Conceptualization and Measurement in the Social Sciences*. Beverly Hills, CA.: Sage Publications, 1982.

Blau, Peter M. Structural Affects. *American Sociological Review*, 1960, 25: 178-193.

Blau, Peter M. *Exchange and Power in Social Life*. New York: Wiley, 1964.

Blau, Peter M. *Inequality and Heterogeneity: A Primitive Theory of Social Structure*. New York: The Free Press, 1977(a).

Blau, Peter M. A Macrosociological Theory of Social Structure. *American Journal of Sociology*, 1977(b), 83 (1): 26-54.

Blau, Peter M. Introduction: Diverse Views of Social Structure and Their Common Denominator. In: Peter M. Blau and Robert K. Merton (eds.), *Continuities in Structural Inquiry*, pp. 1-23. London and Beverly Hills: Sage Publications, 1981.

Bluedorn, A. C. The Theories of Turnover: Causes, Effects, and Meaning. *Research in the Sociology of Organizations*, 1982, 1: 75-128.

Blumer, Herbert. Collective Behavior. In: A. M. Lee (ed.), *Principles of Sociology*. New York: Barnes and Noble, 1951.

Blumer, Herbert. Collective Behavior. In: J. B. Gittler (ed.), *Review of Sociology: Analysis of a Decade*, pp. 127-158. New York: John Wiley and Sons, 1957.

Bohm, David. *Wholeness and the Implicate Order*. London, Boston and Henley: Routledge and Kegan Paul, 1980.

Boissevain, J. Preface. In: J. Boissevain and J. C. Mitchell (eds.), *Network Analysis: Studies in Human Interaction*, pp. vii-xiii. The Hague: Mouton, 1973.

Boissevain, J., and J. C. Mitchell (eds.). *Network Analysis: Studies in Human Interaction*. The Hague: Mouton, 1973.

Boorman, S. A., and Harrison C. White. Social Structure from Multiple Networks: II. Role Structures. *American Journal of Sociology*, 1976, 81 (6): 1384-1446.

Bord, Richard, J. Toward a Social Psychological Theory of Charismatic Social Influence Processes. *Social Forces*, 1975, 53 (3): 485-497.

Boudon, Raymond. *The Uses of Structuralism*. Donald MacRae (trans.). London: Heinemann, 1971.

Boulding, Kenneth E. *Ecodynamics: A New Theory of Societal Evolution*. London and Beverly Hills: Sage Publications, 1978.

Bradley, Raymond T. Social Skills and the Social Organization of the Modern Urban Community. *Pacific Viewpoint*, 1974, 14 (2): 137-158.

Bradley, Raymond T. Some Network Characteristics of Interpersonal Power and Loving Relationships in Charismatic Communes. Paper presented to Annual Meetings of Public Choice Society, Chicago, 1975.

Bradley, Raymond T. Pyramids of Power and Communion: The Structural Properties of Charismatic Communes. Doctoral dissertation. New York: Columbia University, 1980(a).

Bradley, Raymond T. Charisma and Leadership in the Urban Commune. Paper presented to the Fourth Annual Max Weber Colloquium, The William Patterson College, New Jersey, 1980(b).

Bradley, Raymond T., and Timothy Owens. Social Structure and Individual Performance. Paper presented to Annual Meetings of the Sociologists of Minnesota, Saint Paul, 1980.

Bradley, Raymond T. Towards an Integrated Strategy for Relational Analysis. Paper presented to Annual Meetings of the American Sociological Association, Toronto, 1981.

Bradley, Raymond T. Ethical Problems in Team Research: a Structural Analysis and an Agenda for Resolution. *The American Sociologist,* 1982, 17 (May): 87-94.

Bradley, Raymond T. Relational Properties of Charismatic Organization: Results from a Study of 57 Communal Organizations. Paper presented to Symposium on Charisma, Academy of Management Annual Meetings, Boston, 1984.

Bradley, Raymond T. Holonomic Social Organization: An Empirical Test. Paper presented to Symposium on Hologramic Theory: a New Perspective on Organization, Academy of Management Annual Meetings, San Diego, 1985(a).

Bradley, Raymond T. Book Review of *The Age of Charisma,* by Arthur Schweitzer (1984), Chicago: Nelson. In: *Contemporary Sociology,* 1985(b), 14 (2): 242-243.

Bradley, Raymond T., and Nancy C. Roberts. Transformation and Holonomic Social Order. In: Robert E. Quinn and Kim S. Cameron (eds.), *Paradox and Transformation: Towards A New Theory of Organization,* Chapter Three. Cambridge, Mass.: Ballinger Publishing Company, forthcoming.

Braitenberg, Valentino. *Vehicles: Experiments in Synthetic Psychology.* Cambridge, Mass., and London: The MIT Press, 1984.

Briggs, John P., and F. David Peat. *Looking-Glass Universe: The Emerging Science of Wholeness.* New York, Cornerstone Library, Simon and Schuster, Inc., 1984.

Bugliosi, Vincent, with Curt Gentry. *Helter Skelter: The True Story of the Manson Murders.* New York: Bantam Books, 1974.

Burns, James MacGregor. *Leadership.* New York: Harper and Row, 1978.

Burt, Ronald S. Positions in Multiple Network Systems, Part One: a General Conception of Stratification and Prestige in a System of Actors Cast as a Social Typology. *Social Forces,* 1977, 56: 106-131.

Burt, Ronald S. "Models of Network Structure," *Annual Review of Sociology 6,* 1980: 79-141.

Camic, Charles. Charisma: Its Varieties, Preconditions, and Consequences. *Sociological Inquiry,* 1980, 50 (1): 5-23.

Campbell, F. W., and J. G. Robson. Application of Fourier Analysis to the Visibility of Gratings. *Journal of Physiology,* 1968, 197: 551-566.

Campbell, F. W., and B. G. Cleland, G. F. Cooper, and C. Enroth-Cugell. The Angular Selectivity of Visual Cortical Cells to Moving Grating. *Journal of Physiology,* 1968, 198: 237-250.

Carlton-Ford, Steven L. The Effects of Ritual and Charisma: The Creation of Collective Effervescence and the Support of Psychic Strength. Doctoral dissertation. Minneapolis: University of Minnesota, 1986.

Cartwright, Dorwin, and Frank Harray. Structural Balance: A Generalization of Heider's Theory. *Psychological Review,* 1956, 63: 277-293.

Cartwright, Dorwin. The Nature of Group Cohesiveness. In: D. Cartwright and A. Zander (eds.), *Group Dynamics: Research and Theory,* 3rd. ed., pp. 91-109. New York: Harper and Row, 1968.

Catton, William R., Jr. The Development of Sociological Thought. In: Robert E. C. Faris (ed.), *Handbook of Modern Sociology,* pp. 912-950. Chicago: Rand McNally, 1964.

Cell, C. Charismatic Heads of State: The Social Context. *Behavior Science Research,* 1974, 9: 255-305.

Christianson, Gale E. *In the Presence of the Creator: Isaac Newton and His Times.* New York: The Free Press, 1984.

Coleman, James S. Relational Analysis of Networks Using Survey Methods. *Human Organization,* 1954, 17 (4): 28-36.

Coleman, James S. *The Mathematics of Collective Action.* Chicago: Aldine, 1973.

Coleman, James S. Social Theory, Social Research, and a Theory of Action. *American Journal of Sociology,* 1986, 91(6): 1309-1335.

Collins, Randall. *Conflict Sociology: Toward an Explanatory Science.* New York: Academic Press, 1975.

Collins, Randall. Is 1980's Sociology in the Doldrums? *American Journal of Sociology,* 1986, 91(6): 1336-1355.

Comte, Auguste. *Outline of the Positive Philosophy,* Volume 3. 1830-42.

Comte, Auguste. *System of Positive Polity,* Volume 2. Frederic Harrison (trans.), 1851-54.

Coser, Lewis. *Greedy Institutions: Patterns of Undivided Commitment.* New York: The Free Press, 1974.

Daugman, John G. Uncertainty Relation for Resolution in Space, Spatial Frequency, and Orientation Optimized by Two-dimensional Visual Cortical Filters. *Journal of the Optical Society of America* (A), 1985, 2 (7): 1160–1169.

Davis, James A. Clustering and Hierarchy in Interpersonal Relations: Testing Two Graph Theoretic Models on 742 Sociograms. *American Sociological Review,* 1970, 35: 843-852.

Davis, James A., and Samuel Leinhardt. The Structure of Positive Interpersonal Relations in Small Groups. In: J. Berger et al. (eds.), *Sociological Theories in Progress: Volume Two*, pp. 218-257. New York: Houghton-Mifflin, 1972.

DeValois, K. K., R. L. DeValois, and E. W. Yund. Responses of Striate Cortex Cells to Grating and Checkerboard Patterns. *Journal of Psychology,* 1979, 291: 483-505.

Dow, T. E., Jr. The Theory of Charisma. *Sociological Quarterly,* 1969, 10 (Summer): 306-318.

Durkheim, Emile. *The Rules of Sociological Method.* Chicago: University of Chicago Press, 1938.

Durkheim, Emile. *Suicide.* Glencoe, Ill.: Free Press, 1951.

Durkheim, Emile. *The Elementary Forms of Religious Life.* New York: The Free Press, 1965.

Edelman, G. M., and V. B. Mountcastle. *The Mindful Brain.* Cambridge, Mass.: MIT Press, 1978.

Eich, Janet M. Levels of Processing, Encoding Specificity, Elaboration, and CHARM. *Psychological Review,* 1985, 92 (1): 1-38.

El Sawy, Omar A. From Separatism to Holographic Enfolding: The Evolution of the Technostructure of Organizations. Paper presented to the TIM/ORSA Conference, Boston, 1985.

Erickson, V. Lois. Leadership Theory: From Structural Ego Psychology to Vision Through Intuition. Paper presented to the Annual Meeting of the International Association of Political Psychology, Oxford University, England, 1982.

Etzioni, Amitai. *A Comparative Analysis of Complex Organizations.* New York: The Free Press, 1961.

Etzioni, Amitai. Dual Leadership in Complex Organizations. *American Sociological Review,* 1965, 30: 688-699.

Evans, D. C. Computer Logic and Memory. *Scientific American,* 1966, 215: 74-85.

Fabian, J. Charisma and Cultural Change. *Comparative Studies in Society and History,* 1969, 11: 155-173.

Fabian, J. *Jamaa: A Charismatic Movement in Katanga.* Evanston: Northwestern University Press, 1971.

Fabian, J. Kazi: Conceptualizations of Labor in a Charismatic Movement among Swahili-Speaking Workers. *Cahiers d'Etudes Africaines,* 1973, 13 (2): 293-325.

Falter, Jurgen W. Some Theoretical and Methodological Problems of Multilevel Analysis Reconsidered. *Social Science Information,* 1978, 17 (6): 841-869.

Feinberg, S. E., and S. S. Wasserman. Categorical Data Analysis of Single Sociometric Relations. In: S. Leinhardt (ed.), *Sociological Methodology 1981,* pp. 156-192. San Francisco: Jossey-Bass, 1981.

Festinger, L., S. Schachter, and K. W. Back. *Social Pressures in Informal Groups.* Stanford, CA: Stanford University Press, 1950.

Fischer, C. S., R. M. Jackson, C. A. Stueve, K. Gerson, L. M. Jones, with M. Baldassare. *Networks and Places: Social Relations in the Urban Setting.* New York: The Free Press, 1977.

Fischer, C. S. *To Dwell Among Friends: Personal Networks in Town and City.* Chicago: University of Chicago Press, 1982.

Fischer, Louis. *The Life of Mahatma Gandhi.* New York: Harper and Row, 1950.

Flament, Claude. *Applications of Graph Theory to Group Structure.* Englewood Cliffs, New Jersey: Prentice-Hall, 1963.

Fortes, M. *The Web of Kinship Among the Tallensi.* London: Oxford University Press, 1949.

Frank, Ove. *Statistical Inference in Graphs.* Stockholm: forsvarets Forskninganstalt, 1971.

Frank, Ove. Sampling and Estimation in Large Social Networks. *Social Networks,* 1978, 1: 91-101.

Frank, Ove. Estimation of Population Totals by Use of Snowball Samples. In: S. Leinhardt and P. W. Holland (eds.), *Perspectives in Social Network Research,* pp. 319-347. New York: Academic Press, 1979.

Fraser, J. T. *The Genesis and Evolution of Time: A Critique of Interpretation in Physics.* Amherst: The University of Massachusetts Press, 1982.

Friedell, Morris. Organizations as Semilattices. *American Sociological Review,* 1968, 32 (1): 46-54.

Friedland, W. H. For a Sociological Concept of Charisma. *Social Forces,* 1964, 43: 18-26.

Friedrich, Carl J. Political Leadership and the Problem of Charismatic Power. *Journal of Politics,* 1961, 23: 3-24.

Gabor, D. A New Microscopic Principle. *Nature,* 1948, 161: 777-778.

Gabor, D. Holography, 1948-1971. *Science,* 1972, 177: 299-313.

Galanter, Marc. Charismatic Religious Sects and Psychiatry: An Overview. *American Journal of Psychiatry,* 1982, 139 (12): 1539-1548.

Galanter, Marc. Unification Church ("Moonie") Dropouts: Psychological Readjustment After Leaving a Charismatic Religious Group. *American Journal of Psychiatry,* 1983, 140 (8): 984-989.

Glazer, R. A Holographic Theory of Decision Making. Unpublished paper, Graduate School of Business, Columbia University, New York, 1986.

Glock, Charles Y., and Robert Bellah (eds.). *The New Religious Consciousness.* Berkeley: University of California Press, 1976.

Gluckman, Max. *The Judicial Process Among the Barotse of Northern Rhodesia.* Manchester: Manchester University Press, 1955.

Gluckman, Max. Les Rites de Passage. In: M. Gluckman (ed.), *Essays in the Ritual of Social Relations.* Manchester: Manchester University Press, 1962.

Goffman, Erving. *Relations in Public.* New York: Basic Books, 1971.

Goode, William J. The Theoretical Importance of Love. *American Sociological Review,* 1959, 24 (February): 38-47.

Goode, William J. The Place of Force in Human Society. *American Sociological Review,* 1972, 37 (October): 507-519.

Goode, William J. Homan's and Merton's Structural Approach. In: Peter M. Blau (ed.), *Approaches to the Study of Social Structure,* pp. 66-75. New York: The Free Press, 1975.

Goode, William J. *The Celebration of Heroes.* Berkeley and Los Angeles: University of California Press, 1978.

Goodman, Leo. Snowball Sampling. *Annals of Mathematical Statistics,* 1961, 32 (1): 148-170.

Granovetter, Mark. The Strength of Weak Ties. *American Journal of Sociology,* 1973, 78: 1360-1380.

Granovetter, Mark. Network Sampling: Some First Steps. *American Journal of Sociology,* 1976, 81 (6): 1287-1303.

Granovetter, Mark. The Theory-gap in Social Network Analysis. In: S. Leinhardt and P. Holland (eds.), *Perspectives in Social Network Research,* pp. 501-518. New York: Academic Press, 1979.

Griffin, Donald R. *The Question of Animal Awareness: Evolutionary Continuity on Mental Experience.* New York: The Rockefeller University Press, 1981.

Grinder, John, and Richard Bandler. *Trance-formations: Neuro-Linguistic Programming and the Structure of Hypnosis.* Moab, Utah: Real People Press, 1981.

Hallinan, Maureen T. *The Structure of Positive Sentiment.* New York: Elsevier, 1974.

Harray, Frank, Robert L. Norman, and Dorwin Cartwright. *Structural Models: An Introduction to the Theory of Directed Graphs.* New York: John Wiley, 1965.

Heider, F. Attitudes and Cognitive Organization. *Journal of Psychology,* 1946, 21: 107-112.

Heider, F. *The Psychology of Interpersonal Relations.* New York: Wiley, 1958.

Hernes, Gudmund. Structural Change in Social Processes. *American Journal of Sociology,* 1976, 82 (3): 513-547.

Hill, Michael. *A Sociology of Religion.* New York: Basic Books, 1973.

Hinde, R. A. *Towards Understanding Relationships.* London: Academic Press, 1979.

Hofstadter, Douglas R. *Gödel, Escher, Bach: An Eternal Golden Braid.* New York: Vintage Books, 1979.

Hofstadter, Douglas R., and Daniel C. Dennett (eds.). *The Mind's I: Fantasies and Reflections on Self and Soul.* New York: Basic Books, 1981.

Holland, Paul W., and Samuel Leinhardt. A Method of Detecting Structure in Sociometric Data. *American Journal of Sociology,* 1970, 76 (3): 492-513.

Holland, Paul W., and Samuel Leinhardt. The Structural Implications of Measurement Error in Sociometry. *Journal of Mathematical Sociology,* 1973, 3: 385-11.

Holland, Paul W., and Samuel Leinhardt. Local Structure in Social Networks. In: *Sociological Methodology 1976,* D. R. Heise (ed.), 1–45. San Francisco: Jossey-Bass, 1976.

Holland, Paul W., and Samuel Leinhardt. Social Structure as a Network Process. Paper presented to the International Conference on Mathematical Approaches in Social Network Analysis. Bad Homburg, West Germany, 1977.

Holland, Paul W., and Samuel Leinhardt. An Exponential Family of Probability Distributions for Directed Graphs. *Journal of the American Statistical Association,* 1981.

Homans, George Casper. *The Human Group.* New York: Harcourt Brace, 1950.

Homans, George Casper. *Social Behavior: Its Elementary Forms.* New York: Harcourt Brace Jovanovich, 1954.

Homans, George C. What Do We Mean by Social Structure? In: Peter M. Blau (ed.), *Approaches to the Study of Social Structure,* pp. 53-65. New York: The Free Press, 1975.

House, R. J. A 1976 Theory of Charismatic Leadership. In: J. G. Hunt and L. L. Larson (eds.), *Leadership: The Cutting Edge,* pp. 189–207. Carbondale: Southern Illinois University Press, 1977.

Hummel, Ralph P. Freud's Totem Theory as Complement to Max Weber's Theory of Charisma. *Psychological Reports,* 1974, 35: 683-686.

Hummel, Ralph P. Psychology of Charismatic Followers. *Psychological Reports,* 1975, 37: 759-770.

Jantsch, Erich. *The Self-organizing Universe: Scientific and Human Implications of the Emerging Paradigm of Evolution.* Oxford: Pergamon Press, 1980.

Johnson, D. P. Dilemmas of Charismatic Leadership: The Case of the People's Temple. *Sociological Analysis,* 1979, 40 (4): 315-323.

Jung, C. G. *Memories, Dreams, Reflections.* New York: Pantheon Books, 1961.

Jung, C. G. *The Archetypes and the Collective Unconscious.* Second Edition. New Jersey: Princeton University Press, 1969.

Kanter, Rosabeth M. *Commitment and Community: Communes and Utopia in Sociological Perspective.* Cambridge, Mass.: Harvard University Press, 1972.

Kanter, Rosabeth M. (ed.). *Communes: Creating and Managing Collective Life.* New York: Harper and Row, 1973.

Katz, Richard. Education for Transcendence: !Kia-healing with the Kalahari Kung. In: R. B. Lee and I. DeVore, (eds.), *Kalahari Hunter-Gathers.* Cambridge, Mass.: Harvard University Press, 1976.

Katz, Richard. The Painful Ecstasy of Healing. In: D. Coleman and R. Davidson (eds.), *Consciousness.* New York: Harper and Row, 1979.

Katz, Richard. *Boiling Energy: Community Healing Among the Kalahari Kung.* Cambridge, Mass.: Harvard University Press, 1982.

Keller, Evelyn Fox. *A Feeling for the Organism: The Life and Work of Barbara McClintock.* New York and San Francisco: W. H. Freeman and Company, 1983.

Killworth, P. D., and H. R. Bernard. Informant Accuracy in Social Network Data. *Human Organization,* 1976, 35: 269-86.

Knoke, D., and J. H. Kuklinski. *Network Analysis.* Beverly Hills, CA: Sage Publications, 1982.

Kohlberg, L., and R. Kramer. Continuities and Discontinuities in Childhood and Adult Moral Development. *Human Development,* 1969, 12: 93-120.

Kohlberg, Lawrence, and Clark Power. Moral Development, Religious Thinking, and the Question of a Seventh Stage. *Zygon,* 1981, 16 (3): 203-259.

Krishnamurti, J. *Freedom from the Known.* New York: Harper and Row, 1969.

Krishnamurti, J., and David Bohm. *The Ending of Time.* San Francisco: Harper and Row, 1985.

Lakatos, I. Falsification and the Methodology of Scientific Research Programmes. In: Imre Lakatos and Alan Musgrave (eds.), *Criticism and the Growth of Knowledge,* pp. 91-196. London: Cambridge University Press, 1970.

Lashley, K. S. In Search of the Engram. In: F. A. Beach, D. O. Hebb, E. T. Morgan, and H. W. Nissen (eds.), *The Neuropsychology of Lashley.* New York: McGraw-Hill, 1960.

Lashley, K. S. The Problem of Cerebral Organization in Vision. In: P. C. Dodwell (ed.), *Perceptual Processing: Stimulus Equivalence and Pattern Recognition,* pp. 12-27. New York: Appleton-Century-Crofts, 1971.

Laumann, Edward O. *Bonds of Pluralism: The Form and Substance of Urban Social Networks*. New York: Wiley, 1973.

Laumann, Edward O., Lois Verbrugge, and Franz U. Pappi. A Causal Modelling Approach to the Study of a Community Elite's Influence Structure. *American Journal of Sociology*, 1974, 39: 162-174.

Laumann, Edward O., and Franz U. Pappi. *Networks of Collective Action: A Perspective on Community Influence Systems*. New York: Academic Press, 1976.

Lazarsfeld, P., and R. K. Merton. Friendship as a Social Process: A Substantive and Methodological Analysis. In: M. Berger, R. Abel, and C. Page (eds.), *Freedom and Control in Modern Society*, pp. 18-67. New York: Octagon Books, 1954.

Leach, Edmund R. *Political Systems of Highland Burma*. London: G. Bell and Sons, 1954.

Lee, R. B., and I. Devore. *Kalahari Hunter-Gathers: Studies of the !Kung San and Their Neighbors*. Cambridge, Mass.: Harvard University Press, 1976.

Lee, R. B. *The !Kung San: Men, Women and Work in a Foraging Society*. Cambridge: Cambridge University Press, 1979.

Leger, Daniele. Charisma, Utopia and Communal Life: The Case of Neorural Apocalyptic Communes in France. *Social Compass*, 1982, 29 (1): 41-58.

Leith, E. N., and J. Upatnieks. Wavefront Reconstruction with Diffused Illumination and Three-Dimensional Objects. *Journal of the Optical Society of America*, 1964, 54: 1295-1301.

Leith, E. N., and J. Upatnieks. Photography by Laser. *Scientific American*, 1965, 212: 24-35.

Levett, Allan E., and Raymond T. Bradley. Networks and Social Status in Urban Wellington. In: S. D. Webb and J. Collette (eds.), *New Zealand Society: Contemporary Perspectives*, pp. 60-67. Melbourne: John Wiley and Sons, 1973.

LeShan, Lawrence. *The Medium, the Mystic, and the Physicist*. New York: Ballantine, 1972.

Levi-Strauss, Claude. *Structural Anthropology*. Trans. by Claire Jacobson and Brooke Gundfestschoepf. New York: Basic Books, 1963.

Lieberson, Stanley. *Making it Count: The Improvement of Social Research and Theory*. Berkeley and Los Angeles, CA.: University of California Press, 1985.

Lifton, Robert Jay. *Revolutionary Immortality: Mao Tse-tung and the Chinese Cultural Revolution*. New York: Vintage Books, 1968.

Lincoln, Yvonna S. (ed.). *Organizational Theory and Inquiry: The Paradigm Revolution*. Beverly Hills: Sage Publications, 1985.

Lindzey, G., and D. Byrne. Measurement of Social Choice and Interpersonal Attractiveness. In: G. Lindzey and E. Aronson (eds.), *Handbook of Social Psychology*, Vol. 3. Reading, MA: Addison-Wesley, 1968.

Lofland, John. *Doomsday Cult: A Study of Conversion, Proselytization and Maintenance of Faith*. Englewood Cliffs, NJ: Prentice-Hall, 1966.

Loevinger, J., and R. Wessler. *Measuring Ego Development*, Vols. I and II. San Francisco: Jossey-Bass, 1970.

Loevinger, J. *Ego Development*. San Francisco: Jossey-Bass, 1976.

Loevinger, Jane. *Ego Development: Conception and Theories*. San Francisco: Jossey-Bass, 1982.

Loye, David, *The Sphinx and the Rainbow: Brain, Mind and Future Vision*. New York: Bantam Books, Inc., 1983.

Loye, David, and Riane Eisler. Chaos and Transformation: Implications for Disequilibrium Theory for Social Science and Society. *Behavioral Science*, in press.

MacFarland, D., and D. J. Brown. Social Distance as a Metric: A Systematic Introduction to Smallest Space Analysis. In: E. O. Laumann, *Bonds of Pluralism*, pp. 213-253. New York: John Wiley and Sons, 1973.

Madsen, Douglas, and Peter G. Snow. The Dispersion of Charisma. *Comparative Political Studies*, 1983, 16 (3): 337-362.

Manchester, William. *The Last Lion: Winston Spencer Churchill*. Boston-Toronto: Little, Brown and Company, 1983.

Marcelja, S. Mathematical Description of the Responses of Simple Cortical Cells. *Journal of the Optical Society of America*, 1980, 70: 1297–1300.

Marcus, John T. Transcendence and Charisma. *The Western Political Quarterly*, 1961, 14: 236-241.

Marr, David. *Vision: A Computational Investigation into the Human Representation and Processing of Visual Information*. San Francisco: W. H. Freeman and Company, 1982.

Mayhew, Bruce H. Structuralism versus Individualism: Part 1, Shadowboxing in the Dark. *Social Forces*, 1980, 59, 2: 335-375.

Merton, Robert K. Structural Analysis in Sociology. In: Peter M. Blau (ed.), *Approaches to the Study of Social Structure*, pp. 21-52. New York: The Free Press, 1975.

Merton, Robert K., with Elinor Barber. Sociological Ambivalence. In: Robert K. Merton, *Sociological Ambivalence: And Other Essays*, pp. 3-31. New York: The Free Press, 1976.

Messeri, P. *DAMP* — Define Adjacency Matrix Program. Unpublished computer program, Urban Communes Project. New York: Center for Policy Research and Columbia University, 1975(a).

Messeri, P. *STAM — STatistical Analysis of Matrices*. Unpublished computer program, Urban Communes Project. New York: Center for Policy Research and Columbia University, 1975(b).

Miller, Arthur I. *Imagery in Scientific Thought: Creating 20th-Century Physics*. Boston: Birkhauser, 1984.

Mitchell, J. Clyde. The Concept and Use of Social Networks. In: J. C. Mitchell (ed.), *Social Networks in Urban Situations*, pp. 1-50. Manchester: Manchester University Press, 1969.

Mitroff, Ian I. *Stakeholders of the Organizational Mind: Toward a New View of Organizational Policy Making*. San Francisco: Jossey-Bass, 1983.

Mitroff, Ian. Radically Changing Images of Productivity. *ReVision*, 1985, 7 (2): 101-106.

Moreno, J. L. *Who Shall Survive?* Washington, D.C.: Nervous and Mental Disease Publishing Company, 1934.

Morgan, Gareth, and Rafael Ramirez. Action Learning: a Holographic Metaphor for Guiding Social Change. *Human Relations*, 1984, 37 (1).

Morgan, Gareth. *Images of Organization*, Chapter 4, "Towards Self-organization: Organizations As Brains," pp. 77–109. Beverly Hills and London: Sage Publications, 1986.

Movshon, J. A., I. D. Thompson, and D. J. Tolhurst. Receptive Field Organization of Complex Cells in the Cat's Striate Cortex. *Journal of Physiology*, 1978, 283: 79–99.

Murdock, Bennet B. Convolution and Matrix Systems: A Reply to Pike. *Psychological Review*, 1985, 92 (1): 130-132.

Nadel, S. F. *The Theory of Social Structure*. London: Cohen and West, 1957.

Nagel, E. On the Statement 'The Whole is More than the Sum of Its Parts'. In: P. F. Lazarsfeld and M. Rosenberg (eds.), *The Language of Social Research*, pp. 519-527. New York: The Free Press, 1955.

Nettler, G. A Measure of Alienation. *American Sociological Review*, 1957, 22: 670-677.

Nicolis, Grégoire and Ilya Prigogine. *Self-organization in Nonequilibrium Systems: From Dissipative Structures to Order Through Fluctuations*. New York: Wiley-Interscience, 1977.

Oomen, T. K. Charisma, Social Structure and Social Change. *Comparative Studies in Society and History*, 1967, 10 (1): 85-99.

Pais, Abraham. *'Subtle is the Lord ...': The Science and the Life of Albert Einstein*. New York: Oxford University Press, 1982.

Parsons, Talcott. *The Structure of Social Action, Volume II: Weber*. New York: The Free Press, 1937.

Parsons, Talcott. Introduction. In: Max Weber, *The Theory of Social and Economic Organization*, pp. 3-86. Glencoe, Ill: The Free Press, 1947.

Parsons, Talcott. *The Social System*. New York: The Free Press, 1951.

Parsons, Talcott, and R. F. Bales. *Family, Socialization and Interaction Process*. Glencoe, Ill.: Free Press, 1955.

Piaget, Jean. *On Affectivity and Intelligence*. New York: Academic Press, 1983.

Piaget, Jean. *Structuralism*. Translated and Edited by Chaninah Maschler. New York: Basic Books, 1970.

Pietsch, Paul. *Shufflebrain: The Quest for the Hologramic Mind*. Boston: Houghton Mifflin Company, 1981.

Pribram, Karl H. Some Dimensions of Remembering: Steps Toward a Neuropsychological Model of Memory. In: J. Gaito (ed.), *Macromolecules and Behavior*, pp. 165-187. New York: Academic Press, 1966.

Pribram, Karl H. The Neuropsychology of Remembering. *Scientific American*, January, 1969, 73-86.

Pribram, Karl H. *Languages of the Brain: Experimental Paradoxes and Principles in Neuropsychology*. New York: Brandon House, 1971.

Pribram, Karl H., M. Nuwer, and R. Baron. The Holographic Hypothesis of Memory Structure in Brain Function and Perception. In: R. C. Atkinson, D. H. Krantz, R. C. Luce, and P. Suppes (eds.), *Contemporary Developments in Mathematical Psychology*, pp. 416-467. San Francisco: W. H. Freeman, 1974.

Pribram, Karl H. Localization and the Distribution of Function in the Brain. In: J. Orbach (ed.), *Neuropsychology After Lashley*, pp. 273-296. New York: Erlbaum, 1982.

Pribram, Karl H. The Brain, Cognitive Commodities, and the Enfolded Order. In: K. E. Boulding and L. Senesh (eds.), *The Optimum Utilization of Knowledge: Making Knowledge Serve Human Betterment*, pp. 29-40. Boulder, CO: Westview Press, 1983.

Pribram, Karl H. and E. H. Carlton. Imaging. Unpublished manuscript, Departments of Psychology and of Psychiatry and Behavioral Science. Stanford, CA: Stanford University, 1985(a).

Pribram, Karl H., and E. H. Carlton. Object Perception. Unpublished manuscript, Departments of Psychology and of Psychiatry and Behavioral Science. Stanford, CA: Stanford University, 1985(b).

Prigogine, Ilya, and Isabelle Stengers. *Order out of Chaos: Man's New Dialogue with Nature*. New York: Bantam Books, 1984.

Radcliffe-Brown, A. R. On Social Structure. *Journal of the Royal Anthropological Institute*, 1940, 70: 1-12.

Radcliffe-Brown, A. R. *A Natural Science of Society*. Glencoe, IL: The Free Press, 1957.

Ratman, K. J. Charisma and Political Leadership. *Political Studies*, 1964, 12: 341-354.

Ravn, Ib. Creating Futures, Constructing Realities. *General Systems Yearbook*, 1985 (in press).

Ravn, Ib. The Construction of Social Order: A Holonomic Perspective. Paper presented to the Annual Meeting of the American Society for Cybernetics, Virginia Beach, Virginia, 1986.

Rigby, Andrew. *Alternative Realities: A Study of Communes and Their Members.* London: Routledge and Kegan Paul, 1974.

Roberts, Nancy C. Transforming Leadership: A Process of Collective Action. *Human Relations*, 1985(a), 38 (1): 1023-1046.

Roberts, Nancy C. Power Structures in Work Groups: A Test of Hologramic Theory. Paper presented to the Symposium on Hologramic Theory: A New Perspective on Organization, Academy of Management Annual Meetings, San Diego, California, 1985(b).

Roberts, Nancy C. Organizational Power Styles: Collective and Competitive Power Under Varying Organizational Conditions. *Journal of Applied Behavioral Science*, 1986, 22 (4).

Rogers, E. M., and D. L. Kincaid. *Communication Networks: Toward a New Paradigm for Research.* New York: The Free Press, 1981.

Roth, G. Socio-historical Model and Development Theory: Charismatic Community, Charisma of Reason, and the Counterculture. *American Sociological Review*, 1975, 40: 148-157.

Runyon, Richard P., and Audrey Haber. *Fundamentals of Behavioral Statistics.* Reading, Mass.: Addison-Wesley Publishing Company, Inc., 1967.

Schiffer, Irvine. *Charisma: A Psychoanalytic Look at Mass Society.* New York: The Free Press, 1973.

Schlesinger, Arthur, Jr. On Heroic Leadership and the Dilemma of Strong Men and Weak Peoples. *Encounter*, 1960, 15 (6): 3-11.

Schlesinger, Leonard A., Robert G. Eccles, and John J. Gabarro, *Managing Behavior in Organizations: Text, Cases, Readings.* New York: McGraw-Hill, 1983.

Schmalenbach, Herman. The Sociological Category of Communion. In: Talcott Parsons et al. (eds.), *Theories of Society*, pp. 331-347. New York: The Free Press, 1961.

Schwartz, J. E. An Examination of CONCOR and Related Methods for Blocking Sociometric Data. In: D. R. Heise (ed.), *Sociological Methodology 1977*, pp. 255-82. San Francisco: Jossey-Bass, 1977.

Schweitzer, Arthur. Theory of Political Charisma. *Comparative Studies in Society and History*, 1974/5, 16: 150-181.

Schweitzer, Arthur. *The Age of Charisma.* Chicago: Nelson-Hall, 1984(a).

Schweitzer, Arthur. From Pure to Synergistic Charisma. Revised version of paper presented to the Research Committee on the History of Sociology, International Sociological Association Meetings, Munich, West Germany, 1984(b).

Sennett, Richard. Destructive Gemeinschaft. In: Kurt Back (ed.), *In Search for Community.* Boulder, CO: Westview Press, 1978.

Shapley, R. and P. Lennie. Spatial Frequency Analysis in the Visual System. *Annual Review of Neuroscience,* 1985: 547-583.

Sheldrake, Rupert. *A New Science of Life: The Hypothesis of Formative Causation.* Los Angeles: J. P. Tarcher, Inc., 1981.

Shey, Thomas. Why Communes Fail. *Journal of Marriage and The Family,* 1977, 39 (August): 605-613.

Shils, Edward. The Concentration and Dispersion of Charisma: Their Bearing on Economic Policy in Underdeveloped Countries. *World Politics,* 11: 1-19.

Shils, Edward. Charisma. In: *International Encyclopedia of the Social Sciences,* Vol. 2: 386-390. New York: MacMillan Company and The Free Press, 1968.

Shils, Edward. Charisma, Order and Status. *American Sociological Review,* 1965, 30: 199-213.

Simmel, G. *The Sociology of Georg Simmel.* Trans. by Kurt H. Wolff. New York: The Free Press, 1950.

Simmel, G. *Conflict and the Web of Group Affiliations.* Trans. by Kurt H. Wolff and Reinhard Bendix. New York: The Free Press, 1955.

Skocpol, Theda. *States and Social Revolutions: A Comparative Analysis of France, Russia, and China.* Cambridge: Cambridge University Press, 1979.

Slater, Philip E. *Microcosm: Structural, Psychological and Religious Evolution in Groups.* New York: John Wiley and Sons, Inc., 1966.

Smelser, Neil J. *Theory of Collective Behavior.* London: Routledge and Kegan Paul, 1962.

Spencer, M. E. What is Charisma? *British Journal of Sociology,* 1973, 24 (3): 341-354.

Stark, Stanley. Toward a Psychology of Charisma: III. Intentional Empathy, Vobilder, Fuehers, Transcendence-Striving, and Inner Creation. *Psychological Reports,* 1977, 40: 683-696.

Stincombe, Arthur L. *Constructing Social Theories.* New York: Harcourt, Brace and World, 1968.

Suttles, Gerald D. *The Social Construction of Communities.* Chicago: University of Chicago Press, 1972.

Swanson, Guy E. *The Birth of the Gods: The Origins of Primitive Beliefs.* Ann Arbor: The University of Michigan Press, 1960.

Swanson, Guy E. Travels Through Inner Space: Family Structure and Openness to Absorbing Experiences. *American Journal of Sociology,* 1978(a), 83 (Jan.): 890-919.

Swanson, Guy E. Trance and Possession: Studies of Charismatic Influence. *Review of Religious Research,* 1978(b), 19 (Spring): 253-278.

Teilhard de Chardin, Pierre. *Human Energy.* New York: Harcourt and Brace, 1972.

Teilhard de Chardin, Pierre. *The Future of Man.* New York: Harper Colophon Books, 1964.

Theobold, Robin. The Role of Charisma in the Development of Social Movements: Ellen G. White and the Emergence of Seventh-Day Adventism. *Archives de Sciences Sociales des Religions,* 1980, 25: 49-1, Jan-Mar.: 83-100.

Thibaut, John, and Harold Kelley. *The Social Psychology of Groups.* New York: John Wiley, 1959.

Tucker, Robert C. The Theory of Charismatic Leadership. *Daedalus,* 1968, 97 (3): 731-756.

Turk, Herman. Emotion, Value and Charisma: Theoretical Union at Several Levels. In: Herman Turk and Richard Simpson (eds.) *Institutions and Social Exchange.* New York: Bobbs-Merrill, 1971.

Turner, R., and C. Killian. *Collective Behavior.* Englewood Cliffs, New Jersey: Prentice-Hall, 1957.

Turner, Victor W. *The Ritual Process: Structure and Anti-Structure.* Chicago: Aldine Publishing Company, 1969.

Turner, Victor W. *Dramas, Fields and Metaphors: Symbolic Action in Human Society.* Ithaca and London: Cornell University Press, 1974.

Wallace, Walter L. Structure and Action in the Theories of Coleman and Parsons. In: Peter M. Blau (ed.), *Approaches to the Study of Social Structure,* pp. 121-134. New York: The Free Press, 1975.

Wallace, Walter L. *Principles of Scientific Sociology.* New York: Aldine Publishing Company, 1983.

Wallerstein, Immanuel. Marxism as Utopias: Evolving Ideologies. *American Journal of Sociology,* 1986, 91(6): 1295-1308.

Wallis, R. 'Goal Displacement' and 'Routinization of Charisma' in the Nationwide Festival of Light. *Scottish Journal of Sociology,* 1977, 1 (1): 81-93.

Weber, Max. *From Max Weber: Essays in Sociology.* Trans. by Hans Gerth and C. Wright Mills. New York: Oxford University Press, 1946.

Weber, Max. *The Theory of Social and Economic Organization.* Trans. by A. M. Henderson and Talcott Parsons. New York: The Free Press, 1947.

Weber, Max. *The Methodology of the Social Sciences.* Trans. by Edward Shils and Henry A. Finch. Glencoe, IL: The Free Press, 1949.

Weber, Max. *The Sociology of Religion.* Trans. by Ephriam Fischoff. Boston: Beacon Press, 1963.

Weber, Max. *Max Weber on Charisma and Institution Building.* Edited by S. N. Eisenstadt. Chicago: University of Chicago Press, 1968.

Weber, Max. *Economy and Society: An Outline of Interpretive Sociology,* Vols. 1 and 2. Edited by Guenther Roth and Claus Wittich. Berkeley, Los Angeles, and London: University of California Press, 1978.

Webster, M., Jr. Psychological Reductionism, Methodological Individualism, and Large-Scale Problems. *American Sociological Review,* 1973, 38 (April): 258-273.

Wellman, Barry. A Guide to Network Analysis. Paper presented to Annual Meetings of American Sociological Association, New York, 1980.

White, Harrison C., Scott A. Boorman, and Ronald Breiger. Social Structure from Multiple Networks. I. Block Models of Roles and Positions. *American Journal of Sociology,* 1976, 81 (4): 730-780.

Whitehead, A. N. *Process and Reality: An Essay in Cosmology.* New York: The Free Press, 1969.

Wilber, Ken (ed.). *The Holographic Paradigm and Other Paradoxes: Exploring the Leading Edge of Science.* Boulder and London: New Science Library, 1982.

Willner, Ann Ruth. *Charismatic Political Leadership: A Theory.* Princeton: Princeton University Press, 1968.

Willner, Ann Ruth. *The Spellbinders: Charismatic Political Leadership.* New Haven and London: Yale University Press, 1984.

Wilson, Bryan R. *The Noble Savages: The Primitive Origins of Charisma and its Contemporary Survival.* Berkeley: University of California Press, 1975.

Wilson, E. O. *Sociobiology.* Cambridge, Mass: Harvard University Press, 1980.

Winograd, Gaynelle R. A Holonomic Interpretive Approach To Critique Organizational Cultures For Effectiveness, Change, and Communication Competency. Doctoral dissertation. University of Boulder, Colorado, 1986.

Worsley, Peter. *The Trumpet Shall Sound: A Study of Cargo Cults in Melanesia,* Second Edition. New York: Schocken Books, 1968.

Zablocki, Benjamin D. *The Joyful Community.* New York: Penguin Books, 1971.

Zablocki, Benjamin D. Alienation and Investment of Self in the Urban Commune. N.I.M.H. Research Proposal, 1974.

Zablocki, Benjamin D. *Alienation and Charisma: A Study of Contemporary American Communes.* New York: The Free Press, 1980.

INDEX

355